Societies and Political Orders in Transition

This book series presents scientific and scholarly studies focusing on societies and political orders in transition in Central and Eastern Europe but also elsewhere in the world, contemporary and historical. By comparing established societies, characterized by well-established market economies and well-functioning democracies, with post-socialist and other societies, often characterized by emerging markets and fragile political systems, the series identifies and analyzes factors influencing change and continuity in societies and political orders. These factors include state capacity to establish formal and informal rules, democratic institutions, forms of social structuration, political regimes, levels of corruption, specificity of political cultures, as well as types and orientation of political and economic elites.

Societies and Political Orders in Transition welcomes monographs and edited volumes with diverse empirical and theoretical approaches from a variety of disciplines, including political science, economics and social sciences in general, as well as comparative politics, political history, political theory, comparative social research, and comparative economics in particular.

Topics may include, but are not limited to, democratization, regime change, changing social norms, migration, etc.

All titles in this series are peer-reviewed.

This book series is indexed in Scopus.

For further information on the series and to submit a proposal for consideration, please contact Johannes Glaeser (Senior Editor Economics and Political Science) Johannes.glaeser@springer.com.

Carina Barbosa Gouvêa ·
Pedro H. Villas Bôas Castelo Branco

UN Interventions and Democratization

Case Studies of States in Political Transition

Springer

Carina Barbosa Gouvêa
Federal University of Pernambuco
Recife, Brazil

Pedro H. Villas Bôas Castelo Branco
State University of Rio de Janeiro
Rio de Janeiro, Brazil

Translated by Rafael Tayar Scarfon and Carina Barbosa Gouvêa

ISSN 2511-2201 ISSN 2511-221X (electronic)
Societies and Political Orders in Transition
ISBN 978-3-031-32714-8 ISBN 978-3-031-32715-5 (eBook)
https://doi.org/10.1007/978-3-031-32715-5

This Springer imprint is published by the registered company Springer Nature Switzerland AG
The registered company address is: Gewerbestrasse 11, 6330 Cham, Switzerland

Foreword

The work that now comes to the English-speaking reader is the result of the interpretation of Carina Barbosa Gouvêa and Pedro H. Villas Bôas Castelo Branco and the presentation that I make to the reader by honorable invitation of its authors focuses on exposing on its innovation and its interpretation.

One of the essential conditions to produce research is the factor of novelty. Either you ask a question that has not yet been asked or a response that has not yet been given to an already formulated problem.

When analyzing dogmatic research in Constitutional Law, it is usual to observe innovations in answers to the questions already formulated several times over time—since they are challenges that present themselves over time. This research differed in the academic scenario because not only proposed a question not yet been made, but also made use of empirical methods applied rigorously, which connected the reality analyzed the theoretical model.

In this sense, to the question of how UN intervention in the process of constitutional construction of countries in political transition manifests, the author analyzed several scenarios, enabling it to describe what democracy is projected by the UN, what mechanisms are used to introject in the local culture the said democratic project, as well as the problems of such grafted project.

The authors' work proposal also has a proposal for a method of analysis of influences in the process of constitutional construction, which represents a milestone in the empirical analysis of Constitutional Law in all systems that are intended to study the formulation of a constitutionalism. In this system, the authors establish the pre-constituent phase, which analyzes the elements of support for elections as well as awareness campaigns and popular participation; the constituent phase, where it analyzes the influence in the creation of the design of the constituent process and in the enunciation of the constitutional content, as well as in the composition of the constituent assembly aiming at seeking constitutional legitimacy, as well as the proposition of a thesis of substantial democracy; finally, the post-constituent phase, where it analyzes constitutional development and effectiveness.

Such an innovation in constitutional empirical analysis is associated with substantial consideration of the role of the UN in the process of political transitions as well as the design of what is presented as Democracy to states experiencing such transitions.

With this, I would like to emphasize to the readers that they are facing a key work in understanding contemporary constitutional law and in the work that best introduces Carina Gouvêa e Pedro Castelo Branco's thought, marked by substantial theoretical deepening that dialogues with the constitutional experience of our times.

I wish the readers that reading be as enjoyable as I have had, and that may provoke the new and necessary reflections of our common theoretical sense in Constitutional Law.

São Paulo, Brazil
2023

Henderson Fürst
Ph.D. in Philosophy of Law at PUC-SP, Ph.D. and M.Sc. in Bioethics at CUSC, LLB at UNESP

Professor of post-graduate programs at PUC-Campinas, Brazilian Academy of Constitutional Law and Israeli Hospital Albert Einstein

Scientific Editor at National Editorial Group and lawyer

Contents

1 Introduction 1

2 Democracy in Contemporaneity: Building Identity 7
2.1 Semantic Agreement: A Process Subject to a Continuous Invention and Reinvention 7
2.2 An Understanding of the Democratic Regime: A Method for Construction of the Game Rules 10
2.3 The Need to Conform the Constitutional Sign: The Roads of Representation, Deliberation and Participation 15
2.4 A Critical Analysis: Democracy as a Living Organization that Represents Decentralization of Power and Development 22
References 26

3 Construction of an Environment that Maintains Democracy Through Democratic Constitutionalism 29
3.1 Constitution and Constitutionalism: Understanding Its Essence 29
3.2 Developing New Categories of Constitutionalism: An Essential Exercise for the Living of the Constitution 36
3.2.1 Transitional Constitutionalism 36
3.2.2 Transformation Constitutionalism 40
3.2.3 Democratic Constitutionalism 44
References 49

4 The Role of the UN in the Consolidation of Democracy and the Constitution-Making 53
4.1 An United Nations Approach Concepting Democratization and Democracy 53
4.2 Democracy and Human Rights: Independent and Related 61
4.3 Change of Perspectives on the Role of the UN: The Political-Legal Structuring 64

4.4 The Foundational Charter: A Pre-requisite to Achieve the Development of Nations ... 71
References ... 76

5 A Constitution-Making Analysis from the Un Intervention: The Difficulties of Materialization of the Constitutionalism of Transition and Transformation ... 79
5.1 Constitution-Making ... 79
5.2 Intervention in the Pre-constituent Phase ... 81
5.2.1 Support for Election Campaigns ... 81
5.2.2 Intervention in Educational Campaigns and Popular Participation ... 85
5.3 Intervention in the Constituent Phase ... 87
5.3.1 The Contribution in the Design of the Constituent Process and the Enunciation of the Constitutional Content ... 87
5.3.2 The Composition of the Constituent Assembly: Looking for Constitutional Legitimacy ... 89
5.3.3 Substantive Democracy Thesis ... 91
5.4 Intervention in the Post-constituent Phase ... 94
5.4.1 Constitutional Development ... 94
5.4.2 Constitutional Effectiveness ... 97
5.5 Un Intervention Through a Practical Perspective ... 99
References ... 106

6 Hybrid Constituent Power as a Subcategory of the Original Constituent Power ... 109
6.1 Conception of Hybrid Constituent Power ... 109
6.2 Empirical Experiences of Hybrid Constituent Power ... 121
6.2.1 Cambodia ... 123
6.2.2 Bosnia and Herzegovina ... 130
6.2.3 East Timor ... 136
6.2.4 Afghanistan ... 141
6.3 Hybrid Constituent Power: The Role of the UN as a Political Actor ... 149
6.3.1 Hybrid Constituent Power: Materializing Your Senses ... 150
References ... 157

7 Case Study of the UN Intervention in the Political-Legal Structure of the East Timor ... 161
7.1 East Timor: Characteristics and Nature of Conflict ... 161
7.2 The UN Intervention in the Pre-Constituent Phase ... 164
7.3 UN Intervention in the Constituent Phase ... 165
7.4 The UN Intervention in the Post-Constituent Phase ... 172

7.5 The Constitutionalism of Transition, Transformation, and the Democratic and the Legitimacy of the East Timor Constitutional Charter 177
References 184

8 Conclusion 187

Afterword 199

About the Authors

Carina Barbosa Gouvêa Professor of the Post-Graduate Program in Law Master's and Doctorate of the Federal University of Pernambuco (PPGD/UFPE); Post Doctorate in Constitutional Law of the Federal University of Pernambuco (PPGD/UFPE); Doctor and Master's Degree in Law of UNESA; Coordinator of the Study and Research Group "Separation of Powers Theory and Crisis of the Brazilian Democratic System" linked to PPGD/UFPE; Vice Leader of the Research Group International Law and Human Rights (UFPE), CNPq. e-mail: carina.gouvea@ufpe.br

Pedro H. Villas Bôas Castelo Branco Associate Professor at the Institute of Social and Political Studies at the State University of Rio de Janeiro (IESP-UERJ); Professor of the Postgraduate Program in Law at the Veiga de Almeida University (PPGD/UVA). Doctor in Political Science of past IUPERJ current IESP-UERJ, Master in Theory of State and Constitutional at the PUC-Rio. Coordinator of the Laboratory for Political Studies on Defense and Public Security (LEPDESP) linked to UERJ and High War College (ESG). e-mail: pvbcastelobranco@iesp.uerj.br

Abbreviations and Acronyms

ACDI	Canadian Agency for International Development
ADPF	Argument of Non-compliance with Fundamental Precept
APODETI	Timorese People's Democratic Association
ASDT	Timorese Social Democratic Association
ASEAN	Association of Southeast Asian Nations
AU	African Union
BRABAT	Brazilian Peace Force Battalion
CAECOPAZ	Argentine Joint Training Center for Peace Operations
DPA	Department of Political Affairs
DPKO	Department for Peacekeeping Operations
EU	European Union
EUFOR	European Union Force
FRETILIN	Independent Revolutionary Front of Timor-Leste
GDP	Gross Domestic Product
IDEA	Institute for Democracy and Electoral Assistance
IDLO	International Law Development Organization
INTERFET	International Force East Timor
MA	American Military
MBR1	Brazilian Military 1
MBR2	Brazilian Military 2
MBR3	Brazilian Military 3
MBR4	Brazilian Military 4
MBR5	Brazilian Military 5
MFO	Multinational Force & Observers
MINUSCA	United Nations Multidimensional Integrated Stabilization Mission in the Central African Republic
MINUSTAH	United Nations Stabilization Mission in Haiti
MONUA	United Nations Observer Mission in Angola
NATO	North Atlantic Treaty Organization
NOG	Non-governmental organization
NYU	New York University

OAS	Organization of American States
OHCHR	Office of the High Commissioner on Human Rights
OSCE	Organization for Security and Co-operation in Europe
PED	Strategic Development Plan
SFOR	Stabilization Force in Bosnia and Herzegovina
SG/OAS	Secretary-General of the Organization of American States
SRSG	Special Representative of the UN Secretary-General
UDT	Timorese Democratic Union
UN	United Nations Organization
UN WOMAN	United Nations Entity for Gender and the Empowerment of Woman
UNAMET	United Nations Mission in East Timor
UNAVEM III	United Nations Angola Verification Mission III
UNDEF	United Nations Democracy Fund
UNDP	United Nations Development Programme
UNHCR	United Nations High Commissioner for Refugees
UNICEF	United Nations Children's Fund
UNIPSIL	United Nations Integrated Peacebuilding Office in Sierra Leone
UNITA	National Union for the Total Independence of Angola
UNMIK	United Nations Interim Administration Mission in Kosovo
UNMIS	United Nations Mission in Sudan
UNMISET	United Nations Mission of Support in East Timor
UNMIT	United Nations Integrated Mission in East Timor
UNMOGIP	UN Military Observer Group in India and Pakistan
UNODC	United Nations Office on Drugs and Crime
UNOTIL	United Nations Office in East Timor
UNSMIS	United Nations Supervision Mission in Syria
UNTAC	United Nations Transitional Authority in Cambodia
UNTAET	United Nations Transitional Administration in East Timor
UNTAG	United Nations Transition Assistance Group
UNTSO	UN Truce Supervision Organization
USA	United States of America
USIP	United States Institute of Peace

Chapter 1
Introduction

We have lost our identity, we are dead!
No, we are OK, and better than before!
Courageous leadership.
Has brought us security and peace!
Together, side by side.
We have made the sun shine!
(Ka Mate, Maori Song, translated by John Archer).

Democracy, in theory and in practice, is the subject of many debates and a vast field of study that encompasses the most varied areas, among which we could mention constitutional law, political science, and international law. Liberal constitutional democracies became global as they spread across continents, especially after the 1960s. Their guidelines against arbitrariness and authoritarianism began to be widely recognized to the point of reaching, for many, the status of a fundamental and universal value, especially for the United Nations (UN). In this sense, the UN started to contribute its expertise to the promotion of democracy and democratization in different cultural and political contexts. In order to contribute to the expansion of these meanings, the work presents as its fundamental objective to understand the main dimensions of UN interventions in the constitution-making process in states that undergo a process of political transition and its role in the rescue of the liberal-democratic order.

The liberal-democracy doctrine for the UN constitutes a condition of political possibility aimed at the protection, promotion, and effective realization of human rights and justice. Thus, an objective assessment of the degree of respect for human rights, the theory of separation of powers, and the rule of law in constitutions allow a closer analysis of the level of democracy achieved by a given country. In particular, the adoption of procedures and institutions that allow the participation, exercise, and control of political power, such as the institution of fair, free, and competitive elections, provide tangible indications of the values, effectiveness, and achievement of democratic governance.

For the UN, weak or dysfunctional institutions are some of the most serious challenges to democracy. These problems can stem from an autocratic executive, an ineffective or unresponsive parliament, attempts to manipulate constitutional order

C. B. Gouvêa and P. H. V. B. Castelo Branco, *UN Interventions and Democratization*, Societies and Political Orders in Transition,
https://doi.org/10.1007/978-3-031-32715-5_1

and election results, violence, extremist political polarization, the corrosive effects of corruption, civil unrest, inversion of the civil-military relationship, among others.

In this sense, international commitment and assistance become incessant and indispensable. That is why the institutionalization of strategic peace processes in conflict and post-conflict societies has a significant effect: the prevention of violence and its management. The human suffering resulting from the uncertainties and arbitrariness of oppressive governments provoked a wave of formulations of new constitutional charters, especially encouraged by the UN, for which they are the best resources to support and guide human conduct and create predictable and stable conditions of governance.

The peacekeeping mandates entrusted to the UN include the restoration of democracy and the protection of human and fundamental rights. Departments, agencies, and programs were named to help states write constitutions, create independent systems for the administration of justice, demilitarize politics, institute and strengthen the rule of law, establish national institutions, among others. Supporting constitution-making processes centered on national ownership is a critical component of UN Department of the Rule of Law.

For the UN, the design of a constitution can play an important role in political transitions, post-conflict peacebuilding and play a critical role in preventing future atrocities. Among the ways of assistance, it could be mentioned the decision-making processes, including political rights and their strategies; the development of institutional capacities; financial, logistical, and administrative supports. Constitution maker is an online constitutional assistance resource center that has a variety of academic and professional sources, developed by the Department of Political Affairs and the UN Development Program for United Nations staff.

The road to democracy is idiosyncratic and surrounded by a series of political, cultural, and national concerns that are specific to each political organization or ethnic group. Therefore, this book presents four studies of cases selected to cover a perspective that includes different phases of constitutions development. These studies involve three continents and four countries: Cambodia, Bosnia-Herzegovina, East Timor, and Afghanistan. Many of the issues addressed in this paper will be submitted to empirical testing to verify how constitutions are implemented.

It seeks to analyze the way the UN intends to offer appropriate and shared responses to the challenges presented by non-democratic nations so that they can face their own weaknesses. Before this complex scenario, the paper shows the difficulty that the UN finds in aligning new aspirations that the democratic constitutional culture intends to promote with the old traditions and national cultural barriers.

The issue related to the creation and implementation of a constitution necessarily involves understanding what is the role to be played by the constitutional charter in times of crisis or re-democratization and that ends up leading to the center of the debate the challenge of trying to promote a constitution that is the result of the options resulting from that population and, at the same time, promote its development through its institutional archetype. Creating these favorable conditions to achieve this end is one of the UN objectives.

The empirical experiences of constitution-making carried out by the UN in countries such as East Timor, Haiti, Sudan, Afghanistan, Bosnia, Nepal, Cambodia, Egypt, and Iraq demonstrate that such practices, although with common goals, that is, democratization, are in an evolutionary process and need improvement—whether in pre-constituent, constituent or post-constituent processes. The constitution forged under the auspices of the UN consists of a set of intentions that apply a theoretical-abstract model of constitutionalism in tune with the categories of transition, transformation, and democratic constitutionalism.

The development of the construction of constitutions by different procedures, pursued with the use of systematized transition formulas, in an analysis line, demonstrates a close relationship between the intended type of justice and the relevant limiting political conditions.

On one hand, the intervention highlights the difficulties that different social realities present, such as to promote popular participation; as well as an increasing westernization, meaning that too much international influence can be detrimental to constitutional process and content, once the result can be inadequate to local needs. This standard may assume a paradoxical response to the UN's commitment to human rights and democracy.

If for the UN the recognition of democracy through the constitution is the consolidation of the logic of democratization, which has human rights as its central element and, with that, imposes constitutional action on this same final vector; however, for caution, it is necessary to take into account the risk that such a proclamation results in a merely symbolic/rhetorical response that adds little or nothing to the newly democratic nation, mainly to the promotion of its development.

The issue surrounding this study is the verification of the institutional ability of the UN to contribute to the generation of a legitimate constitutional order in those countries in stages of re-democratization from the way it a applies constitution-making.

The book sought to understand the UN intervention process that involved the study of the democracy and democratization. In the conception espoused by the UN, three meanings can capture its substance and practice: the protection of democratic institutions; the responsibility of power holders; and the respect for and the protection of the Rule of Law and human rights. Democracy is stronger and more resistant when it is based on legitimate representative mechanisms and socio-political interaction that ends up becoming a stronger model to guarantee a framework of freedoms. There is not a model to be copied, but a goal to be achieved, although some elements are essential: the holding of free and fair elections; the management of transparent rules and effective regulations bringing out the participatory dynamic; the promotion of rights and freedoms, among others. Based on this notion it was possible to characterize the intended constitution model in a substantial and organic way, still maintaining a dialog with the classic and contemporary thought of constitutionalism and the constitution and its functions.

Another aspect of the analysis refers to specific contexts that will allow the understanding of the terms and interventional phases pre-constituent, constituent, and post-constituent with the objective of brighten up the efforts. The book explores and questions UN intervention modalities to analyze their effectiveness and controversies and examines whether an "external political actor" can have a substantial impact on the development of democratic governance. It adopts the comparative method to contrast different studies. These approaches will be materialized in the following ways: literature review, semi-structured research, and applied case studies.

Thematic studies will analyze how the UN operates from the perspective of comparative constitutional law and democracy theory in implementing the theoretical and practical perspective on promoting liberal democracy. It also explores changing perspectives regarding its role: the political-legal structuring of a nation that encompasses the substantial and formal content of a constitution; its reforms; process formulations at the operational level; and complementary laws.

The chapters will also focus on specifically technical approaches such as Security Council Resolutions, Transitional Authorities, and institutional design options chosen by the UN. Its structure is composed of a structuring analysis and involves the following chapters: contemporary democracy and the construction of identities; the development of the categories of contemporary transitional, transformational, and democratic constitutionalism; the role and rules of the UN in consolidating democracy and constitutions; critical analyses of the construction of constitutions from their interventions in the pre-constituent, constituent, and post-constituent phases; the hybrid constituent power that represents the direct and indirect intervention of the UN in the constituent phase and the case studies of Cambodia, Bosnia-Herzegovina, East Timor, and Afghanistan; and, the case study of the intervention in the political-legal structure of East Timor, which involves the pre-constituent, constituent, and post-constituent phases.

The first chapter addressed a wide range of issues involving democracy in contemporary times and the construction of identities from its theoretical dimension. The chapter explores the concept of democracy and the journey that marked contemporaneity from a perspective of building semantic meanings to allow for a better understanding of the rules of the democratic game. In its evolution, democracy, conceived to resist time, conflict, and crisis, started, contemporaneously, to also invest in the popular autonomy, representing, therefore, a cooperative democracy, since it has an end and a means at the same time. It has an end because it has the purpose of aggregating several recipients and accommodating the fundamentals of an equal and participatory society; and a means because it will require several interpreters and mechanisms for its realization and development.

In the second chapter the development of the categories of contemporary constitutionalism is discussed: transitional, transformational, and democratic. These categories will be used in the constitutions to verify their effective potential for the contribution of social development in flagellated nations.

In the third chapter the way the UN effective the constitution-making in countries in political transition stages will be exposed. The purpose is to describe the role played by the UN in the consolidation of democracy and democratization, which includes the process of building constitutions claimed by the new apology of "democracy". This changing function of changing perspective is perceived in the development of its role: from humanitarian action to political-legal structure. It is necessary to emphasize its involvement in the processes of elaboration of a constitution in the pre-constituent, constituent, and post-constituent phases. Empirical data supporting these claims have been extracted exclusively from its publications, reports, and official experiences. This option proved to be adequate, since it essentially sought to reflect its principles, foundations, and objectives, including the critical aspects of its own approach. The also has, to illustrate the theoretical arguments, a semi-structured interview, carried out with six military personnel (five from Brazil and one from USA), aiming to collect data and experiences in UN missions.

The fourth chapter of the book allowed to verify how the international organization acts in the consolidation of democracy through the political-legal structuring that is connected to three distinct phases: the pre-constituent, constituent, and post-constituent. Thus, the need to analyze the ability to obtain a constitutional text coated with legitimacy from the constitution-making process carried out by the UN was observed. The work explores its potentialities, as well as a critical appreciation of the design of the constituent process, the institutional modeling and the content of rights, which revealed the difficulties of materializing the transitional and transformational constitutionalism, offering some contributions related to this great challenge.

The five chapters conceptualize hybrid constituent power that opens a new door to reflection on the theory of original constituent power. The idea of internationalization of constituent power represents the approach of the influence of international law on the normative content of constitutional law, causing the rules that should order citizens' activities not to be produced only by the national legislator, which creates a problem of legitimacy for the regulatory bodies, corresponding to an increasingly high degree of penetration of International Law in Constitutional Law.

It can be mentioned that the hybrid constituent power causes a distortion of the institutional balance of the State because international norms interfere in the formation of material or procedural internal norms, affecting State structures, namely: the political organization and the distribution of competences. Among the experiences of the hybrid constituent power, from the consummated UN interventions, some lessons were learned through the practical perspective by those who were directly or indirectly involved in peacebuilding operations, in which one of the objectives was to consolidate democracy. To delimitation of the research object and contributing to the construction of the legitimacy and effectiveness of the constitution, we proposed some guidelines that can be outlined for the improvement and legitimacy of the hybrid constituent power. Case studies that provided an overview of the role of UN constitutional assistance, in the constituent phase were also presented: Cambodia, Bosnia-Herzegovina, East Timor, and Afghanistan. Thus, the overview of the legal framework was addressed; the description of the process, considering the degree of inclusion, transparency, and participation of the local population; the focus and ways of intervention. The case studies presented do not, however, represent a definitive answer to what the broad set of UN experiences in the field of hybrid constituent power meant.

The final chapter presents a case study in the legal political intervention of East Timor. This country had the direct support of the UN for the development of the adopted constitution model, which can be considered a paradigmatic case since this intervention lasted at least 12 years and was consummated in the three intervention phases. This investigation enabled to explore the possible patterns of constitutional resistance and the legitimacy of its constitution.

The UN is considered the largest global provider of democracy and human rights, but little has been written about how it directly and indirectly assists in the construction of constitutions in the conceptual, theoretical, and practical forms which are being studied in this book. More than simply offering conclusions about UN methods, this work seeks to clarify the existing ambiguities and, in the end, create a resource that will serve as an auspicious guide in the field to understand the whole process as well as its unresolved internal tensions.

Chapter 2
Democracy in Contemporaneity: Building Identity

2.1 Semantic Agreement: A Process Subject to a Continuous Invention and Reinvention

Embracing the idea of structuring social life in collectivities as a necessity, the dilemma related to the way of formulating the choices related to this same grouping and the eventually democratic character of this mechanism of specification of collective options is put forth.

Identifying who the people, the foundations and the structures that hold the authority (internal or external) and the mechanisms according to which the group's choices can materialize is a central element to this construction of a collective life.

The cover that covers any semantic determination tends, in a way and, to limit the amplification of the meaning of a word in analysis.[1] The scope of the etymological definition of democracy can be understood through its descriptive use which, in turn, is subdivided into the *democracy of the ancients*—dictating the power of the *demos*, and of the moderns—as the determining power of the representatives of the *demos.*

Constant,[2] exploring the course of man's struggle for freedom, States that for the ancients, democracy is reflected in participation in decisions taken within the city, whereas for the moderns it is characterized by the distance of the people from the political elites.

The rule of law and democracy correspond to two ways of seeing freedom: in the so-called "rule of law", it is predominantly placed in its negative, defensive character, which curves power, blocking its intervention. Already in the "Democratic State", we have the same attribute now manifest in its positive aspect, based on the exercise of power and will be the one that legitimates authority.[3]

---

[1] DEMOCRACY in: (2009).

[2] Benjamin Constant (1985).

[3] J.J. Canotilho (2003).

C. B. Gouvêa and P. H. V. B. Castelo Branco, *UN Interventions and Democratization*, Societies and Political Orders in Transition,
https://doi.org/10.1007/978-3-031-32715-5_2

According to Constant,[4] the ancient peoples formed an isolated line, the enemy of other families; now a mass of men exist under different names, under various modes of social organization, but essentially heterogeneous. The results of these differences can be perceived in the extent of a country, which can greatly diminish the political importance that distributive touches everyone. The darkest Republican of Rome and Sparta was an authority. Not the same with a citizen of Brazil. His personal influence is an imperceptible element of the social that will impresses the government on his direction.

It is perceived the plurality of cores that undergoes the historical conditions and changes naturally with the transition from the political conjuncture of one reality to another. It has had life for at least 2,500 years translating different meanings for the people, times and places.[5]

At the same time, legal consciousness has invested much more energy on the values of democracy to link the legitimacy of governance to generalized suffrage extended on equal terms than in the conceptions of self-government of the XVIII and XIX centuries.[6]

By allowing democracy, the goal of many constitutions and underpinning substantial preconditions and formal structures of democratic politics, the notion of a policy is based on equal participation of all and is expressed through any regular vote.[7] It encompasses both the notion of participation in the direction of public policies and the ability to act by controlling the powers of government.

Although the popular government is the subject of many Magna Charters, cannot be interpreted exclusively by its "original" meaning. Words written in a formal document cannot reach all, their dictates. They are not totally determined or totally indeterminate.

It is Jackson's claim that the view of constitutional law must perceive democracy as "a living tree." A metaphor that captures the idea that a "living" document is not limited by its origins. The interpretation of any democracy must vary through legal sources and various understandings, conveying the idea of equilibrium so that the tree cannot fall structures that are too rigid tend to have the time factor, and their revitalization requires pruning. And this is concretized by the intervention of human strength.

This allowed us to broaden the view that democracy today is not only achieved by the possibility of choosing political actors, but also includes a constitutional protection that affirms: the superiority of the fundamental charter; the existence of fundamental rights; the legality of State actions; a system of legal and procedural safeguards[8]; the decentralization of power. Constitutions may be concerned not only with the authority to legislate but allow democracy to play its role, which is multidimensional.

[4] Benjamin Constant (1985).

[5] Robert A. Dahl (2001a, 2001b).

[6] Vicki Jackson (2006).

[7] Vicki Jackson (2010).

[8] Bernardo Fernandes Gonçalves (2011).

Since the concept of democracy is still the main engine of the mode of government,[9] the great difficulty is to determine "what is" and "what would be" in this new regime. This is because its development is not "linear, because it is always subject to stumbling and setbacks.[10]

It means that it is not enough to mention his name to legitimize his performance. To perceive the unrealism of this simple and unitary notion that does not form in a collection of individuals among them, but having as its destination a complex set of classes, races, clans, States, religious groups, whose power and influence vary enormously from time to time and from country to country.[11]

Conceptual evolution also allowed us to find representation through external inputs, that is, of international organizations. For the United Nations, democracy embodies in its heart the forging of a charter of rights and guarantees; contributes to the preservation of peace and security; ensures justice and human rights and promotes economic and social development.[12] It means that it has the firm purpose of establishing a "democratic culture" in societies devastated by war and for the purpose of establishing sustainable peace.[13] This particularity will be further discussed in chapter three.

There is no doubt that democracy has become a dominant belief in the contemporary world, and for Sen[14] it is a demanding system, not just a mechanical condition. Seen from this perspective, its merits and its claims can enrich citizens' lives, considering that political freedom is crucial for the development of individuals as social beings; has an important instrumental value, which reinforces the hearing through which people can express their claims; and its practice feeds collective learning and helps society to shape its values and priorities. It has a constructive importance, especially with the guarantee of open discussion, debate, criticism and dissent, which are fundamental to the process of making choices.

At the present time, it is to be understood as an open model, "a process subject to a continuous invention and reinvention", allowing to be questioned, at any time, the forms of social coexistence.[15] It would be a great misconception to believe that democracy, as the constitutional reason for a political regime, has an immutable and eternal essence, who's ideal inspired all democratic models of government of peoples.[16] The being in transformation is its natural and dynamic State.

---

[9] Democracy for the United Nations is a universal ideal and is one of the fundamental values that make up the organization.

[10] Bernardo Fernandes Gonçalves (2011).

[11] Fábio Konder Comparato (1989).

[12] Boutros Boutros-Ghali (1996).

[13] Peter Harris, Ben Reilly, Daniel Zovatto (2001).

[14] Amartya Sen (1999).

[15] DEMOCRACY in: (2009).

[16] Simone Goyard-Fabre (2003).

2.2 An Understanding of the Democratic Regime: A Method for Construction of the Game Rules

The evolution of the study devoted to the concept under analysis was opposed to the modern (representative) view of the ancients (direct), according to Bobbio.[17] By "democratic regime" it is understood a set of rules that involve procedures for the formation of collective decisions, which will be foreshadowed the widest possible participation of the interested parties. If, in this general concept, the strategy and the compromise between the parties are included in the formation of a majority through free debate, Bobbio's definition[18] better reflects the reality of democracy defined as representative. Another possible definition, according to the author,[19] is the one that puts evidence the substitution of the techniques of the force for the persuasion as a means of resolving conflicts.

In this second stage, the theme of building the rules of the game has gained greater prominence. The institutional design was designed primarily to organize the State, not only in defining its competencies, but also assigning functions to specific bodies. This principle, called tri-partyism, not only prohibits the creation of new organs and functions but also limits the possible development of new alternatives to reciprocal controls. Today is a growing demand dictated by the complexity of functions in the contemporary State.

Each of the functions performed is established with a gradual concentration and consists in giving those who administer each department the necessary constitutional means and the reasons for not interfering in the performance of their actions.[20] They will equip the various actors that make up the government system, of autonomy and authority to exercise their attributions and will provide defense mechanisms for this exercise to be complete.

The historical emergence of current democratic regimes, also called the "democratic political system", can be divided into distinct phases.[21] At the national level of government, the first phase appeared in the United States at the end of the XVIII century. In the following centuries, democratic regimes gradually emerged in northern and western Europe, in British regimes, and in a few Latin American countries.

According to Huntington[22] and in summary form, in the first period, between 1820 and 1920, occurred the growth of the democracy; in the second, between 1920 and 1942, totalitarian regimes began to flourish in the world, culminating in the conflict of World War II; in the third, between 1942 and 1953, there was its expansion; and

[17] Norberto Bobbio (1986).

[18] Norberto Bobbio (1986).

[19] Norberto Bobbio (2008).

[20] James A. Gardner (2005).

[21] Samuel P. Huntington (1984).

[22] Samuel P. Huntington (1984).

finally, between mid-1953 and 1980, there were no strong trends for either expansion or democratic decline.

The situation was reversed in many aspects of this growth among the independent nations of the world. During the 1930 and 1940s, the democratic index decreased in Germany, Italy, Austria, Poland, the Baltic States, Spain, Portugal, Greece, Argentina, Brazil and Japan. The war that took place to make a safe world for democracy seemed instead to have brought its progress to a limit, which has given rise to social movements of the right and left with the intention of destroying it.

The battles of World War II marked another dramatic multiplication of democratic regimes. With the help of their allies, the United States imposed democracy in West Germany, Austria, Italy, and Japan.

Coincidentally, the process of decolonization went its way with the newly independent nations, initially adopting a form of policy of the imperial powers. In at least some cases, such as India, Israel, Ceylon and the Philippines, the form of democracy was accompanied by its substantial content. Other countries, such as Turkey and some Latin American States, have followed the political models of the victorious Western powers. A dominant situation: the extension of democracy between the periods 1820–1920 and 1942–1953 and the reduction in 1920–1942. At each stage, there were very few significant regime changes against the dominant regime. The thirty years that followed 1950 until the early 1980s, however, were not characterized by a strong movement in either direction. Trends were mixed—so the numbers of democratic regimes seemed to expand from the 1950s to the early 1960s; from the 1960s to the 1970s; and then increase again, from 1970 to 1980.[23]

In general, changes in the State of democracy in the world was not very large. It was difficult to argue that the world was democratic in 1984 than it had been in 1954. The indicative of this relative stability was given by "Freedom House's".[24] According to this organization, as of January 1973, 32% of the world's population was living in States considered free. In that year, the percentage increased to 36%. Over the next 10 years, this percentage did not change, ranging from 37 to 35%. In January 1984, it was 36%, exactly as it had been 10 years ago.

The general stability of the extension of democracy has brought important development in both directions. Any future estimate must find its roots in explaining why these mixed tendencies prevailed between 1950 and 1980, and therefore the overall stability in the prevalence of democratic regimes in the world will continue. As a method, democracy is open to all possible contents, but it is also very demanding when asking for respect for institutions, precisely because they are supported by all the advantages of the technique—among them are the political parties as the only subjects allowed as a connection between individuals and the government.[25] This

[23] Samuel P. Huntington (2014).

[24] Freedom House'*s* is an independent surveillance organization dedicated to expanding the world's freedom. Founded in 1941, it was the first American organization to defend the advancement of freedom in the world against major threats to democracy and the defense of citizens to exercise their fundamental rights. http://www.freedomhouse.org.

[25] Norberto Bobbio (1986).

concept has been progressively extended, given that it was not sufficient to promote progress.

Based on this perspective, there is a difficulty in knowing how new institutions and practices can be strengthened or consolidated, so that they will stand the test of time, political conflict and crisis.[26]

The discussion of power in the post-war globalized world is centered on the forms of resistance exercise,[27] political emancipation and the subject, their definition and the forms of power of this citizen.[28] In times of bureaucratization, unbridled corporatism and assemblage, nothing more complex than enforcing the rules of the game.[29]

The concept of a "liberal democracy" seemed to triumph in the Western world—England, United States, France[30]—enshrined in the idea of freedom and equality recognized by the Declaration of American Independence of 1776 and the Declaration of Human Rights and Citizenship proclaimed in France in 1789: "men are born and remain free and equal in rights."

The existence of regimes called "liberal democratic" or "liberal democracy" leads us to believe that liberalism and democracy are interdependent.[31] In the first case, it is understood a certain conception of State, where it has limited powers and functions; in the second, we mean various forms of government, particularly those in which power is not in the hands of one or a few, but of all.

As Hobhouse[32] reported, the first condition of free government is not made by arbitrary determination but consolidated by rules of law that will lead to the subjection of the ruler. Both observations echo what was said by Locke[33]—the natural freedom of man is nothing more than not subject to any terrain and not subject to the will or legislative authority of man other than that established by the consent of the community. Liberalism asserts that freedom from the attacks of people and tyrannical caprices cannot exist without the rule of law.[34]

There is a view[35] that this theory is also based on the following postulates: politics is a means for the pursuit of ends, these being rooted in a sphere of social freedom pre-existent to politics itself; the democratic process serves to place the State at the service of society, which will become an administrative apparatus, structuring itself as an economic system based on trade between private persons; the policy must be

---

[26] Robert A. Dahl (2001a, 2001b).

[27] The Constitution of East Timor, for example, States in its Article 11 the valorization of resistance as a recognition against foreign domination and the contribution of all who fought for national independence.

[28] Gabriel Méndez Hincapie, Ricardo Sanín Restrepo (2012).

[29] Norberto Bobbio (1986).

[30] Simone Goyard-Fabre (2003).

[31] Norberto Bobbio (2000).

[32] Leonard T. Hobhouse (1964).

[33] John Locke (2010).

[34] Brian Z. Tamanaha (2008).

[35] J.J. Canotilho (2003).

geared towards pursuing these interests before an administration that has become a specialized power for collective purposes.

Also considered a conception that establishes limits to the regime with respect to its powers as well as its functions, translated in the idea of "Minimum State".[36] In the Rule of Law, there is the subordination of public powers of any degree to the general laws of the country, constituting a purely formal limit. But there is also the subjection of laws to material sources, recognizing some fundamental rights guaranteed by the constitution and therefore inviolable.

In a strong sense, which is proper to the liberal doctrine, are integral parts of the constitutional mechanisms that prevent or hinder the arbitrary and illegitimate exercise of power. Its control by autonomous and independent specialized arms (legislative, executive and judiciary) is born with a strong ethical load, with the criticism of paternalism, having its main reason to be in defense of the autonomy of the human person.

Participation within political power is resolved through many individual freedoms, claimed and won by citizens. It can also be understood as a manifestation of that freedom that achieves the right to meet or to associate to influence the politics of the country itself.[37]

The development of representative regimes is gaining strength, where, from these ideas, the limited powers of the State can appear in two directions: gradual extension of the right to vote, which was initially restricted to a part of the citizens, based on well-founded criteria on the census, the culture, the sex, extending from a gradual evolution for all; and in the multiplication of representative organs, these composed of elected members.[38]

This process is part of the structure of the State as guarantee, consisting of a more quantitative rather than qualitative transformation of the representative regime. This does not mean that it falls within the proper line of democracy in upholding individual freedoms and setting limits for public powers, I consider that equality of rights—which would logically imply universal suffrage—sometimes finds its property as a guarantor.[39]

Throughout the XIX century, the debate around democracy was developing mainly through a confrontation between the dominant political doctrines at the time: liberalism and socialism.[40] This is perceived by the insurmountable contradiction between freedom and equality, which ends up explaining the basis of a belief in social progress that seeks to seal a close alliance between doctrines.[41] It was the upward socialization that brought to the constitutional height, during the second half of the XX century, the fundamental rights of the second dimension. In fact, the whole process of the open society, consecrating the participatory society, becomes unfeasible and doomed

---

[36] Norberto Bobbio (2000).

[37] DEMOCRACY AND SOCIALISM (1998).

[38] DEMOCRACY AND SOCIALISM (1998).

[39] Simone Goyard-Fabre (2003).

[40] DEMOCRACY AND LIBERALISM (1998).

[41] Simone Goyard-Fabre (2003).

to failure if there is no consequence, the advent of institutional frameworks propitiating a system that incorporates in its bases the principles of justice that are inborn to that State modality.[42] These principles are objectively developed to concretize the declaratory discourse of fundamental rights. And, according to Bonavides,[43] there will only be functioning if there is a tarrying in political institutions alongside participatory democracy, which is, in theory and in practice, the executing agency.

There is not much difference in the relationship between democracy and socialism, whose democratic ideal is an integral and necessary element, but it is not constitutive.[44] Integral, because there is a strengthening of the popular base in the State and necessary, because without this effort there would be no possibility of reaching that deep transformation of society from the perspective of the Socialists.

The egalitarian principle that dominated political life had the consequence of the emergence of social rights. The Social State has its foundations structured in the crisis of the Liberal State, whose standards were not adapted to the collective needs, at a moment when it was admitted that the absenteeism of the State entity needed to be overcome, expanding its action in the social relations and economic spheres.[45]

This process of change from the Liberal to the Social State happens in different ways: through the critique of democracy only representative; the consequent resumption of some themes of direct democracy; and of the demand for popular participation and control of power that, from below, should extend to political decision-making bodies. The change came from political demonstrations and protests throughout Europe by the excluded,[46] in response to social and economic inequality and other reflexes of the Liberal State.[47]

Since then, the notion of opposition between the State and man has been questioned as a subject of rights, whose rights should be fulfilled through State action, responsible for protecting and guaranteeing economic and social well-being.

Some of the distinctive features of this new form of State with respect to the representative regime: the State must be not a parliamentary body, but of work, executive and legislative, at the same time; the electoral system must be extended to all parts of the State apparatus, such as the army, judiciary and bureaucracy; the commune is composed of municipal councilors elected and revocable at any time; the decentralization of their own functions, as in the "rural communes", which would have sent their representatives to a national assembly.[48]

In this way, the new type of empowerment must take place in the very places of production and is exercised not by the abstract citizen of "formal democracy" but by the working citizen through the "factory councils." These bodies will expand in all sectors of society where there are important decisions to make. It would be the

[42] Paulo Bonavides (2009).

[43] Paulo Bonavides (2009).

[44] DEMOCRACY AND SOCIALISM (1998).

[45] Carina Barbosa Gouvêa (2015).

[46] Rogério Gesta Leal (2000).

[47] Vicente de Paulo Barretto (2010).

[48] DEMOCRACY AND SOCIALISM (1998).

State system a federation of unified councils, through ascending regroupings, to the various territorial and administrative levels of the State.[49]

Considering the lessons learned and the way in which opposing theories postulate about fundamental values, it can be understood that liberal and socialist doctrines do not consider democracy incompatible with their own principles—on the contrary, they even understand it as an important part of his peculiar belief.

There would be no reason, therefore, to disregard democratic liberalism and democratic socialism.[50] A theory initially hostile to democracy, like the elitist, has been reconciled with it since a method or set of procedural rules for the constitution of government and an ideology.

Democracy will be compatible with theories of diverse ideological foundations and contents. The characteristics ended up allowing an orientation to certain values, such as the peaceful resolution of social conflicts, the elimination of institutional violence, the relay of the political class, tolerance,[51] among others.

Among the associations of the republican tradition,[52] there is a similarity that goes beyond the mere formal concept in the distinctions: in liberalism, there is a marked presence of the limitation of State power that, for its operationalization, requires an administrative apparatus that becomes specialized power for purposes social issues; in socialism, understanding of the democratic process passes through popular control with decentralization of power. In the end, the essence of the concept of democracy would be to consider not only the element that is the agent—actors of the decision, but also the mechanisms that allow it to be formed.

2.3 The Need to Conform the Constitutional Sign: The Roads of Representation, Deliberation and Participation

Adopting the concept of Bobbio,[53] it can be understood that democracy, from its historical conception, had two dominant meanings: the set of rules whose observance is necessary for political power to be distributed among most citizens, as well as called "rules of the game"; and how democratic government should be influenced by equality, that is, the constriction of power.

---

[49] DEMOCRACY AND SOCIALISM (1998).

[50] FORMAL MEANING OF DEMOCRACY (1998).

[51] FORMAL MEANING OF DEMOCRACY (1998).

[52] For Sellers, it was the study of the ancient republican tradition that brought contemporary theories to constitutional government. And in this conception, he assured that for the advance of any science it is necessary to understand the reason and the reality that it affects. First one thinks of the purpose of government - justice and common good; then in the method - laws; then on the technique to ensure success - control and balance conceived on the constitutional architecture. (Mortimer N.S. Sellers, Niccolò Machiavelli (2015).

[53] Norberto Bobbio (2000).

In contemporary political theory, with the prevalence of a liberal-democratic tradition, the characteristics of institutional design tend to be resolved and depleted in a more or less broad cast, such as: (1) the highest political body is played by the legislative function and should be composed of members directly or indirectly elected by the people, in periodic elections; (2) with the legislative body, there should be other institutions with elected officials, such as local government bodies or the head of State; (3) wide openness to citizens to exercise political rights, as long as they reach the age of majority; (4) voters have equal votes; freedom for the choice of their leaders, according to their own opinion, in a free contest of political parties that fight for the formation of a national representation; (5) any single or blocked list election is excluded as democratic; (6) is the principle of numerical majority, and several forms of majority can be established according to criteria of opportunities not defined once and for all; (7) no decision taken by the majority should limit the rights of the minority, especially the right to become a minority on parity of conditions; (8) government body should enjoy the confidence of the parliament or the head of the executive branch, in turn, elected by the people.[54]

It is observed that the procedures demonstrate how to arrive at the decisions and not "what to decide". Democratic legal science considers the essential precepts of legal individualism to be acquired, but agrees that, once these values are reserved, it is necessary that the law endeavors to place the social in its cogitations.[55] In this way, the set of these rules, by itself, is not able to find all the answers to all the questions that are formulated in the social reality. It is also not possible to define what criteria should be followed for a regime to be considered "democratic". What is certainly possible to affirm is that a form that does not observe any rule cannot be considered democratic, at least until the behavioral meaning of democratic has been defined, in Bobbio's words.[56]

The separation of powers is a technique in decline subject to gradual overcoming, Bonavides[57] warned us, which must be imposed by new requirements of balance and accommodation to constitutional schemes whose thinking is no longer based on preponderant reasons of formalism in the protection of rights, according to with the classical content of its initial elaboration and the primary purpose of the old liberalism.

Another meaning that comprises forms of political regime is one that ascribes a formal and substantial qualifier. The first is characterized by the so-called "universal behaviors," using which diverse decisions can be made, as shown by liberal and democratic regimes, alongside social and democratic ones. The second, because it refers predominantly to certain content inspired by ideals characteristic of the tradition of democratic thought with great emphasis on egalitarianism.

Thus, formal democracy is constructed as the government of the people, and substantial democracy as a government for the people, which is aligned with the

---

[54] SOME TYPOLOGIES OF DEMOCRATIC REGIMES (1998).

[55] Paulo Bonavides (2009).

[56] SOME TYPOLOGIES OF DEMOCRATIC REGIMES (1998).

[57] Paulo Bonavides (2009).

prospects of constriction of power. The concept of "equality" can then be considered as a specific and historically determined form of legal conformity, such as access by all to ordinary jurisdiction. And it applies in rights when it covers all those fundamental sayings, considering the rights that should be enjoyed by all without discrimination. This cast is modified from time to time, from people to people and, therefore, there is no determinability in its fixation.

For men, equality calls for a single, uniform and strong government. This is the government to which nations tend in our day, but individual independence and local freedoms will always be a product of art.[58]

There is differentiation in the process of construction at the beginning of a great democratic revolution or when war between different classes only arises. In the first, the people are strengthened to centralize power and public administration in the hands of the government, to decentralize the power of the "aristocracy." At the end of this revolution, it will be this class, defeated that tries to give the direction to the State, of all the businesses, because it fears the "small tyranny" of the town, that has become its pair and, often, its master.

Representation is one of the parameters considered essential to democracy, today, according to the idea that the rulers receive their mandate from the governed and must act in their place.[59] It reaches its complexity due to the diverse techniques for its development, which have obeyed, in the history of political ideas, two logics that are important to distinguish: imperative and representative mandates.

It is the first of the model recognized by the feudal right—the "imperative mandate"—where the representative or the elected would be the "mouth of the represented", being forced by instructions, without being able to move away from them and getting to perform the act which the client ordered him to execute.

Recognizing the artificialism present in this mandate, since there is no possibility of ascertaining what the will of the represented is, in modern times, the idea of "representation" has been coined according to a logic different from the "imperative mandate"—which does not reflect necessarily a maturation of the notion of democracy as a socio-political ideal.

By the representative route, the rulers occupy a position distinct from the governed, and in this sense the people do not deliberate by itself. However, as elections are repeated, the nation has an effective means of exercising some influence over rulers.

It is a collective delegation granted by the people to the group that will represent them. In this idea, there is an affinity of values between a certain social segment and the respective representatives. The elected is the representative from the point of view of the value inclusion of the one who elected him.

This principle is based on the following postulates, according to Canotilho[60]: constitutionally authorized legal exercise of "domain functions", made in the name of the collectivity, by organs of State sovereignty; direct or indirect derivation of the

[58] Alexis de Tocqueville (2000).

[59] Simone Goyard-Fabre (2003).

[60] J.J. Gomes Canotilho (2003).

legitimacy of domination of the principle of popular sovereignty; exercise of power to pursue the ends or interest of the community.

It reaches its foundation in popular correspondence, but it can also be considered a "substitution of the sovereignty of the people", which eliminates its critical, political and exclusive character and imposes a legal subject with limited political rights, among them the vote, densely controlled by the constitution and bylaws.[61] Generally, collective deliberations are taken by those who are part of it—people elected for this purpose.

This juridical turn is the exponential identification of "democracy in liberalism", that is, a progressive tendency capable of changing the political discussions to the constitutional limits that must be natural for this ideal.

The nature of government cannot be understood without reference to its temporality according to Manin.[62] The author believes that leaders, besides being distinct individuals that occupy a differentiated position, also maintain in their decisions a certain independence before the will of the governed ones. They do not represent a regime that strictly enforces their wishes, as the indirect form of government by all.

Deliberative autonomy is not absolute, and there is ample freedom of initiative. Obviously, decisions must be taken in such a way as not to lead to a rejection of voters at the end of the term. But they can, for example, on their own initiative and against the will of their representatives, adopt a policy that, once implemented, will not provoke disapproval. The constitutional provision of this government confers an influence on the course of politics and gives citizens a retrospective judgment of the rulers' actions.

On the other hand, the idea of deliberative democracy is linked above all to the school of "liberal republicanism," which starts with the republican ideal of the self of government—people govern themselves through political action and the laws that they themselves give to themselves.[63]

A deliberative democratic system, for Madison,[64] would be intended to apply equally to ordinary and constitutional policy of control, whose general contours, once properly understood, seem potentially relevant today as they were before. Politics and society have changed, and the "people" have expanded to include new "men" in the context of the modern State.

Madison[65] began to find an answer to reach a way to choose representatives able to govern without succumbing to the corrupting influence of specific groups by the insularity and desire for popularity or power.

The result: a deliberative democracy in which elections are structured to sift through an elite that can choose in our favor, free of irrationality and self-interest, realizing popular politics without persecution.

---

[61] Gabriel Méndez Hicapíe, Ricardo Sanín Restrepo (2012).

[62] Bernarb Manin (1995).

[63] J.J. Canotilho Gomes (2003).

[64] James Madison (1998).

[65] James Madison (1998).

This does not mean that in politics doing the best for the people means transferring responsibility to a group represented, moving as far as possible from popular control and influence. This is a misrepresentation of Madison's will, who was above all a committed Republican who believed in popular government and that people should control government and laws all the time.

In synthetic terms, the theoretical premises return to the following: deliberative politics is structured in the idea of "civic virtue"; equality of participants in the political process; possibility of universal consent in normative disputes through practical reason; citizens' right to participate in public life and control of representatives.[66]

It presupposes a dialogic conception of politics and its consideration as a rational process of discussing problems and alternatives to obtain fair or at least reasonable solutions to the ordering of community life and not only to provide procedural openness to the pursuit of private interests or the optimization of subjective preferences. There is no indication of the mode or place to be considered where the discussion should take its place in government. Should it be present at all stages of the decision or only in some? This is one of the questions put forward by Manin,[67] where criticism is opposed to the simple doctrinal definition.

It ends up hiding the fact that, in this form of government, the power to deliberate fulfills a specific function that is not to produce the decision, nor necessarily to construct the propositions of these, if not to produce, alone, the consent in a situation in which no will has the right to impose itself on the others. The so-called "consensus", before being the reasonable virtue of individuals and groups who agree to discuss their problems and compose their interests, is a determined regime of the sensitive, a particular way of visibility of law and its identity.[68]

As the proposals do not necessarily have their origin in the instance under discussion, no proposition is adopted if it has not been submitted to a judgment in the field under discussion. The positive characteristic lies in the central role played by the judgment of the collectivity, as in the elective process of designating the representatives. The mass of the people occupies the position of judge or a jury, arbitrating between different individuals. Therefore, it is not a regime in which the collectivity self-governs, if not a system in which everything that corresponds to the government is submitted to the collective court.

The centrality of democracy is characterized by the existence of a mass that has sovereignty over everything in its power.[69] This need not necessarily be connected to representative political power or the State; it is observed that this is an immanent tendency of political life combined in the social sphere. It represents an ethical and political space that does not depend for its existence on any reference to a legislative dimension, being, according to Hincapie and Restrepo,[70] "a space where relations and

[66] J.J. Canotilho Gomes (2003).

[67] Bernarb Manin (1995).

[68] Jacques Rancière (1996).

[69] Gabriel Méndez Hincapie, Ricardo Sanín Restrepo (2012).

[70] Gabriel Méndez Hincapie, Ricardo Sanín Restrepo (2012).

meetings are manifested without the need to evoke an external source of legitimation or meaning the plan overlaps itself with the organization's plan".

As Rancière[71] explains, in democracy the subject defines himself, from his central place in political activity. Not only is it a break from the logic of absolute separation between rulers and governed, but the rupture of the idea that all kinds of power distribution means a preexisting model.

There is no better remedy against the abuse of power in any form than the direct or indirect participation of citizens, the greater number of constitutional persons, in the formation of laws. Liberal ideals and democratic methods have gradually come together. The development of democracy has become and is the main instrument for the defense, be it of the rights of liberties, or those born of revolutions.[72] In this logic, the citizen and society hold legitimate expectations in the sense that the State must offer concrete benefits that guarantee the quality of life, both now and for the future.[73]

Thus, the insertion of pluralism of political or cultural ideas does not mean denying the existence of the State or renouncing the goal of equilibrium. Nascimento[74] presents the concept of formulating a constitutional theory that legitimizes and recognizes the existence of diverse groups of interests, integrated in the conception of the political phenomenon and with nexuses that interconnect individuals to the State, without implicating in the disappearance or disintegration between State and society, which follow influencing each other, reciprocally. A State in which people are individually part. Opens the way to the conception of participatory democracy.

In this conception, the whole will be constructed by constitutional persons endowed with legitimacy before the perception of the content of a democratic constitution, it is a matter of "organizing the State so that it can represent a guarantee against the abuse of its own power and, at the same time, caution against diverging social forces".[75]

Relations built in the public arena that consider the plurality of interests represented will contribute to the formation of a truly emancipated society, responsible and promoter of rights and guarantees, as well as determine and control public action, including the action of the judiciary power[76] itself.

Thus, understood as the new theory of emancipation, presented by Souza Santos,[77] revalues the principle of community, society-providence (citizens and constitutional persons), not dismissing the obligations imposed on the State by the constitutional charter, but opening the field to a responsible participation of those inserted in the territory, knowing that the sovereignty and actions of the State are not absolute, but relative and popular.

---

[71] Jacques Rancière (2001).

[72] Norberto Bobbio (2000).

[73] Carina B. Gouvêa, Alfredo Canellas G. da Silva (2014).

[74] Rogério Bento do Nascimento (2012).

[75] Rogério Bento do Nascimento (2012).

[76] José Adércio Leite Sampaio (2010).

[77] Boaventura Souza Santos (2010).

In these redefining foundations, what is sought is a rational constitution of the will clearly recognized insofar as the organized formation of society, which generates responsible decisions within the State organs, remains permeable in the face of the values, themes and arguments that hatch in the political communication of its surroundings, which, as such and, cannot be only institutional.[78]

Hence, other political actors are recognized who bring significant expressions of popular wills, such as non-governmental organizations, civil associations, non-institutionalized social movements, volunteers that can alter the social reality of care delivery, assigning to these subjects rights to participation and direct competition in the deliberation process, as well as in its solutions. For all, a new model of constitutionalism is needed that legitimates social action, embodied in democratic practice that reflects communicative interlocution.

Thus, the theory of justice as fairness, idealized by Rawls,[79] has taken place, since contemporary societies are multicultural and must allow the coexistence of very diverse groups. The main economic, social and political institutions will be a unified system of cooperation. In this way, it validates the diversity and plurality of conceptions for the construction of a democracy that must be shaped by contestation, persuasion and the formation of the new consensus.

This stems from the fact that it is the product of the meanings that encompass democracy that are both political values and reflexes of power struggles—dynamic and, above all, constructed by political and social actors daily.[80] For Palamo,[81] one of these constitutive elements encompasses the collective practice that comes to be called "political culture", which corresponds to a symbolic code that defines the range of possible alternatives to choose the course of action. Hence, its concept in a particular historical and political context must also be understood as a reflection of the conflicts that occur in society both within and outside the strictly institutional.

This perspective reconstructs the dynamics of transformation for the challenges facing a regime that will be defined as democratic.

The criteria to which a democratic process would have to correspond to satisfy the requirement that all members be equally able to participate in decisions, according to Dahl,[82] would be:

(a) effective participation—before a policy is chosen by the association, all members should have equal and effective opportunities to get other members to know their opinions about what this policy should be;
(b) equality of vote—in decision making, everyone should have equal and effective voting opportunities, and everyone should be counted as equal;
(c) clear understanding—within reasonable time limits, each member should have an equal and effective opportunity to learn about important alternative policies and their likely consequences;

---

[78] Rogério Gesta Leal (2009).

[79] John Rawls (2002).

[80] Damiano Palano (2015).

[81] Damiano Palano (2015).

[82] Robert A. Dahl (2001a, 2001b).

(d) control of the planning program—members should have the opportunity to decide how and what issues should be put into planning. Thus, the process required by the previous criteria is never closed;
(e) Inclusion of adults—all, however, resident and permanent, should have the full right implicit in the first criterion.

The old formulas, in times of revaluation of democratic essences, deserve a remodeling so that it can be attributed to the different realities.

2.4 A Critical Analysis: Democracy as a Living Organization that Represents Decentralization of Power and Development

Democratic regimes are fraught with social conflicts. Since the governing role is to resolve disagreement to make it possible to coexist between individuals and groups, which have different interests, the more conflicts increase, the greater the difficulty in mastering them.[83]

For Bobbio,[84] in a pluralistic society, such as the one in which a democratic system lives and flourishes, where the class struggle is multiplied by a myriad of smaller corporate disputes, the opposing interests are almost infinite, and it is not possible to satisfy one without offend the other.

On the reasons for the emergence of democratic regimes, there are two focuses: an approach focused on the preconditions of society for development, such as economic health and equality, social structure, external environment and cultural context; and the other focus, on the nature of the political processes by which development has taken place.[85]

The political reality is multiple; men are different and complementary to each other, so in its naturalness, this reality is always plural, diversified and even composite because of the heterogeneity of the elements that make it up.[86] The aspiration is for the gradual renewal of society through the free debate of ideas and the change of mentalities and way of life: this is a permission granted only to democracy, as it allows the expansion of the silent revolutions, as observed in the last decades, the transformation of relations between sexes.[87]

Society is a system of four subsystems, according to Comparato,[88] which includes participatory, which determines who is or is not a member and under what conditions; the cultural, which regulates symbols and beliefs; the economic, which determines

[83] Norberto Bobbio (2000).

[84] Norberto Bobbio (2000).

[85] Samuel P. Huntington (1984).

[86] Simone Goyard-Fabre (2003).

[87] Norberto Bobbio (1986).

[88] Fábio Comparato et al. (1985).

the mode of production, and; the political one, that regulates, by commands, the collective activities. For the author, one of the reports of the principle of congruence is the existence of relations of conformity between the degree of observable democracy in civil society and in the political system. This results from effective practices in the relationship of people in occupational relationships.

The political system results from norms and practices that regulate popular participation, the form of verification and exercise of power and authority, in addition to the sense that they are applied, both in general terms and the interests of classes and policies in progress. The rates of democracies of civil society and the political system show significant differences.

This pluralism allows us to understand the freedom of dissent. For Bobbio,[89] this, since it is kept within certain limits defined by the "rules of the game", is not an annihilator of society, but a facilitator. Where the contest is not admitted, there is a society that is dead or destined to die.

Rethinking democracy in the molds forged, controlling power by its own power, the idea of popular sovereignty and representativeness, justifies a purely theoretical doctrine for the government.

The representative was designed only for the action of the political framework in the State; already deliberative must be participatory and this participation must influence both the State coordination and the performance of private agents, companies, non-governmental organizations, social movements, whose interests and performance the State coordinates.

The advent of differences is not the obstacle to be always overcome in the enlargement of the active people, but it is also constitutive for the renewal and continuation of the democratic process.[90]

A constitution that is forged to give vent to the wills of the center of the political space must be open from the medium understanding of its dispositions, so that this community can interact with the constituted powers and achieve the protection of their rights, the inclusion of their identities and his own defense. There is a range of principles, guarantees and rights in the literature that make it difficult for individuals and groups to understand their content. The process of democratization cannot be taken for granted,[91] it is a dynamic process that undergoes.

There are many problems to be solved, such as that of the "non-politicized" constitutional person, "where the only way to make a subject become a citizen is to attribute to him those rights that the writers of public law of the last century had called *activae civitatis*".[92] Education for citizenship would arise in the very body of democratic practice. It is an endless process, which never comes to a term, can never be a total politicization.[93]

[89] Norberto Bobbio (1986).

[90] Friedrich Müller (2011).

[91] Norberto Bobbio (1986).

[92] Norberto Bobbio (1986).

[93] Friedrich Müller (2011).

The systematization of ideas that will be presented in the later chapters represents attempts to improve the democratic principle in the regime that is intended to be democratic, reshaping and adjusting its value.[94]

If constitutions build the political body of the State, there is an urgent need to address the constitutional role of democratic politics to see, for example, that it is not the separation of powers, but rather the alternation between them that strengthens the best defense of rights.[95]

In addition, the so-called "distributive democracy", by Souza Santos,[96] makes sense because democratic forces will have to focus their struggles for a democratic fight that will be organized through the democratization of coordination tasks.

To admit the value and contribution that society and institutions can offer to the debate of the constitutional sense is "a phenomenon that lies in an indisputable upward line," as Valle[97] has said. This phenomenon, for the author, seems to show a perception that the path to the consolidation of the Democratic State, since its representative dimension, involves employment in the participatory facet of public choices, "stage of development of society that will involve still plenty of inductive activity ".

It seeks to improve the reflection around the construction of a channel of dialogic and participative communication through the institutional spheres. To increase the possibilities, that is, the range of agents that can contribute to the elucidation of the constitutional sign, which is alive and in constant transformation—this is a step towards adopting the open society of interpreters, a logic that the constitution can present as a true social construct and not only a technical document to be unveiled in its sense by holders of a particular expertise.

The constitutional interpretation depends on a process of political discussion that must recognize in its nucleus, in a way not unique but indispensable for the claims and convictions of citizenship "standing up" to externalize their positions on the matter.[98]

The joint existence of diversified tendencies in the same society is part of the essence of democracy, so that the institutional design of the arms of organized political power still predominantly reflects the logic of the supremacy of the majority represented by "low vocalization in favor of political minorities; of non-response as a legitimate mechanism of power; of the disqualification of the desire of the minority".[99]

---

[94] The way constitutional democracy was conceived, whether in classical and legal constitutionalism, ends up providing its meaning as a "higher law" maintained by the Constitutional Courts. (Richard Bellamy 2006a, 2006b). What invites us to reflect on the remembrance of democratic processes.

[95] Richard Bellamy (2006a, 2006b).

[96] Boaventura Souza Santos (2002).

[97] Vanice Regina Lírio do Valle (2013).

[98] Roberto Gargarella (2011).

[99] Vanice Regina Lírio do Valle (2013).

How to promote social and democratizing transformations? The constitutional system is a process that needs to somehow allow the expansion of the horizons of a society that wants to be more democratic and reinforce its practical commitments to individual autonomy and collective self-government.[100]

It informs us that the air of time proposes a response to this paradox, since democratic wisdom would not be centered so much on scrupulous attention to the representative institutions that guarantee the power of the people, but on the adequacy of the forms of exercising the politician to the way of being a society, the forces that move it, interests and the crisscross needs that forge it.[101]

In addition, historical achievements of the human trajectory, which have been deeply debated, especially in scenarios that are not in complete harmony with the daily life of the different actors, since material inequality and pluralism show the fragilities of the old formulas policies.[102] For Valle,[103] this "paradox brings to the center of the debate the challenge of a new stage to conquer; the formulation of a potentially agglutinating idea of human capacity "to wish to be in an environment that would allow them to mobilize.

As an object of many constitutions, democracy aims at sustaining substantial preconditions and formal policy structures that are based on a universal principle of equal participation, including by the United Nations. For the UN, among its nuclei, it can be highlighted: it is unlimited; does not have a single source of interpretation; the constitution serves as a skillful means for its materialization—formal and substantial; is a guarantee of human rights and justice; promotes development. For Gargarella,[104] it is essential to think about the relationship between democracy and constitution. The distinction between dogmatic that embraces the rights and organic that involves the "machinery of power" reflects the main tension that exists in any constitution.

According to the author,[105] the constitutions were forged with two souls. One looks at the rights part and another at the relation to the organization of power. These two parts were not designed to perfectly articulate with one another, were built to function autonomously.

Since democracy does not constitute rhetoric and needs promotion, therefore, it is not enough to simply enunciate its name to denominate a democratic environment. Being a hybrid, it is both an end and a middle. The end is because it will accommodate the main foundations of an equal and participative society and a middle because it will require a variation of interpreters and mechanisms for its realization and promotion of human development.

The UN has impregnated with senses "new democracies" and this comes from the fact that its merits are able to enrich the political life of the nation. But this is not a mechanical condition and may end up representing a setback.

[100] Lucas Arrimada (2011).

[101] Jacques Rancière (1996).

[102] Vanice Regina Lírio Valle (2011).

[103] Vanice Regina Lírio Valle (2011).

[104] Roberto Gargarella (2015).

[105] Roberto Gargarella (2015).

If end and middle, at the same time, need to have a connection between the law and the formal structures of power, we may think here in a cooperative democracy. What would be an alternative to address issues of common interests.

The forms of constitutionalism that have been presented frame a framework in which the re-discussion of the "old democracy" can expand, which has not shown itself enough to guarantee the legitimacy, the fundamentality and the effectiveness of the rights then enshrined, by acting of these formal instances of representation.

Exploring the potential advances proposed by these challenges allows us to move towards meeting new categories of constitutionalism to build an enabling environment for cooperative democracy.

References

Alexis de Tocqueville. (2000). A democracia na América: sentimentos e opiniões: de uma profusão de sentimentos e opiniões que o Estado social democrático fez nascer entre os americanos, pp 366–369 (Martins Fontes).

Amartya Sen. (1999). Democracy as a universal value. *Journal of Democracy, 3–17* (May 04th 2013). Retrieved from http://www.unicef.org/socialpolicy/files/Democracy_as_a_Universal_Value.pdf.

Benjamin Constant. (1985). Of the freedom of the ancients compared to that of the moderns. *Revista de Filosofia Política, 1* (Apr. 16th, 2014). Retrieved from http://caosmose.net/candido/unisinos/textos/benjamin.pdf.

Bernardo Fernandes Gonçalves. (2011). Curso de Direito Constitucional, 209 (3rd ed. Lumen Juris).

Bernarb Manin. (1995). La democracia de los modernos: los principios del gobierno representativo. *Revista Sociedad da Facultad de Ciencias Sociais (UBA), 1–20* (Jan. 03rd, 2014). Retrieved from http://fadeweb.uncoma.edu.ar/carreras/materiasenelweb/abogacia/derecho_politico_II/biblio/unidad3/Manin%20Principios%20del%20gobierno%20representativo.pdf.

Boaventura Souza Santos. (2010). Pela mão de Alice: o social e o político na pós-modernidade, 256 (13th ed. Cortez).

Boutros Boutros-Ghali. (1996). An agend for democratization. UN: NY, pp. 4–6.

Boaventura Souza Santos. (2002). Reinventar a democracia, pp. 60–61 (2nd ed. Gradiva).

Brian Z. Tamanaha. (2008, January). The dark side of the relationship between the rule of law of land and liberalism. Saint John's Legal Studies Research, Paper n. 08–0096 1–37 (May. 14th, 2013). Retrieved from http://ssrn.com/abstract=108702.

Canotilho Gomes, J. J. (2003). Direito Constitucional e Teoria da Constituição, p. 1416 (7th ed. Coimbra: Edições Almedina).

Canotilho, J. J. (2003). Direito Constitucional e Teoria da Constituição, pp. 99 (7th ed. Coimbra).

Carina B. Gouvêa, Alfredo Canellas G. da Silva. (2014). Building elements of the effectiveness of deliberative democracy in a nation of constitutional persons. CONPEDI; Uninove. (Org.). *Direitos fundamentais e democracia II. Florianópolis*/SC: FUNJAB, pp. 156–178.

Carina Barbosa Gouvêa. (2015). O direito fundamental à saúde, um olhar para além do reconhecimento: building on the effectiveness that operates in favor of democracy and institutional design, p. 33 (Gomes & Oliveira).

Damiano Palano. (2015, August). La democrazia dei pochi l'eredità dell'anti-elitismo e le sfide alla teoria democratica. Quaderni di Scienza Politica, pp. 174–234 (Apr. 15th, 2015). Retrieved from https://www.academia.edu/12410163/La_democrazia_dei_pochi_L_eredità_dell_anti elitismo_e_le_sfide_alla_teoria_democratica_in_Quaderni_di_Scienza_politica_2015_n._2_pp._173-234.

Democracy and liberalism. (1998). In: Vol. 1, Norberto Bobbio, Nicola Matteucci, Gianfranco Pasquino. Dicionário de Política, p. 323 (11th ed. Universidade de Brasilia).
Democracy and socialism. (1998a). In: Vol. 1, Norberto Bobbio, Nicola Matteucci, Gianfranco Pasquino. Dicionário de Política, p. 324 (11th ed. Universidade de Brasilia).
Democracy in: Vicente de Paulo Barretto. (2009). Dicionário de Filosofia do Direito, p. 190 (Renovar).
Fábio Konder Comparato. (1989). Para viver a democracia, p. 70 (Brasiliense).
Fábio Comparato et al. (1985). Brasil, sociedade democrática, p. 114 (José Olympio).
Formal meaning of democracy. (1998b). In: Vol. 1, Norberto Bobbio, Nicola Matteucci, Gianfranco Pasquino. Dicionário de Política, p. 326 (11th ed. Universidade de Brasilia).
Friedrich Müller. (2011). Quem é o povo? A questão fundamental da democracia, p. 38 (6th ed. Revista dos Tribunais).
Gabriel Méndez Hicapíe, Ricardo Sanín Restrepo. (2012, July–December). La constitución encriptada: nuevas formas de emancipacíon del poder global. Revista de Derechos Humanos y Estudios Sociales, p. 107 (Sep. 20, 2013). Retrieved from http://www.uaslp.mx/Spanish/Academicas/FD/REDHES/Documents/Número%208/Redhes8-05.pdf.
Jacques Rancière. (1996). O desentendimento: política e filosofia, p. 101 (Editora 34).
Jacques Rancière. (2001). Ten theses on politics. Theory & Event, pp. 1–16 (Oct. 17th, 2013). Retrieved from http://www.after1968.org/app/webroot/uploads/RanciereTHESESONPOLITICS.pdf.
James A. Gardner. (2005). Democracy without a net? Separation of powers and ideia of self-sustaining constitutional constraints on undemocratic behaviour. Saint Jhon's Law Review, pp. 293–317 (Jun. 24th, 2013). Retrieved from http://ssrn.com/abstract=599982.
James Madison. (1998, 18, October). The Federalist n 10. Constitution Society (Oct. 01, 2013). Retrieved from http://www.constitution.org/fed/federa10.htm.
John Locke. (2010). Segundo tratado sobre o governo, p. 27 (Martin Claret).
John Rawls. (2002). Justiça e democracia, pp. 201–241 (Martins Fontes).
José Adércio Leite Sampaio. (2010). Direitos fundamentais (2nd ed. Del Rey).
Leonard T. Hobhouse. (1964). Liberalism (1911). Reprint. New York: Oxford University, p. 17.
Lucas Arrimada. (2011). La democracia como precondición del constitucionalismo: práticas democráticas y reforma constitucional. La constitución em 2020: 48 propuestas para una sociedad igualitaria, p. 236 (1st ed. Siglo Veintiuno Editores).
Mortimer N.S. Sellers. (2015, October). Niccolò Machiavelli: father of modern constitutionalism. University of Baltimore Legal Studies, pp. 1–11 (Oct. 21st, 2015). Retrieved from http://ssrn.com/abstract=2676078.
Norberto Bobbio. (2008). A era dos direitos, p. 191 (8th ed. Elsevier).
Norberto Bobbio. (1986). O futuro da democracia: uma defesa das regras do jogo (6th ed. Paz e Terra).
Norberto Bobbio. (2000). Liberalismo e democracia, p. 7 (6th ed. Brasiliense).
Paulo Bonavides. (2009). Do Estado liberal ao Estado social 10 (9th ed. Malheiros).
Peter Harris, Ben Reilly, Daniel Zovatto. (2001). Democracia constituição y conflictos profundamente arraigados: opciones para la negociación, p. vii (Estocolmo: International Institute for Democracy and Electoral Assistance).
Richard Bellamy. (2006a). Constitucionalism and democracy. Internacional Library of Essays in Law Theory Second Series, pp. 11–68 (Jun. 08th, 2013). Retrieved from http://papers.ssrn.com/sol3/papers.cfm?abstract_id=1571492.
Richard Bellamy. (2006b). Constitucionalism and democracy. Internacional Library of Essays in Law Theory Second Series, pp. 11–68 (Jun. 08th, 2013). http://papers.ssrn.com/sol3/papers.cfm?abstract_id=1571492). What invites us to reflect on the remembrance of democratic processes.
Robert A. Dahl. (2001a). Sobre a Democracia, p. 12 (Universidade de Brasília).
Robert A. Dahl. (2001b). Sobre a Democracia 13 (Universidade de Brasília, 2001b).

Roberto Gargarella. (2011). Democracia, representacíon y participacíon política. La constitución em 2020: 48 propuestas para una sociedad igualitaria, p. 231 (1st ed. Siglo Veintiuno Editores).
Roberto Gargarella. (2015). Qué són los derechos? Canal Justicia (Mar. 20th, 2015). Retrieved from https://youtu.be/-x3CzQbQgYU.
Rogério Gesta Leal. (2000). Perspectivas hermenêuticas dos direitos humanos e fundamentais no Brasil, p. 41 (Livraria do Advogado).
Rogério Bento do Nascimento. (2012). Repensando o conceito de responsabilidade nos marcos de um constitucionalismo democrático deliberativo. Matheus Vidal Gomes Motnteiro, Renan Aguiar, Ivan Simões Garcia. Estado, direito e democracia: perspectivas contemporâneas, pp. 349–350 (Lumen Juris).
Rogério Gesta Leal. (2009). Fundamentos Redefinitórios do Direito Fundamental de Participação Política no Brasil: movimentos sociais e administração pública. Temas sobre direitos humanos: em homenagem Professor Vicente de Paulo Barretto, p. 180 (Lumen Juris).
Samuel P. Huntington. (1984). Will more countries become democratic. Political Science Quarterly, pp. 193–218, (Apr. 16, 2014). Retrieved from http://www.chsbs.cmich.edu/fattah/courses/pols535/huntington.pdf.
Simone Goyard-Fabre. (2003). O que é democracia, p. 127 (Martins Fontes).
SOME TYPOLOGIES OF DEMOCRATIC REGIMES. (1998). In: Vol. 1, Norberto Bobbio, Nicola Matteucci, Gianfranco Pasquino. Dicionário de Política, pp. 327–328 (11th ed. Universidade de Brasilia).
Vanice Regina Lírio do Valle. (2013). Backlash à decisão do Supremo Tribunal Federal: pela naturalização do dissenso como possibilidade democrática. II Seminário Internacional de Teoria das Instituições (Oct. 25th, 2014). Retrieved from https://www.academia.edu/5159210/Backlash_%C3%A0_decis%C3%A3o_do_Supremo_Tribunal_Federal_pela_naturaliza%C3%A7%C3%A3o_do_dissenso_como_possibilidade_democr%C3%A1tica.
Vanice Regina Lírio Valle. (2011). Direito fundamental à boa administração e governança 22 (Fórum).
Vicente de Paulo Barretto. (2010). O Fetiche dos Direitos Humanos, p. 195 (Lumen Juris).
Vicki Jackson. (2006). Constitutions as "living trees"? Comparative constitutional law and interpretative metaphors. Fordham Law Review, p. 939.
Vicki Jackson. (2010). Paradigms of public law: transnational constitutional values and democratic challenges. *International Journal of Constitutional Law, 517–562.*

Chapter 3
Construction of an Environment that Maintains Democracy Through Democratic Constitutionalism

3.1 Constitution and Constitutionalism: Understanding Its Essence

Understanding the premise that the concept of democracy has shifted from the purely representative dimension to a broad understanding of the open process of formulating public choices and that needs to materialize in a particular model of constitutionalism that will be the method by which the ideal progressive and transformative.

In a broad conception, the term constitution, initially an empirical concept, went from the scope of nature to that of political-legal language to designate the situation of a country; the way it is constituted by characteristics of its territory and inhabitants; its historical evolution; the relations of power existing in it; its legal norm and its political institutions.[1] This period goes back to before the Modern era.

The attempt to limit the power of the state to the interests of the freedom of subjects has permeated the doctrine of natural law since the mid-eighteenth century.

From the perspective of legal positivism, the term "constitution" comes within the scope of the law, according to Valle,[2] borrowed from the social sciences, and with an essentially descriptive content, and can be identified as a document that formulates the structuring of power. Therefore, the concept is consolidated, as the "set of legal rules defining the relations of political power, the status of governors and governed".

This document, identified by Bonavides,[3] is defined by classical constitutionalism, since it is reduced to a legal instrument that gave jurisdiction to three fundamental organs of the State order, therefore, the divorce between society and the State is established, since its greater expression reflected the legal side of the commitment of power to freedom, with the State and with the individual.

---

[1] Grimm (2009).

[2] Valle (2013a).

[3] Bonavides (2009).

C. B. Gouvêa and P. H. V. B. Castelo Branco, *UN Interventions and Democratization*, Societies and Political Orders in Transition,
https://doi.org/10.1007/978-3-031-32715-5_3

With the advance of the modern constitutionalist movements, the constitution becomes a forum where the political identities are based on two assumptions: politics is a fundamentally collective activity, based on a network of socially constructed meanings, which is subject to your preferences, restrictions and instructions; Second, cultures incorporate social meanings from their political practices and this is a characteristic that distinguishes societies.[4]

It is possible to identify that the theoretical-abstract matrices formulated translate a singular State, with an institutionalized political system, organized functionally and structurally, that protects rights and provides the corresponding guarantees.[5]

In Sartori's view,[6] the constitution as a legitimizing sign affirms the importance of its goal for the matrices of English, American and European constitutionalism, and now, with the purpose of restricting the arbitrary exercise of power, thus guaranteeing a limited government, containing a set of fundamental principles and the structuring of institutional design.

Its content has expanded over time and various theories[7] about its meaning have been constituted. The conception of it becomes a sufficiently elastic concept to insert into its form divergent political, economic, and social contents and to project itself into characterized constitutional types.[8] As it always must be thought in the face of the political, economic, social and cultural reality that underlies it and which is a reality not only of facts, but also of opinions, political positions, civic and constitutional culture.[9]

A relative differentiation of domains requires consideration of the most precious human values and social welfare and individual freedom, depended on a limitation of the government's powers in defense of these rights. The right ceased to be a criterion of eternal validity to become a contingent product of political will.[10] Through the constitution, the legal subjection of power could be reconciled with the irreversible positivation of law. This recognition did not necessarily represent the representation of social reality.[11]

Not everything that presents itself as constitutional deserves to be it, and not everything presented as decreed as constitutional achieves it effectively, be it by inadequacy, imbalance, incapacity of integration, insurmountable contradiction with

---

[4] Vorländer (2012).

[5] Pulcinelli (2015).

[6] Sartori (1962a).

[7] The great doctrinal currents that crossed the XIX, XX and XXI centuries ended identify the constitution from its nature, significance and diverse characteristics and functions. We stand out the concepts naturalistic, positivist, historicist, sociological, Marxist, institutionalist, decisive, deriving from the philosophy of values, structuralisms (Miranda 2011).

[8] Miranda 2011.

[9] Miranda (2011).

[10] Grimm (2009).

[11] The most important condition of effective validity is its consensual basis. Without the general disposition of the political actors to comply with the mandate, without a support of the population, a model is deprived of power or prone to lose it in a crisis (Grimm 2009).

other norms, and so on. It is Miranda's[12] assertion that the new constitutions meet three primary requirements: the highest possible rigor in the precepts pertaining to the fundamental rights and freedoms of man, of the citizen, of the worker and of the groups in which they are inserted, a task of interpretation and regulation; the limits of its normative force, its integrating and inclusive function, the precepts of economic, social and cultural life, subject to the successive modes of concreteness inherent in the manifestations of the constitutionally organized political will; creation of legal and political mechanisms, and procedural guarantee of these norms.

From this point of view, there is a tension between the ideal notion of constitution, reflected through its content and legal and political mechanisms, followed by frailties, whether in terms of its effectiveness or the challenge to this attribute because of the passing of time on an institutional design that was coined at a particular point in the trajectory of a social body.[13]

According to Gargarella,[14] many constitutions, for example, are generous with the recognition of rights, since they have a broad list of economic, social, and multicultural rights and this is related to a democratic-social mode that marks the Latin American constitutionalism from the beginning of the twentieth century. On the other hand, the institutional organization thought from the liberal point of view, of checks and balances, stagnated in nineteenth century.

This robust commitment to rights does not fit the organization of power as we have thought since the middle of the last century. A compromise was formed between liberals and conservatives and the political elites of that era who came from a legacy of violence and confrontation that decided to compromise and, in some way, to share the power.

Two different commitments have been focused on: a list of strong and unconditional rights and democratic organization. At the same time, the constitution establishes in its design a pact with the idea of rights and with democracy. This ended up revealing a part of the wealth and a part of the problem of any constitution.[15] It becomes very difficult to keep these two areas separate, because the rights curtain must connect with the curtain of democracy.[16] This is a commitment to overcome the legacy left by authoritarian governments and the concern for social and human rights, which must be emphasized unconditionally.

The growing development and recognition of constitutional charters eventually gave way to constitutionalism, which was used to oppose to contractualism and popular sovereignty—ideas of the French Revolution, the constituted powers of the State which, although liberal, will not yet be considered democratic, not being of the king or the people, but of the State, as the right.[17]

---

[12] Miranda 2011.

[13] Valle (2013b).

[14] Gargarella (2015).

[15] Gargarella (2015).

[16] Gargarella (2015).

[17] Bercovici 2004.

Reflection emerges around its manifold manifestations, because if there is a consensus around the central element of the term constitution—the limitation of political power in favor of the governed—there is, on the other hand, a very varied repertoire of solutions that are oriented in thesis to materialize this same purpose.[18]

The conceptions of constitutionalism arose with the intention of establishing mechanisms to control the exercise of political power by social groups, as well as being linked to the historical development of the very concept of constitution.[19] For Valle,[20] they are informers and conformers of the content of the constitution and relate to a vision that no longer operates from a total segmentation between law and politics.

It is from Canotilho[21] the affirmation that there is not a single conceptual category but several constitutional movements, with some moments of approximation between them, providing a complex historical-cultural weaving.

This idea, according to Backer,[22] can be understood as a systematization of thought about constitutions founded and its development since the mid-twentieth century from a normative set against which the constitutions are legitimized. Hart[23] warns that the meaning of legitimation fits into a political and legal concept that, in the modern era, is fundamental to the validation of "political and legal" acts.

These different responses to Canotilho[24] are the result of the responsive constitutionalization that guarantees the conditions under which the diverse perspectives of value, knowledge and action can coexist. The constitutions of our time will have to march with their eyes on the past, the present and the future, for one cannot give up the heritage of historical-constitutional experience, as Zagrebelsky[25] warned us. Past and future are linked in a single line, needing an incessant redefinition of the principles of constitutional coexistence, with the continuous re-elaboration of the constitutional roots of the order.

What highlights the dynamic nature of the concept of constitutionalism is highlighted by Backer,[26] who developed it throughout this century, characterizing it as: (i) a classification system; (ii) the main object from which it is possible to define the characteristics of the constitutions (of the document of organization of political power within the institutional apparatus); (iii) determining the legitimacy of the constitutional system as conceived or implemented; (iv) the basis of the rule of law, a fundamental postulate of the government; (v) the basis on a metric of substantive values derived from a source beyond the control of any individual.

[18] Valle (2014).

[19] Pulcinelli (2015).

[20] Valle (2013b).

[21] Gomes Canotilho (2003).

[22] Backer (2009).

[23] Hart (1994).

[24] Gomes Canotilho (2008).

[25] Zagrebelsky (2011a).

[26] Backer (2009).

The changes in contemporary constitutionalism have two paradigm-force ideas in politics and law: human rights and democracy.[27] It is important to note in these changes the constructions that alternate between functions of the State and in the State and, according to Sartori,[28] has a prescriptive purpose.

The insertion of the finalistic value element will revert the logic of classical constitutionalism, as it requires the authority not only to observe procedural parameters, but also to be committed to the objectives it proposes. These juridical mutations, according to Moreira Neto,[29] lie in the secular task of constructing a less authoritarian, more efficient, controlled, human model of political organization, as institutions require—the incorporation of postmodern political values.

These elements produce an ideology of material and procedural limitation on State power, the content of which is the focus of the constitutionalist debate, and from these definitions it is possible to begin to theorize the emerging variants and values based on constitutionalism that have emerged since 1945.

The deconstruction of the idea of antecedence of constitutionalism and the constitution as its consequence established by Pulcinelli,[30] informs us that rationality leads us to: first choose the type of constitutionalism, still in the plane of abstraction, according to the form that wants the politically and with the ideology compatible with that choice, to later normalize it in the constitution.

However, this logic has been reversed in several archetypes. There are States that first consolidated their texts and then demanded from the Constitutionalists the identification or even the construction of a theoretical-abstract model that would justify and support the already systematized[31] proposal. The Timorese[32] Charter brought with it this characteristic during its elaboration process, having been coined directly by the UN intervention. The new Constitution sought to design, in a general way, the form of society that was intended to build carrying the sign of transformation.[33]

In this sense, the theoretical-abstract model, stated in an intuitive way, according to Pulcinelli[34] must be conceived before the constitution is drawn up, but this is not always possible either through the political context or because the charter is a living organism. This definition fits the so-called "open charter"" of Zabrebelsky,[35] which, within limits, allows the spontaneity of social life, such as competition, to assume

27 Diogo de Figueiredo Moreira Neto (2011).

28 Sartori (1962b).

29 Diogo de Figueiredo Moreira Neto (2011).

30 Pulcinelli (2015).

31 Pulcinelli (2015).

32 The description and the process will be exposed in the fifth chapter of this thesis.

33 This goal, according to Pulcinelli, will be characterized as recognizing an extensive role of social, participation, collective, civil and political rights, providing judicial instruments aimed at their effective guarantee, as well as increasing mechanisms for participation and direct deliberation of citizens (Pulcinelli 2015).

34 Pulcinelli (2015).

35 Zagrebelsky (2011).

political leadership as a condition for the survival of a pluralistic and democratic society.

These constitutional inspirations can change over time, bringing a new insight into constitutionalism applied or desired by society.[36] Admitting this exploratory possibility ends up forging different ideologies capable of differentiating "giving a constitution" and "living a constitution"—open concepts to use the construction of consensuses and dissent and admit different developments, enabled to improve the trajectory of the community.

There is no closed concept of neo-constitutionalism, since there is no way to individualize a definition that corresponds to a univocal, clear and cohesive conception.[37] What exists are variations on the transformations of legal thought coined by various theoretical-abstract conceptions about how power will be limited.[38]

One of these categories is a globalization movement of a certain pattern of institutional organization, of a constitutionalism as a theoretical model that inspires,[39] which can prove to be a problem and a retrogression before the initial perspective of development.

The so-called transnational constitutionalism relies on the legitimating and substantial values defined by the consensus of the community of nations, moving in the opposite sense of the traditional sense, which places its source of values in the people of the nation itself, in the national constituent power.

This category, in the words of Backer,[40] has sought to claim the privilege of arbitrating legitimate constitutional values. It is based on the development of a single system designed to give authentic expression to the values of the community of nations that together make up the systems of constitutionalism and legitimate constitutions.[41]

In the same sense, Peters[42] points out that "global constitutionalism" helps to shape complex realities by the phenomenon of globalization, reaching the economic, scientific and political planes, which has increased dependence on international law and the most fundamental norms can represent a cosmopolitan international law. In contrast, one might think that Peters' statement is unattainable,[43] since the universal charters find only a general reference or value, without explicitly defining them.

Thus understood, it becomes the scenario on which the organization of States can be evaluated, legitimized and affected. It suggests both a systematization of the parameters to conceive the constitutions and to respond to the manifestations of constitutional expressions. It does not propose a particular form of governmental

---

[36] Valle (2014).

[37] Sarmento (2008).

[38] Pulcinelli (2015).

[39] Valle (2014).

[40] Backer (2009).

[41] Chapter 3 will present the UN legal-political intervention, whose objective is to implement a democracy in countries without a democratic tradition or affected by internal conflicts.

[42] Peters (2005).

[43] Kirchner (2004).

organization or a single system of substantive principles through which it can be expressed, also distinguishing the forms of organization of legitimate or illegitimate States.

This framework takes on a certain set of behaviors, including democracy, human, social, cultural, economic, labor, religious freedom and other rights, serving as a practice for the perfection of constitutionalism. In addition, a critique by Backer[44] suggests that this constitutionalism has become another means of organizing the great competition among international communities to "legitimize the discourse of political organization"—the language may be the constitution, but the goal is to have control.

Constitutionalism ended up reaching the limits strictly dictated by the international[45] field, especially after the Second World War. The support of international organizations[46] can be verified, as an example, in the preamble of the Japanese Constitution,[47] in the Charter of East Timor, in its Article 9[48] and in the Charter of Haiti, in its Article 139.[49] This narrowing may end up representing a subordination of domestic law to the global community. This basic premise comes from the fact that the international community is governed by rules and principles and not simply by power, and in this sense, it is possible to support, on an emergency basis, the new bases of legitimacy through this system.[50]

National identities develop through complex heterogeneous processes of dissent ranging from individual to collective environments. That is why an "idealized constitutional" community must strive to fit the local community and, therefore, should not be imagined from a global point of view.

---

[44] Backer (2009).

[45] In this view, for example, Friedmann (1964), Macdonald and Johnston (2005).

[46] These countries were cited in an exemplary way since they had direct UN intervention.

[47] "(…) We believe that no nation is responsible only for itself, but that the laws of political morality are universal and that obedience to these laws is incumbent upon all nations to uphold their sovereignty and justify their sovereign relationship with other nations.".

[48] The mentioned article refers to the reception of international law in the internal order, whose item 1 establishes that the Timorese legal order adopts the principles of general or common international law.

[49] The determination of the article is that the President of the Republic must negotiate and sign all international treaties, conventions and agreements and submit them to the National Assembly for ratification.

[50] Peters (2005).

3.2 Developing New Categories of Constitutionalism: An Essential Exercise for the Living of the Constitution

3.2.1 *Transitional Constitutionalism*

The study that involves contemporary constitutionalism can find answers and mechanisms that seek to forge a legitimate, democratic constitution that enables the formation of a collective will, further stimulating the debate around its foundation and its sphere of action.[51] This Charter should aim to be, not a mere document, but an empowering and emancipating instrument of right and of the constitutional person.

The new theoretical propositions or categories of constitutionalism sometimes operate in an exercise that presents itself, according to its characteristics; sometimes descriptive, other times prescriptive.[52] These new incorporations are after the scenario already brought by neo-constitutionalism,[53] making it clear that the intention is the perfecting of legal constitutionalism.

Transitional constitutionalism can be understood as a theoretical category[54] that seeks to explore not the content element of a constitution, but how it will be articulated.[55] It concerns the way in which the process of drafting the document is structured considering the sensitive context of political composition for re-democratization. It addresses, therefore, the dimension of the process of constitutionalization.

The "democratic transitions"[56] have been undertaken by many "new democracies",[57] such as in Central Europe, Asia, Africa and Latin America, and have been presented as one of the main forces behind these profound changes, since its intention is to guarantee the stability of the process of constitutional change. These transitional constitutional changes often came as part of political agreements negotiated

[51] Valle (2014).

[52] Valle (2014).

[53] As stated in item 2.1, represented by the re-constitutionalization that followed the Second World War.

[54] Yeh and Chang (2009), Teitel (2003), Khatiwada (2008), Pulcinelli (2015).

[55] Pulcinelli (2015).

[56] The research does not intend to address the issue of "transitional justice." As an illustration, it should be mentioned that the terminology for Teitel was proposed to account for the self-conscious construction of a distinct conception of justice associated with periods of radical political change. Seen as an important component for the UN, because aspirations can give rise to the demand for a type of adequate accountability to aid in promoting peace and security (Teitel 2008).

[57] Many so-called democratic transitions occurred after the fall of the Berlin Wall, a major symbol of the end of the Cold War and focal point of events as the end of world bipolarization; the bankruptcy of socialist systems; American hegemony and the beginning of dramatic changes around the world. This is not to say that all democratic transitions occurred in the same period. Some Asian countries, such as South Korea, Taiwan, the Philippines, changed their systems in 1987. There is no pretension in this study to present constitutional experiences at certain times or places because it is not an empirical or comparative study. For discussions on democratic transitions, it is recommended to read Huntington (1991), Ackerman (1994).

by previous regimes and current reformers,[58] including with the direct support of international actors.

The transition does not simply imply the period of transposition from one political system to another, it is also associated with the experiences of political and institutional reorganization of countries that came from movements of substantive changes in power, be it by forces of revolutionary movements, independence or emancipation of the areas involved.[59]

On another plane, but related to the order of transition, it is worth noting that transitional restorative justice deals with the theme of the political project through which societies deal with the legacy of human rights violations, with the objective of securing times of peace, justice and protection of individuals.[60]

Because of this, it is the legal and constitutional principles that contribute to solving difficult issues during the constitutional transition context, since the institution of the new regime seeks to break away from the old values and insert new ones, which will be rooted and universally known.

This development, pursued using systematized transition formulas, in the construction of constitutions by different procedures,[61] in a line of analysis, shows a close relation between the type of justice that one wants to achieve and the relevant political limiting conditions.

The first challenge of political composition for the re-democratization was to show a constitutionalism that could lead the new directions of the country and that at the same time was lodged with an adaptability that served the delicate balance necessary for the realization of that crossing towards democracy.[62]

Pulcinelli[63] reveals that this differentiated panorama allows that the bet on the change, also occurring without rupture, is given through a constructive effort, establishing constitutional arrangements facilitating the integration of the society to the new political-legal system, being able even to admit an unconventional judicial adjudication with constitutional contributing through a rational speech, continually perfecting the project and the founding pact, especially since social transformation is a permanent and developing work.

As an instrumental concept functioning as an identifier of institutional mechanisms by which it will be possible to convey the change of the political, economic and social order of a country,[64] nothing stops this constructive effort from coming from both internal and external forces.

---

[58] Yeh and Chang (2009).

[59] Yeh and Chang (2009).

[60] Japiassú and Cruz (2013).

[61] For Widner, the results of written constitutions encompass a set of distinct procedures. In general, they cover a series of functions that are organized in stages: negotiation of basic rights, development of provisional documents, immutable principles, preparation of the initial text, deliberation and approval, ratification and promulgation. These stages will be constructed in various formal ways (Widner 2008).

[62] Valle (2013b).

[63] Pulcinelli (2015).

[64] Pulcinelli (2015).

The UN has been involved in several processes of building a constitution[65] that encompasses formal, substantive content, reforms of existing charters, and even the formulation of the process at an operational level especially in post-conflict settings.

This change will boost the fundamental text in search of a consensus resulting from institutional[66] maturation itself. If this category is related to how the fundamental charter will be translated, numerous techniques can form a constitutional culture, according to Pulcinelli.[67]

In transitional constitutionalism the characteristics of relativization are found in three important aspects: between the procedure of elaboration of the constitution and the process of amendment; between informal processes of dialogue channels; and the idea of "unconventional constitutional jurisdiction".[68]

There is a distinct procedure between amending a constitution that seeks a less difficult legislative course in the transition process. This option is an opening for "weaker" constitutional processes, which ends up reconciling the acceptance of a consensus with opposing forces within the rules of the political game. In a traditional constitutional amendment process, questions concerning the sovereignty of the State, the name, the flag or the territory or questions related to the fixed clauses are not always involved. Substantial or procedural restrictions remain a vital element of the new order. In transitional constitutionalism, this control can be relativized, since it intends, in a time of profound change, to be open to all kinds of institutional possibilities. Some constitutional revisions found no substantive or procedural limits, such as what happened in South Korea. The process of updating the text gave way to a new structure of government with a new constitutional court. The central idea is to operate on the new regime in an entirely new framework.

As for the relativization between formal and informal processes of dialogue channels, these were used as an inducer and facilitator for the new reforms. One of the most famous examples was the "roundtable talk".[69] First introduced in Poland in 1989, then imitated by Czechoslovakia and Hungary and spreading in many transitional democracies. During these panel discussions, critical principles of the new Charter or its revision were established and agreed. In times of turbulent transition, both the old regime and the reformist face great pressure for reform, and these informal mechanisms are important in alleviating political tensions and making peaceful negotiations.

---

[65] This process will be better detailed in Chap. 3.

[66] Pulcinelli (2015).

[67] Pulcinelli (2015).

[68] Yeh and Chang (2009).

[69] This process is well detailed in the book by Elster (1996).

Another feature not less striking is the emergence of "unconventional constitutional jurisdiction", which can be understood in two ways: the creation of a constitutional court with the power of judicial review[70] and the constitutional interpretations[71] from these Courts.

It is expected from the Courts, in the transitional model, that they become partakers of the fundamental changes. This may include interpretation of constitutional principles consistent with liberal democracies, guiding the rights to the free market or the redistribution of powers of the approved government. They are invited to produce changes on constitutional norms from their interpretations and from the political controversies that arise in the transition process.

In this way, it is believed that they can define the constitutional content of what is necessary at the time of transition, or rather, avoid the political vacuum by intervening judicially in the process. Thus, the Courts can inform their decisions with the support of constitutional principles consistent with the liberal democracies and redistribution of political powers for the stabilization of the government approved or in approval.

The Courts are also invited to promote fundamental changes in constitutional norms, based on their interpretation. For this reason, transitional constitutionalism does not dispense with the activism of the courts, which, by overcoming all the risks of popular revolutions and disagreements of the popular representatives, becomes a dominant feature in this historical phase, despite the well-known concern of the counter majoritarian role.[72] Its acting represents an agent of the intended change. The Constitutional Court of South Africa, for example, has exercised this power, even annulling various provisions of the new constitutional bill and sending them back for further reformulations.

This measure is of an exceptional nature, since constitutional revisions represent collective decision-making and must be carried out by elected representatives, which would be most beneficial for the consolidation of democracy in the long term.

Another aspect, constituent of the nature of transitional constitutionalism, is that it subordinates the question of the original legitimacy of the text, admitting that this same sign of empowerment of the charter comes through practice.[73] This exercise will be better evidenced by the presentation of the "democratic constitutionalism" posed by Post and Siegel[74] presented in later sub item.

As already understood, transitional constitutionalism does not represent a finalistic concept, such a movement does not dictate the purposes or objectives to be achieved, but elucidates that this relationship between the conception of power limitation and written text can be elaborated through other forces other than the rational

[70] One can cite, for example, Spain in 1978; South Korea in 1988; Hungary in 1990; Bulgaria in 1991; Romania in 1992; South Africa in 1994. This information was extracted from the link http://www.ccrm.rol.md/wwc . Accessed on March 2014.

[71] There are numerous reference works that deal specifically with these issues, such as courts created or restored in all former communist or authoritarian regimes in the East and Central Europe (Hartwig 1992; Schwartz 1993; Sheive 1995; Maduna 1989; Dickson 1997).

[72] For Bickel the constitutional jurisdiction configures a counter-force in the systems (Bickel 1986).

[73] Pulcinelli (2015).

[74] Post and Siegel (2013, 2007).

design of precedence of choice of pattern.[75] The constitution is used more to promote the stabilization of society and initial beacon of the transformation process. In this sense, it acts as a propeller of the constantly changing consensus from the institutional maturation—in this profile, the character is instrumental with progressive incremental logic.

3.2.2 *Transformation Constitutionalism*

Despite its dynamics and progressiveness, transitional constitutionalism does not individually account for all aspects of political, economic, and cultural change in a society. It is recognized that the exclusive bet on the law can lead to constitutional frustration, because the law is not enough to serve as a model for politics alone, nor a perfect instrument enough to realize social rights—there are elements in other spheres, including cultural ones, that need be developed.[76]

The situation of fragile political stability and, at the same time, of serious social problems, ended up demanding a category that, without neglecting its objectives of re-founding a society based on equality and inclusion, did not enter the trap of a pretension of constitutional detailing law that either made the political agreement unfeasible, or resulted in a merely symbolic text, incapable of guiding the collective.[77]

For example, constitutional changes in different Latin American countries were marked by important differences for at least three reasons: on the one hand, the nature and origin of the process, while in other cases the new constitutions were the natural result of the fall of dictatorships such as Brazil and Paraguay; On the other hand, the reforms sought to strengthen existing democratic regimes with problems of legitimacy, such as Mexico and Colombia; and in a third situation, such as Venezuela, Ecuador, and Bolivia, the new constitution was tied to the collapse of the previous party system and to the rise of new political forces, such as Chavismo in Venezuela, the indigenous movement in Bolivia, or the Correismo in Ecuador.[78]

For Uprinmy,[79] most constitutional texts and reforms substantially modify the understanding of national unity to point out that it is not the result of a homogenization of different cultures, but a marked recognition of differences and a greater appreciation of pluralism in all its shapes.

Thus, the constitutions, mainly the Andean, begin to define their nations as pluriethnic and pluricultural, and establish as a constitutional principle the promotion of diversity. This recognition is accompanied by the consecration of religious freedom and protection to groups traditionally discriminated against, such as indigenous peoples and black communities in Brazil.

---

[75] Pulcinelli (2015).

[76] Pius Langa adds the "transformation of the legal culture" (Langa 2006).

[77] Pulcinelli (2015).

[78] Uprimny (2011).

[79] Uprimny (2011).

In the same way, constitutions have been protective in recognizing constitutional rights, since in addition to incorporating civil and political rights inherited from liberal traditions, such as property, privacy, due process, freedom of expression, have also broadened rights economic, social and cultural rights, such as education, housing and health, and have advanced in the recognition of forms of collective law, especially the right to the environment.

In recognition of this diversity and the consecration of new rights set out in innumerable normative sources, the constitutions express a strong commitment to equality, not only prohibiting discrimination, but also directing special political authorities to affirmative action with the aim of real and effective social rights. Reform agendas retake a status of attachment to a constitutional level.[80]

In this sense, constitutionalism of transformation[81] concerns the substantive content of the proposal of constitutionalism manifested in a text that intends to be the engine of change of a social reality. It has a direct impact on the progress of democracy, characterized by being a dynamic and expansive process.[82]

According to Klare,[83] they designate the efforts that encompass the long-term project of promulgation, interpretation and constitutional implementation, aimed at transforming social relations and institutions of power into a democratic, participatory and egalitarian society.

The functions of the constitution that intends to be transformative must unite the foundationalism and constructivist perspectives so that: (i) it consolidates the revolutionary efforts for the institution of a new democracy; (ii) establishes the connectivity of ideological constitutionalism and social participation as indicative of legitimacy to solidify the new regime; (iii) provides the new institutional design and its preconditions; (iv) represents a continuous and constructive process. In addition to limiting power, the Charter calls for change.[84]

Thus, in addition to law, it is possible to deduce that coercive and comprehensive[85] social facts, endowed with their own independent reality, consist of influential and relevant factors to channel, alongside constitutionalism of transformation, the process of advancing society.

In this way, the right will need the alignment of other social forces to collaborate with the permanent change towards the desirable life by the society that it will compose. Vieira and Ajouz[86] maintain that, although the constitution still holds the status of a fundamental document of political-juridical organization, its writing

[80] Yeh and Chang (2009).

[81] Consult Langa (2006), Klare (1998), Vieira and Ajouz (2013).

[82] Carpizo (2009).

[83] Klare (1998).

[84] Vieira and Ajouz (2013).

[85] According to Rocha, these facts can be understood as a way of acting fixed or not, capable of exerting on the individual an external coercion; or else, which is general in the extension of a given society, presenting an existence of its own, independent of the individual manifestations it may have (Guimarães Rocha 1991).

[86] Vieira and Ajouz (2013).

and—perhaps with greater relevance—its interpretation are focal points aimed at the proposed change. One must therefore consider the influence of the social forces that by policy will contribute to the sphere of law for the transformation itself.

The common attributes of this transformative format can be pointed out by two fundamental elements: the commitment to promote material equality and the emergence of a culture of power justification.[87]

Implementing a substantially parity treatment for all citizens consists of, as a primary goal, modifying a status quo of political segregation, misery and social exclusion. In this model, one thinks of the reconstruction of the State and, consequently, of the society, by crossing the question of the redistribution of resources, as well as of the offer of access to essential goods and services such as health, education, housing, food, water, electricity, as well as the bet of political emancipation. There is scope for consecration of a fundamental right to development.[88]

In the Brazilian Constitution, especially in the clauses that determine the objectives of the Republic and in its fundamental provisions, impositions are found: the enunciation of the aims of promoting the common good, as well as the eradication of poverty and social inequalities and catalog of social rights, with immediate application.[89]

As for the construction of a "culture of justification of power" pointed out by Langa[90] it is expected that the holders of power, including the Court, the responsibility to justify their decisions, to avoid any coercive attempt of imposition of will. It is possible to consider an approach with Gardbaum[91]: all governmental actions that interfere with individual rights or autonomy must be justified in terms of public reason. The new order must be a community built on persuasion rather than coercion.

This category bets on the constitution as a lever of social inclusion, thus, it is necessary that, at this moment founding, institutions play an active and dialogical[92] role. Democratic institutions assume different roles—which does not exclude the assignment of duties to civil society as well.[93]

Most reforms in transformational constitutionalism draw the recognition of fundamental rights, not limited to rhetorical exercise without effectiveness, but rather a practice that extends the mechanisms of protection and guarantee of these rights. One example is the 1991 Colombian Constitution, which provides for direct judicial forms of protection of rights such as *support* and *guardianship.*[94]

---

[87] Langa (2006).

[88] Vieira and Ajouz (2013).

[89] Vieira and Ajouz (2013).

[90] Langa (2006).

[91] Gardbaum (2016).

[92] This characteristic favors the construction of mechanisms that favor a shared interaction between the units of power involved or, at least, define criteria of implementation in collective terms (Vieira and Ajouz 2013).

[93] Vieira and Ajouz (2013).

[94] Cited as an example, the Colombian Constitution of 1991 envisaged, in its Article 86, tutelage as a mechanism for direct protection of fundamental rights, as well as other mechanisms, including

Many countries have created or strengthened their constitutional justice by strengthening constitutional courts or courtrooms. In most cases, the idea seemed to be the same: to give the citizen or certain legitimates effective mechanisms to claim the effective enforcement of their rights, or even to quickly move away the offensive norm from constitutional values of the normative system.

Concerning citizen participation, transformational constitutionalism has also brought important mechanisms that have redesigned decision-making institutions. Most of the reforms were guided by the idea of strengthening representative democracy and, at the same time, building new spaces for participation, basically in two ways: the recognition and expansion of mechanisms for direct participation, such as plebiscites, referendums and popular consultations, and the creation of citizen bodies public management control,[95] without prejudice to the space open to popular participation granted by the legislative[96] and judicial powers.[97]

Some premises are therefore established that the concept enumerates the following preconditions: implementation of equal treatment between citizens; procedure for drafting the constitution, including the amendment process; relativization between the formal and informal channels of dialogue; strengthening of representative and participatory democracy; constitutional moment extending in time, from a logic of progressive development; relativization between the idea of judicial review—with the creation of constitutional courts and the judicial decision—and interpretations from the court.

The promulgation of a text that transmits transformative objects is not enough to configure what is a theoretical appeal, when the text is evolutionist; the hermeneutic is moved to the modifying promotion[98] that does not diminish the extreme importance of the interpretive practices since they are the ones that qualify constitutional living.

If the project of transformational constitutionalism does not have a finish line, it is necessary to adjust the routes of the direction of this theoretical-abstract matrix. Democratic constitutionalism aims to contribute to determine the direction to be followed in a category of construction that invests in constitutional practice.

---

popular actions for the protection of collective rights. In a recent decision, the Colombian Constitutional Court, through action 437/12, regarding the fundamental right to housing, in which it is possible to identify three situations that the judge can grant the guardianship whenever and when the established requirements are met: in the face of the right to a dignified life, it is a State obligation not to disturb the enjoyment of the right in an unjustified way and to protect people from undue interference with the enjoyment of the right to life, granting protection immediately; when there is a request regarding the fulfillment of a subjective right acquired according to the legal and regulatory development of the subject; when the situation of vulnerability is manifestly evident jeopardizing their dignified life.

[95] Uprimny (2011).

[96] In this sense, the Brazilian Constitution enumerates, in its Article 58, Sect. 2, II, the possibility of holding public hearings with civil society entities through the National Congress.

[97] Likewise, the Brazilian judiciary, as established in Article 21, VII, of the Internal Rules of the Federal Supreme Court, has the power to convene a public hearing that is proposed to the expert panel, regulatory entities and representatives of civil society, aiming at obtain technical and factual information regarding the action in.

[98] Vieira and Ajouz (2013).

3.2.3 Democratic Constitutionalism

The term "democratic constitutionalism",[99] as posed in US by Post and Siegel,[100] expresses the paradox that: constitutional authority depends as much on its capacity for democratic response as on its legitimacy as the supreme law. These proposals were presented in a more systematic way in "The Constitution in 2020″ and portray a reflection on the theme of the mechanisms of construction and updating of the American constitutional sense, with the consequence of aggregating legitimacy to decisions (judicial or not) in which the application of the North American constitution is undertaken.[101]

Whether the legal system is founded on common law, in constitutional times of open textures, pluralism and high potential for social controversy, the American debate on the necessary guarantee of updating of constitutional sense[102] continues to be useful for the discussion that involves new tools for the re-democratization process or new democracies, which ends up justifying the analysis of the new category.

This deeper view of democracy is fundamental to meeting the demands of justice, equality and emancipation.[103] It allows connecting constitutionalism and democracy and invests in constitutional law and politics in the process of renewing the founding text.[104]

The broader concept was developed by Post and Siegel[105] and is part of what Balkin[106] describes as a "rebirth of liberal constitutional thinking that has emerged in the last five years".

"Democratic constitutionalism" rejects originalism,[107] because each generation develops the constructions that best meet the needs of the time, remaining faithful to the basic principles, its tradition. This consideration requires that the commitments contained in the document be guaranteed; institutions and people, which, ultimately, determine the interpretation and direction of the works to be performed.

---

[99] In view of the variety of conceptualization and to distinguish the concept of "democratic constitutionalism", considered exclusively by Post and Siegel, quotation marks will be used when the expression refers to the theoretical proposition of those authors. In a sense different from that undertaken by Post and Siegel: Balkin (2007), Ray (2011), Balkin (2009), Berger (1998), Bustamante and Nascimento de Godoi Bustamante (2016) , Gomes Canotilho (2008), Hedrick (2012), Minow (2006), José Guilherme Berman Corrêa Pinto, Controle fraco de constitucionalidade (2013), Thesis (Doctorate in Law)—Post-Graduate Law Program in PUC-Rio, Pontificial Catholic University of Rio de Janeiro (2013), Balkin (2016), Workshop on Constitution Building Processes (2007), Zagrebelsky (2011a).

[100] This proposition was initially presented by Post (2000) and later followed by Siegel (Post and Siegel 2013). There are also some perceptions of this category in the text by Post and Siegel (2007).

[101] Valle (2014).

[102] Valle et al. (2016b).

[103] Hedrick (2012).

[104] Valle (2014).

[105] Post and Siegel (2007).

[106] Balkin (2007).

[107] See Berger (1998).

This deference allows us to visualize two possibilities of perspective: historical and non-historical. The non-historical perspective[108] of society assumes that there is an essence of law and constitution that always presents itself in the same way, that is, there is an a priori, which is always present and does not change with the passage of time.

If, on the other hand, you admit that historicity is relevant, you welcome the influence of that environment and you are receiving the collection of learning that time can bring you. This duality will allow lending flexibility to the institutional design.

Betting on historicity is seeing security in change—Zagrebelsky[109] already said that "open constitutions" are those that allow, within the constitutional limits, both the spontaneity of social life and the competence to assume political leadership. Both conditions for the survival of a pluralistic and democratic society. The "a priori" is a political contingency, with accumulation of past and future experiences; it is social reality; "Unpredictability of problems and social spontaneity".[110]

This capacity for change will have its limits, which do not call into question the "principle of continuity", referring to the constitutive values and principles of the "Western concept of constitution". It has a set of values that it intends to have preserved, of historical conquests, the so-called "nucleus of identity of the constitution". This includes the set of norms and principles that structure a particular legal-constitutional order.[111]

This is also the position suggested by Hedrick[112] when he makes clear his objection to the overly fundamental static models of constitutionalism: the constitution can only be made from rational activity, which will advance and thus mature through legislation, to realize democratic potential.[113]

The main characteristic is the presence of weak mechanisms to control the constitutionality of norms by the judiciary. They receive this name because, they have a word in the subject of constitutionality control, but not necessarily the last one.

This moderate participation of the judges comes to be seen as a proposal able to reconcile the best of both worlds: political and legal constitutionalism; democracy and constitutionalism. An outstanding example is the Canadian Charter of Rights and Freedoms, from the perspective of receiving these rights. Courts and parliament

---

[108] Valle (2013).

[109] Zagrebelsky (2011a).

[110] Zagrebelsky (2011a).

[111] Gomes Canotilho (2008).

[112] Hedrick (2012).

[113] In the same line is the redemptive constitutionalism of Balkin, which recognizes that the constitution has partial commitments. There is a direct connection with constitutional fidelity in that it recognizes that the principles have never been fully realized and that each generation is responsible for trying to create a society that adheres more faithfully to these elements (Balkin 2007) shared vision is that of Ray, where constitutional fidelity and redemption go hand in hand and require a life-view of the constitution. Time is an important ally, since the set of unrealized principles permeate the generations that are committed to maintaining and applying it (Ray 2011).

share the responsibility for judging constitutional values and evaluating the reasonableness of their own functions for these values. Responsibility comes from different perspectives given their institutional characteristics.

All the forms indicated, which permeate "democratic constitutionalism", are focused on the practice that places emphasis on constitutional development outside the courts as well. The focus is on both social and political movements, as well as on the potential of formal institutional structures and practices to distribute the power to interpret the Constitution.

This is also a vision shared by the international community. The term "democratic dialogue" was coined by a group of institutions, the Canadian International Development Agency (CIDA), the Institute for Democracy and Electoral Assistance (IDEA), the United Nations Development Program (UNPD) and has been used in Latin America and the Caribbean region to highlight both the relevance of dialogue and the strengthening of democratic institutions.

The way the dialogue works attracts a wide variety of social actors to engage in conversations that lead to positive change.[114] It was concluded that these conversations are essential to inclusive processes because they are open, sustainable and flexible and can adapt to fluctuating contexts.

For Pruitt and Thomas,[115] decision makers are the people who have a formal responsibility to address the challenges that society faces at various levels—local, national, regional and global—playing an important role in these processes and their outcomes.

In Latin America and the Caribbean, this term was used expressly for the proliferation of dialogue to focus on democratic governance, and three criteria help differentiate it[116]: (i) the goal is to address the complex social problems that existing institutions are not serving properly; (ii) the participants are microcosms of the system that creates the problem and should be part of the solution; (iii) the process is an open and inclusive dialogue, which allows the building of confidence necessary to reach an agreement on concrete actions.

There are three elements that share this idea: dialogue, which represents the gathering of many voices, historical perspectives, exploration, inquiry, shared discoveries, an expanded permission to foster respect and understanding for the formation of shared meaning and knowledge building; the deliberation, which concerns the authority of this argument, being subject to an inclusive and expanded debate; and decision-making, which would include reasonable arguments, analyses of possible solutions, detailed examination of the advantages and disadvantages, and informed judgment.

For Post and Siegel,[117] trust in the constitutional order's responsiveness plays a crucial role in preserving its authority. In addition, ensuring that this relationship can be realized will depend on whether people and all members of the system have

[114] Pruitt and Thomas (2008).

[115] Pruitt and Thomas (2008).

[116] Pruitt and Thomas (2008).

[117] Post and Siegel (2013).

significant opportunities to adopt alternative constitutional understandings. Balkin[118] warns us that there are two different types of contributions to constitutional development: the first is in the official field, the laws, the institutions, and the second is the contributions that come from society through its various vocalizations.

There is a subtle difference between the "democratic constitutionalism" coined by Post and Siegel and the so-called "popular constitutionalism",[119] in which the idealizing conversation of the constitutional sense ideally involves the entire universe of its applicators—constitutional persons and democratic institutions—of substantive content shifts from the "juridentric" model to the conception that values politics and other actors that make up the dialogic arena.

In "democratic constitutionalism", even if the importance of jurisdiction is recognized, it does not necessarily entail transposing in its favor and in an exclusive regime, of the decision center as to the content of the rights guaranteed, especially the fundamental ones.

This category has attributes that favor a culture of constitutional development and the exercise of dissent because it focuses its use on an institutional framework that is fed by internal and external conditions. It analyzes the understandings and practices by which constitutional rights have been historically established in the context of the cultural controversy.

And in this sense, the proposal connects with the idea that the adjudication of rights and the democratic exercise of politics are habits that necessarily keep a mutual interference in the search for a solution of conflicting interests that can present themselves in the daily exercise of constitutional lawmaking.[120]

There are elements common to the genre, which can be assimilated as the advice of an expansion of the universe of interlocutors in this process, understood as a dialogical vision of the concept and, on the other hand, as the nature that values the constitutional document directed to the concretization of the text and of development promotion, postulating the progressive look that is in tune with the transformation project it wants to affect.

In the field of specificities, it recognizes the constitution that is lived and is not the domain of a specific constitutional authority,[121] but finds in it a role of extreme relevance to associate many agents who incorporate this process of revelation of meaning.[122]

Interpretive divergence is a normal condition of constitutional development. Thus, the contest finds its democratic legitimacy whose capacity is to inspire and attribute an identity that is sustained by traditions of popular engagement. It is from this that

[118] Balkin (2016).

[119] The most prominent theorists of this category are Kramer (2004) and Tushnet (2006).

[120] Valle (2016).

[121] As stated by Bustamante, judicial supremacy is experiencing a moment of mistrust as regards the interpretation of the constitution and its content. The principled arguments in the context of constitutional policy are often inconclusive, which ends up making it particularly difficult to justify its authority (Bustamante and Nascimento de Godoi Bustamante (2016).

[122] Valle (2016).

the capacity that empowers the citizens to be part of the process of discovering the constitutional sign comes from. It contributes to social cohesion in a normatively heterogeneous political system because there are in these dispositions a realm of definitions involving expressions of value, equality, freedom, dignity, identity. And it will be from this construction that there will be possibility to form the exercise of persuasion and the formation of the new consensus.

One of the major concerns of Post and Siegel[123] is the updating of the sense of the constitutional text, mainly because the constitutional vision reflects its moment of edification coined in the nineteenth century. Preserving identity and the constitutional vision—that was formulated at the time of the founding act—is a problem because they may be in constant tension. The constitutional subject can no longer find an answer to its wishes, to solve its problems and still consider that the constitution does not recognize it, since, there is no normative predictability that frames it.

According to Barros,[124] some substantive and formal issues in the constitution present relevant challenges. Among them, the most frequent ones are in the distribution of power between the legislative, executive and judiciary; in federalism versus decentralization; in the distribution of revenues; in fundamental rights, including sensitive issues such as religion, homosexual marriage, abortion, gender equity, among others. That is, there are intermittent conflicts.

To try to address these problems, it would be necessary to try to create a vision of constitutionalism and constitutional jurisdiction that would harmonize these two conceptions.

That is, to construct a method of work that allows the updating and development of meaning—preserving both the vision and the constitutional identity—and, at the same time, receives individual and technical perception. These two vectors are important and will somehow have to be integrated into the constitutional response.

Thus, this mechanics will incorporate three biases: contestation, persuasion and the formation of the new consensus. It is important to mention that these elements of construction do not specifically reflect the vision of the democratic constitutional jurisdiction, but rather that of "democratic constitutionalism", which involves a practice of applying the text.

The space for contestation is the same for dissent. To contest is to diverge, that is, part of this possibility as manifestation of dissent because this is the element that will allow identifying that there begins to be the constitutional vision with that of the identity. This is what triggers this permanent exercise of meaning updating.

Why should there be appreciation of this manifestation? Because it is the only way of perceiving that the understanding that is developing in the constitutional court, in the public offices or in the legislative itself no longer attends to the constitutional vision, because it does not generate more identity. There is a divergent voice.

In addition, to be considered democratic, the challenge must correspond to a persuasion. The persuasive exercise—constructed through a mechanism in which

---

[123] Post and Siegel (2007.

[124] Workshop on Constitution Building Processes (2007).

the dialectic is developed—will have to allow the inclusion of several perspectives in relation to the same problem.

Society is plural, interests are polycentric and it is in this modeling that the size of the divergence will be perceived, which will allow, for example, minimalist or macro decision making. It is possible to map the real dissent, through the call of other actors, until the appearance of other situations that were not put in the conflict as it originally emerged.

The size of this new consensus also dictates the extent of the constitutional response. A minimum consensus for deep dissent will not be worth it. If, in the argumentative exercise, one has been persuaded by the other and there was an average consensus, then the answer advances a little more. According to Minow,[125] this practice does not convert all acts of persuasion into legal reforms, since the set of ideals or concepts, to persuade, can lead to logical or coherent limitations. This is a truism that is proper to constitutional practice, being subject to constant and infinite contestation.

The formation of the new consensus and the construction of the decision ultimately give the problem back to society. Moreover, this reflects the constitutional living and allows the development of the updating of the meaning of the text.

There are many unanswered questions, as these will also be found in constitutional practice. An obstacle to the incorporation of this category is found, for example, in the dialectical difficulty between institutions. Other questions that orbit in the construction of its elements are also not ignored: who should compose the exercise of persuasion? Are the representations of social movements important? Would jurisdiction have a more active role? Could the court in thesis, make a question for the practice of persuasion?

However, it is not denied that the ability to conform to dissent, found in Post and Siegel's category of democratic constitutionalism, eventually provides strategies and arrangements that can favor the practice of various social, historical, cultural, and economic realities.

References

Ackerman, B. (1994). *The future of liberal revolution.* Yale University Press.

Balkin, J. M. (2007). Original meaning and constitutional redemption. *Constitutional Commentary*, 427–532 (2007). http://papers.ssrn.com/sol3/papers.cfm?abstract_id=987060.

Balkin, J. M. (2009). *The return of liberal constitutionalism*, Balkinization. http://balkin.blogspot.com/2009/05/return-of-liberal-constitutionalism.html

Backer, L. C. (2012). From constitution to constitutionalism: a global framework for legimity public power systems. *Penn State Law Review*, 101–177 (2009). http://ssrn.com/abstract=1272264

Balkin, J. M. (2016). Constitutional interpretation and change in the United States: the official and the unofficial. *Yale Law School, Public Law Research Paper*, 1–30. http://papers.ssrn.com/sol3/papers.cfm?abstract_id=2594925.

Bercovici, G. (2004). Constituição e política: Uma relação difícil, Lua Nova Revista. *Cultura e Política, 5.*

[125] Minow (2006).

Berger, R. (1998). Originalism's pretenses. *Cornell Law Review*, 350–358. http://scholarship.law.cornell.edu/cgi/viewcontent.cgi?article=3347&context=clr

Bickel, A. M. (1986). *The least dangerous branch—the supreme court at the bar of politics* (2nd ed., Vol. 16). Yale University Press.

Bonavides, P. (2009). *Curso de Direito Constitucional* (24th ed., Vol. 94). Malheiros.

Bustamante, T., & Nascimento de Godoi Bustamante, E. (2016) *Jurisdição constitucional na era Cunha: entre o passivismo procedimental e o ativismo substancial na jurisprudência do Supremo Tribunal Federal.* Direito & Práxis, pp 346–338. http://www.e-publicacoes.uerj.br/index.php/revistaceaju/article/view/17530/15891).

Canotilho Gomes, J. J. (2008). *"Brancosos" e interconstitucionalidade: itinerários dos discursos sobre a hitoricidade constitucional* (Vol. 121). Almedina.

Carpizo, J. (2009). Tendencias actuales del constitucionalismo latinoamericano. *Revista Derecho del Estado*, 7–36.

Dickson, B. (1997). Protecting human rights through a constitutional court: The case of South Africa. *Fordham Law Review*.

Diogo de Figueiredo Moreira Neto. (2011). *Poder, Direito e Estado: o direito administrativo em tempos de globalização* (pp. 71–72). Fórum.

Elster, J. (1996). *The roundtable talks and the breakdown of communism* (Vol. 21). The University of Chicago Press.

Friedmann, W. (1964). *The changing structure of international law*. Columbia University Press.

Gargarella, R. (2015). Qué són los derechos? Canal Justicia. https://youtu.be/-x3CzQbQgYU

Gardbaum, S. (2016). Positive and horizontal rights: Proportionality's next frontier or a bridge too far? *Forthcoming UCLA School of Law Research*, 1–35. http://papers.ssrn.com/sol3/papers.cfm?abstract_id=2726794

Grimm, D. (2009). *Constitucionalismo y derechos fundamentales* (Vol. 30). Editorial Trotta.

Gomes Canotilho, J. J. (2003). *Direito Constitucional e Teoria da Constituição* (7th ed., Vol. 51). Edições Almedina

Guimarães Rocha, E. P. (1991). *O que é etnocentrismo* (Vol. 27). Brasiliense.

Hartwig, M. (1992). The Institutionalization of the rule of law: the establishment of constitutional courts in the eastern European countries. *U. J. INT'L L. & POL'Y*, pp. 449–50.

Hart, H. L. A. (1994). *The concept of law* (2nd ed., Vol. 100). Oxford University Press.

Hedrick, T. (2012). Democratic constitutionalism as mediation: the decline and recovery of an idea in critical social theory. *Constellations*, 382–400. http://onlinelibrary.wiley.com/doi/10.1111/cons.12002/ful

Huntington, S. (1991). *The third wave: Democratization in the late twentieth century*. University of Oklahoma Press.

Japiassú, C. E. A., & Cruz, E. (2013) Justiça de Transição. R. L. do Valle (Eds.), *Justiça e constitucionalismo em tempos de transição* (Vol. 34). Fórum.

Klare, K. (1998). Legal culture and transformative constitutionalism. *South African Journal on Human Rights, 149*. http://heinonline.org/HOL/LandingPage?collection=journals&handle=hein.journals/soafjhr14&div=17&id=&page=

Kramer, L. (2004). *The people themselves. Popular constitutionalism and judicial review*. Oxford University Press.

Khatiwada, A. (2008). Constitutionalism of transition. *Kathmandu Law Review*, 1–17. http://ssrn.com/abstract=1500826

Kirchner, K. (2004). Relative normativity and the constitutional dimension of international law: a place for values in the international legal system. *European & International Law, 49*.

Langa, J. P. (2006). Transformative constitutionalism. *Stellenbosch Law Review* 351–360. http://sun025.sun.ac.za/portal/page/portal/law/index.afrikaans/nuus/2006/Pius%20Langa%20Speech.pdf

Maduna, P. M. (1989). Judicial review and protection of human rights under a new constitutional order in South Africa. *Human Rights Law Review, 66*.

Macdonald, R. St J., & Johnston, D. M. (2005). *Towards world constitutionalism: issues in the legal ordering of the world community*. Martinus Nijhoff Publishers.

Minow, M. (2006). Constituting our constitution, constituting ourselves: comments on Reva Siegel's constitutional culture, social movement conflict and constitutional change. *California Law Review, 1457*. http://scholarship.law.berkeley.edu/cgi/viewcontent.cgi?article=1246&context=californialawreview

Miranda, J. (2011). *Teoria do Estado e da Constituição* (3rd ed., Vol. 206). Forense.

Orländer, H. (2012). *On the meaning of constitutional culture, Constitutional cultures: On the concept and representation of constitutions in the Atlantic world* (Vol. 25). Cambridge Scholars Publishing.

Peters, A. (2005). Global constitutionalism revisited. In M. N. S. Sellers (Eds.) *Why obey international law? International Legal Theory* (Vol. 11, pp. 10–41).

Post, R. (2000). Democratic constitutionalism and cultural heterogeneity. *Australian Journal of Legal Philosophy*. http://ssrn.com/abstract=229161

Post, R., & Siegel, B. R. (2007). Roe rage: Democratic constitutionalism and backlash. *Harvard Civil Rights-Civil Liberties Law Review, 289*. http://digitalcommons.law.yale.edu/fss_papers/169?utm_source=digitalcommons.law.yale.edu%2Ffss_papers%2F169&utm_medium=PDF&utm_campaign=PDFCoverPages.

Post, R., & Siegel, B. R. (2013). Democratic constitutionalism. In J. M. Balkin, R. Siegel (Eds.) The constitution in 2020 (pp. 25–34). Oxford University Press. http://www.constitution2020.org/chapters/3_Democratic%20Constitutionalism.pdf

Pruitt, B., & Thomas P. (2008) Diálogo democrático um manual para practicantes, Agencia Canadiense de Desarrollo Internacional (ACDI), Instituto Internacional para la Democracia constituição la Asistencia Electoral (IDEA), Secretaría General de la OEA (SG/OEA), Programa de las Naciones Unidas para el Desarrollo (PNUD), no page.

Pulcinelli, E. (2015). STF como indultor da mudança no constitucionalismo de transformação. Thesis Doctorate In Law—Post Graduate progmme In Law of Estácio de Sá University (Vol. 220).

Ray, B. (2011). Demosprudence in comparative perspective. *Stanford Journal of International Law*, 111–173. http://ssrn.com/abstract=1649034

Sartori, G. (1962a). Constitucionalism: a preliminary discussion. *American Political Science Review, 853*.

Sartori, G. (1962b). Constitucionalism: a preliminary discussion. *American Political Science Review*, 853–864.

Sarmento, D. (2008). O neoconstitucionalismo no Brasil: riscos e possibilidades. G. S.Leite, & I. W. Sarlete (Eds.), *Direitos Fundamentais e estado constitucional: Estudos em homenagem a J.J. Gomes Canotilho* (pp. 9–10). RT.

Schwartz, H. (1993). The new East European constitutional courts. In A. E. Dick Howard (Eds.), Constitution making in eastern Europe (Vol. 26).

Sheive, S. W. (1995). Central and Eastern European Constitutional Courts and the anti-majoritarian in South Africa. *Law & Pol'y Int'l bus, 21.*

Teitel, R. G. (2003). Transitional justice genealogy. *Harvard Human Rights Journal*, 69–94. http://www.law.harvard.edu/students/orgs/hrj/iss16/teitel.pdf

Teitel, R. (2008). Transitional justice globalized. *Transitional Justice Institute Research Paper*, 1–4.

Tushnet, M. (2006). Popular constitutionalism as political law. *Chicago-Kent Law Review*, 991–1006 (2006). http://scholarship.law.georgetown.edu/cgi/viewcontent.cgi?article=1238&context=facpub

Uprimny, R. (2011). Las transformaciones constitucionales recientes em América Latina: Tendencias y desafios. César Rodríguez Garavito, El derecho en América Latina: un mapa para el pensamiento jurídico del siglo XXI 109. Siglo Veintiuno Editores.

Valle, V. R. L. (2013a). Classes notes, Research Group New Perspectives in Constitutional Jurisdiction/UNESA (Estácio de Sá University, Rio de Janeiro Jun 6th, 2013a).

Valle, V. R. L. (2013b). Constitucionalismo c Transição: sobre a arte de reconciliar o aparentemente inconciliável. Regina Lírio do Valle, Justiça e constitucionalismo em tempos de transição 91 (Fórum).
Valle, V. R. L. (2013c). Constitucionalismo e Transição: sobre a arte de reconciliar o aparentemente inconciliável, Justiça e constitucionalismo em tempos de transição, 88–119.
Valle, V. R. L. (2014). Constitucionalismo democrático: sobre como reside no poder a aptidão para limitar a si mesmo. In J. R. Vieira, M. M. L. Camargo, V. R. L. do Valle, et al. (Eds.), Diálogos constitucionais e as relações entre os poderes: V Fórum de Grupos de Pesquisa em Direito Constitucional e Teoria do Direito (Text provied by the author).
Vieira, J. R., & Ajouz, I. (2013). O Constitucionalismo transformador e o papel institucional do Poder Judiciário. V. R. L. do Valle (Eds.), *Justiça e Constitucionalismo: em tempos de transição* (pp. 165–186). Fórum.
Valle, V. R. L., Pulcinelli, E., & Maneiro, R. J. (2016a). Contestação, persuasão e consenso no STF: construindo um constitucionalismo democrático.
Valle, V. R. L., Pulcinelli, E., & Maneiro, R. J. (2016b). Constestação, persuasão e consenso no STF: construindo um constitucionalismo democrático.
Widner, J. (2008). Constitution writing in post-conflict settings: an overview. *William & Mary Law Review,* 1522.
Workshop on Constitution Building Processes. (2007). Workshop Report. Nova Jersey: Bobst Center for Peace & Justice, Princeton University, International IDEA, New Jersey
Yeh, J.-R. V., & Chang, W.-C. (2009). The changing landscape of modern constitutionalism: transitional perspective. *National Taiwan University Law Review*, 145–183. http://ssrn.com/abstract=1482863
Zagrebelsky, G. (2011a). Historia y constitución (Vol. 13). Trotta.
Zagrebelsky, G. (2011b). El derecho dúctil: ley, derechos e justiça 14 (Editorial Trotta).

Chapter 4
The Role of the UN in the Consolidation of Democracy and the Constitution-Making

4.1 An United Nations Approach Concepting Democratization and Democracy

In the face of internationally mediated peace agreements, with the aim of promoting a real national rebuilding and the establishment of democratic regimes,[1] we can see the importance of international organizations in this process, specifically the United Nations (UN) that also acts in the technical support to the development of future national constitutions.

This text may or may not be endorsed by the supported population. If there is significant conflict within society or government as to the root of the supremacy of the base text, then this document can become a "facade constitution". Even if it comes to harbor aspirational principles and adopt structures of power for the functioning of government, such provisions and principles are ineffective, but potentially illegitimate.

In the difficult time of national refoundation, international pressures may, in fact, influence the production of constitutional results more accepted by foreign actors. However, how would this result of incorporating constitutional attributes regarded as desirable affect the local population and the potential for the success of these constitutions? The questioning is based on whether this model would reduce the violence and internal conflicts of the country in question, generating a stable socio-political environment; and if he would be able to allow the generation of institutionality and a society that respects fundamental rights. Sometimes, even with empirical analysis, it is not possible to provide "best practice" statements regarding the drafting of a written constitution, especially in the context of high levels of violence. There is variation in relation to procedural details structuring the modeling of institutional design, besides the multifaceted cultural manifestations.

[1] As in the case of East Timor, Haiti, the Balkans, Cambodia, Lebanon, Rwanda, Mozambique, among others.

C. B. Gouvêa and P. H. V. B. Castelo Branco, *UN Interventions and Democratization*, Societies and Political Orders in Transition,
https://doi.org/10.1007/978-3-031-32715-5_4

With the aim of following its main guideline, the United Nations Charter aims at preserving future generations from the scourge of war and affirming faith in the fundamental rights of man, in the dignity and worth of the human being, in the equality of rights of men and women, as well as large and small nations. It also aims to establish conditions for justice and respect for obligations arising from treaties and other sources, as well as to promote social progress and better living conditions within a broad freedom. In addition, for such purposes, practice tolerance, live in peace with one another, and join forces to maintain international peace and security.

Since its establishment in 1945, the UN has helped to end various conflicts, usually via Security Council[2] resolutions. Peace operations are a unique and dynamic instrument designed to help countries devastated by conflict to create the conditions for lasting and lasting peace.

Over the years, its operation has evolved to meet the needs of different types of conflicts and political scenarios. Their missions are considered multidimensional and were created not only to ensure the implementation of comprehensive agreements, but also to help institute governments, monitor human rights compliance, secure and reform institutional sectors, and so on.

Thus, the book "An Agend for Democratization",[3] published by the UN, coined the conceptual difference between democracy and democratization. This last concept consists of a process that leads to a more open, more participative environment. A method that leads to a system of government that incorporates a variety of institutions and mechanisms, the ideal of political power based on the will of the people.[4] The meaning of the term "democracy" has varied considerably in world affairs. In 1945, it had a clear concept, defined by the allied nations oppositional to fascism.

Although there is no mention of the word "democracy" in the United Nations Charter, the opening words "We the people" reflect its fundamental principle. The will of all is the source of legitimacy of sovereign States and therefore of the UN.

This statement is also based on the 1948 Universal Declaration of Human Rights, which sets forth the rights that are essential for effective political participation. This declaration has inspired the creation of constitutions around the world and has contributed to the global acceptance of democracy as a universal value. The Declaration on the Granting of Colonial Countries and Peoples adopted by the General Assembly in 1960 reaffirms the right of peoples to self-determination. Therefore, this normative triad provides a clear and solid basis on the roles and responsibilities of the United Nations in promoting democratization.

---

[2] The Security Council has normative predictability in the United Nations Letter in Art. 23 to 32. Its main responsibility is to maintain international peace and security. In carrying out its duties, the Council shall act in accordance with the purposes and principles of the United Nations.

[3] This book, published by the United Nations, was presented to the General Assembly by then General Secretary Boutros-Ghali on 20 December 1996 as a supplement to two previous reports on democratization. Resolution A/51/761, of December 20, 1996. The United Nations system has been distributed as an official document (United Nations Organization 1996b) at the 51st session, the theme of which was "Support from the United Nations system for the efforts of governments to promote and consolidate new or restored democracies" (Boutros-Ghali 1996).

[4] Boutros-Ghali (1996).

Today presents a new facet of the traditional concept. The different economic, social, cultural, and historical circumstances of the world's societies have become responsible for the conceptualization of the term because there are significant differences between democracy as perceived in one or another society. Increasingly, there is greater recognition that it addresses a wide range of human concerns and is essential for the protection of human rights.

This system of government is not immune to criticism, such as there can be no democracy in times of trouble or war; it leads to disorder; reduces efficiency; violates the rights of minorities and communities; one must wait until development is fully achieved. Nevertheless, on the other hand, it finds a deeper truth, according to the UN: it contributes to maintaining peace and security, securing justice and human rights, and promoting economic and social development.

> It is a universal value based on the free expression of peoples to determine their political, economic, social and cultural systems and their full participation in all aspects of their lives.[5]

Authoritarian governments, which lack legitimacy, too often resort to intimidation and violence to suppress domestic disagreement. They tend to reject institutions, the free press, and the independent judiciary. The atmosphere of tension and oppression that is felt in neighboring countries can intensify the fear of war. Therefore, while the criticism echoes, there are potential justifications for this value to become universal.

Institutions in democratic processes channel interests on a deliberation ground and offer means of compromise that can be respected by all participants in the debates, thus reducing the risk that differences or controversies will trigger conflicts or armed confrontations. Also by being freely elected by regular and genuine elections by their citizens, they end up promoting and respecting the rule of law, and the rights of individuals and minorities. Moreover, they effectively cope with social conflicts, as they absorb migrant populations and respond to the needs of marginalized groups.

It is true that the introduction of democratic practices strengthens civil society and governability. This assertion is also capable of promoting imminent danger, especially in underdeveloped societies because government capacity can be devoted entirely to the promotion of the basic needs of the population and this can promote the reverse of the democratic sense.

From the external point of view, intuitions and democratic processes can foster peace between States. The legitimacy conferred on democratically elected governments means that they enjoy respect for peoples and boost expectations of negotiation, agreements, and international relations.

In this conception, democracy is an attribute of the political regime capable, therefore, of providing an environment for the protection and effective realization of human rights enshrined in the Universal Declaration of Human Rights, developed in the International Covenant on Civil and Political Rights, which contains a series of directives that sustain significant democracies.

It is a pioneering experience of the UN in this body of international restructuring from the construction of the League of Nations and the logic of its alliance framed

[5] United Nations (2012).

in the aftermath of the First World War. The pact thus concluded was designed to ensure protection against the dangers of frustrated nationalism by respecting self-determination; balance power through a shared security system; reverse the arms race through the policy of disarmament; and replace the secret treaties with open diplomacy. It was understood as the link capable of uniting efforts.[6]

The UN action to broker the achievement of these goals through the Report of the Office of the High Commissioner for Human Rights,[7] dated 2012, reflects the efforts that the United Nations has made to guarantee democracy from a human rights perspective. It is concluded that ensuring this regime is a continuous exercise and these challenges can arise both in politically stabilized and transition countries.

In parts of Latin America, Africa, Europe, and Asia, numerous authoritarian regimes have given way to increasingly sensitive democratic forces and increasingly open societies. In some, the transition process took place through democratization for the first time; in others, the changes restored their roots.[8]

This democratic resumption is considered essential for the advancement of a wide range of human interests and protection of human rights. It is undeniable that there is no model of "democratization" or "democracy" suitable for all societies. The reality is that communities, individually, must decide when to begin their process, including their nature, historical circumstances, economic situation, political will, and commitment of their members. The persistence of democracy itself requires a permanent process of renewal and political development.

By the UN definition, each society must be able to choose the form, foundation, timing, and character of its process. The imposition of foreign models not only violates the Charter of Principles of Human Rights, but also the principle of nonintervention in the internal affairs of each country.[9] This assertion stems from the fact that this determination not only contrasts with the principle enshrined in the Charter, but also of "non-interference in internal affairs", and it can generate resentment both in the State and in the population, which can fuel internal forces contrary to democratization and the idea of democracy.

Its primary purpose is to help each State to follow its own path through support based on their experiences through counseling or assistance. This support expressly requires an official request by the requesting State. According to Boutros-Ghali,[10] a community that develops democratization ends up taking responsibility and compromising with the senses that come from it. The activities and functions of the United Nations are parallel and complementary to state development activities and responsibilities, as it seeks to: provide, contribute, and coordinate assistance to those who

[6] Boutros-Ghali (1996).

[7] This study was approved by the Human Rights Council on 23 March 2012 through Resolution 19/36, which recognizes that by promoting the normative content and realization of human rights enshrined in various international instruments, it could play a role in the development and promoting compliance with the principles, norms and standards that would be the basis of democracy and the rule of law (United Nations Organization 2002a).

[8] Boutros-Ghali (1996).

[9] Boutros-Ghali (1996).

[10] Boutros-Ghali (1996).

request and seek to create a favored context in which those who ask for help and who provides a fruitful outcome.

With this method, who wins is democracy, because it can evolve and assume many faces, which will depend, effectively, on the characteristics of each society. This process needs a continuous mechanism for political renewal and development.

Although civilizations exhibit different forms of regime, the concept of democracy itself is disputed and there is a multiplicity of perspectives in understanding its inherently problematic content.

In the conception espoused by the UN, three elements can capture its content and its practice: the protection of institutions; accountability of those in power; respect for and protection of the rule of law and human rights. To ensure a more effective outcome to democratic reconstruction, it is necessary to establish an emerging consensus on democracy and its practical importance and what is the concern of the United Nations towards this same goal.

Although there is a conclusion that there is no preeminent tradition that imposes itself and is not tied to a more specific cultural context than another, strengthening local infrastructures strengthens the overall progress of the institutional reordering project. Thus, according to the UN, democracy is stronger and more resilient when it is based on legitimate representative and fair mechanisms of socio-political interaction and ends up becoming a stronger model to guarantee a framework of freedoms.[11] The purpose of the United Nations is not to persuade States to institute the regime, to apply external models or to borrow "strange" forms of government.[12]

The mechanisms adopted to give meaning to this practical support by the UN come in different forms. As noted by General Secretary Ban Ki-moon,[13] there is no model to be copied but a goal to be achieved. Some elements are essential, such as the holding of free and fair elections; the administration of transparent rules and effective regulations bringing the participatory dynamics to the fore; the promotion of rights and freedoms governed by the rule of law, among others.

This phenomenon of revalorization of constitutional democracy has a significant impact on the United Nations—just as the new States have called for support during the era of decolonization, following a new era of adherence to a State and independent policies, States are turning to Organization to request support in democratization.[14]

The new "apology for democracy" and the recent recognition of the role that the United Nations can play in democratization processes have been clearly manifested by the increased interest shown by the General Assembly in recent years and by

---

[11] This global spread can be perceived, since most States have adhered to the international instruments that establish the values of democracy such as the Universal Declaration of Human Rights, the International Covenant on Civil and Political Rights and the International Covenant on Economic, Social and Cultural.

[12] Boutros-Ghali (1996).

[13] Ban Ki-moon is the 8th Secretary-General of the UN, succeeded by Ghanaian Kofi Annan in 2007. In 2011, he was re-elected by the General Assembly by acclamation for a second term at the head of the organization by the end of December 2016.

[14] Boutros-Ghali (1996).

the increased effectiveness of the principle of the holding of periodic and authentic elections.[15]

Being democratization a new area of expertise in the context of technical assistance, since traditionally support used to be provided in the context of economic and social development, with the main emphasis on building and strengthening physical infrastructure.

After its founding and in the ensuing era of decolonization and transition, the UN began to oversee plebiscites and referendums around the world, becoming a reliable impartial actor for so-called democratic change.[16]

The evolution of this electoral reform process coincided with a major reorientation of requests for technical assistance from member States reflecting the growing interest of United Nations agencies and programs in the social dimension of development and management of public affairs. Assistance was provided before and after the elections, to ensure the continuation and consolidation of the process.[17]

Report A/51/512[18] presents in detail the types of assistance that can be provided, from guiding the creation of a political mindset to the holding of democratic elections, as well as providing advice for the creation of institutions to support the process of democratization.

Aid to create a democratic mindset can take many forms and in principle and often the milestone lies in "electoral assistance", although it is not limited and should not be limited to this context.

In Cambodia (1993) and El Salvador (1994), the UN helped the parties to hold an impartial electoral campaign, free of party intimidation, with the help of diplomacy, civic education programs, and activities to ensure equitable access to the media. In Mozambique (1994), they helped transform the National Resistance of Mozambique into a political party and facilitated the country's transition from a one-party system to a multi-party system.

On the other hand, UN programs for the return of refugees and displaced persons to their homelands have contributed greatly to the restoration of a political environment in which the possibility of establishing a democratization process can be seriously considered.

In its quest to improve democracy and institutions, the UN in 2000 recommended a series of important legislative, institutional, and practical measures to consolidate democracy through Resolution 2000/47, and in 2002 the following were declared essential: elements: respect for human rights and fundamental freedoms; freedom of association; freedom of expression and opinion; access to power and its exercise, in accordance with the rule of law; holding of free, fair and periodic elections, by

---

[15] Confirmed by the General Assembly in December 1988 through Resolution 43/157.

[16] United Nations (2012).

[17] United Nations Organization (1993).

[18] According to this report, the promotion of a democratic culture includes: political parties and movements and the mobilization of civil society; election assistance; free and independent media; creation of a political culture through observance and supervision of human rights; improved accountability and quality of public sector management and democratic governance structures; strengthening the rule of law (United Nations Organization 1996a).

universal suffrage and by secret vote, as an expression of the will of the people; pluralist system of political parties and organizations; separation of powers; independence of the judiciary; transparency and accountability in public administration; and free, independent and pluralistic media. The community activities carried out between 1994 and 2006 illustrate, among other processes, an international interest in the expansion of democracy.

Support for the diffusion of the democratic mentality is fundamental, especially for the maintenance of democratic politics after the celebration of the first referendum or election. The United Nations is committed to increase confidence, both in political processes and in national long-term capacity. It is vital to prepare, renew, and continuously strengthen the institutional foundations on which democratization can take shape.

In this way, United Nations departments, agencies, and programs are called upon to assist in the construction of constitutional projects; to create independent systems for the administration of justice; to provide police force with a view to comply and make ensure that others comply with the rule of law; to depoliticize military institutions; to establish national institutions for the promotion and protection of human rights.

This international organization is not the only actor to support democratization on the international scene. For example, in cases where the United Nations was mandated to establish or maintain peace to help achieve national reconciliation and consolidation of democracy, the establishment of informal and special groups to support its activities has contributed to and to achieve, among other things, a coordinated approach to promoting a democratic mindset.

This was the case when the "Group of Friends of the Secretary General for Guatemala" and the "Group of Friends of the Secretary General for Haiti" were established. In these cases, the UN and the Organization of American States have implemented a joint civilian mission for human rights.

This advance, by bringing a proliferation of actors, including international and regional intergovernmental organizations, individual members, non-governmental organizations, who have engaged in this effort, has formed a large global enterprise. As an example, the Organization for Security and Co-operation in Europe (OSCE), the Organization of American States (OAS), the African Union (AU), the Association of Southeast Asian Nations (ASEAN), among others. Special reference is made to The Institute for Democracy and Electoral Assistance (IDEA), the Center for Constitutional Transitions of the New York University (NYU) Law School, the Max Planck Institute, the Forum of Federations, the International Law Development Organization (IDLO) and the US Institute for Peace.

The last two decades have been an undeniable advance in their experiences, as they have provided various forms of electoral assistance to more than 100 countries, including, but not limited to, consulting, logistics, training, civic education, and computer applications. Efforts have been made to design instruments to promote a common understanding of the principles, norms, standards, and values that underpin democracy, with the aim of guiding Member States in the development of national democratic traditions and in commitment to human rights and development.

This process was also seen, influenced, and driven largely by the dialog established in the International Conferences. The first and second International Conferences of New or Restored Democracies were held in Manila in June 1988 with thirteen participating countries, respectively, and in Managua in July 1994 with 74 participating countries and at the World Conference on Human Rights, organized by the United Nations in Vienna in June 1993.

The result of all this was the creation of a post in charge of coordinating requests for electoral assistance within the UN Department of Political Affairs and an Electoral Assistance Division.

The Office of the High Commissioner on Human Rights (OHCHR) and the United Nations Development Program (UNDP) seek to address democratic deficit challenges through their advisory services and technical cooperation programs.

Other partners also provide extremely important support and are becoming instrumental in helping and perfecting the mechanisms for forging a fundamental charter.

Given its breadth, UNDP is the international primary provider for the promotion of good governance and democracy around the world, notably in terms of elections, parliamentary effectiveness and accountability, civil society participation, and the training of government officials.

In 2005, the United Nations Democracy Fund was created to support projects to build and strengthen institutions and ensure the participation of all in the process, as well as the creation of a global network of information on assistance. The leaders of the nations pledged to spare no effort to promote democracy and strengthen the rule of law.

This orientation towards democratization, according to the UN,[19] is aligned with the theme of building "democratic governance",[20] which is a food for economic and social policies to respond to the aspirations of those who seek to eradicate poverty and expansion of choices and must respect the needs of future generations.

These difficult issues in democracy and democratization suggest important lessons. The first is that it is essential for each State to decide the form, pace, and character of its democratization process.

Second, democratization must begin with an effort to create a culture of democracy. Characterized by the communication, dialog, and openness of the world's ideas and activities.

---

[19] United Nations (2012).

[20] Democratic governance is closely related to the definition of "good governance". For Valle, a fundamental right to good administration will have to understand, as a result of the protective function, a space free from the actions of the holders, who, free of any interference, have the right to formulate their own choices; the guarantee of individual intervention in the formation of the will of the public authorities; and the conditions propitiated by the public powers to overcome personal condition that prevents them from exercising values of private morality. Therefore, democratizing public administration requires implementing reflection on governance, from a participatory, inclusive and procedural perspective. It will include the "orientation to the construction of citizenship, the expansion of the public sphere of decision" that can only be reached "from the effective presence of citizenship as a co-author of public choices" (do Valle 2011).

Third, it must seek to achieve an institutional balance between the State and society. Finally, support must be followed by development, so that socio-economic, civil, and political rights are respected.

4.2 Democracy and Human Rights: Independent and Related

The link between democracy and human rights can be seen in Article 21 (3) of the Universal Declaration of Human Rights, which states:

> The will of the people will be the basis of the authority of the government; this will be expressed in periodic and legitimate elections, which must be by universal and equal suffrage, to be held by secret vote or process equivalent to the freedom to vote.

It was in 1993 that the Vienna Declaration and the program of action adopted by the World Conference on Human Rights affirmed that democracy, respect for human rights, and development are interdependent and mutually reinforcing and that the international community should support its strengthening and promotion.[21]

The rule of law is anchored in a system of government that aims to establish equality, limiting control, and guaranteeing freedom and representative government and is seen as the production of a fair model.

Democratic doctrine for the UN is a natural environment for the protection, promotion, and effective realization of human rights and justice. Thus, an objective assessment of the degree of respect for human rights and the rule of law allows for a correct analysis of the level of democracy in each country. Evidence of access and participation in public affairs and the expression of the people's sovereign choice provide tangible indications of the values and effectiveness of governance institutions under an order.

For the United Nations,[22] weak or dysfunctional institutions are among the most serious challenges to democracy. These problems can arise from an autocratic executive, an inefficient or not responsible parliament, attempts to manipulate the constitutional order and the results of the elections, the violence, and the corrosive effects of corruption, among others.

In this sense, social and incessant commitment is indispensable, so the institutionalization of strategic peace processes in conflict and post-conflict societies has a significant effect on both sides: prevention of violence and its management.

Transitions to democracy are intrinsically disordered and multifaceted. They are a deliberate course of sequential social transformation and this allows the proper integration and application of the normative values of human rights and the rule of law.

---

[21] United Nations Organization (2002b).

[22] United Nations Organization (2002b).

This fundamental change revolves around the adoption of adequate institutions for advancement, that is, the need to redistribute political power with a view to ensure effective government through constitutional reform. According to the UN, growing inequalities represent a particularly acute challenge and there is no miraculous response.

At the Second International Conference on New Democracies and Restored Democracies, held in Managua in 1994, the vulnerability that new democracies face can be observed. In short, the problems encountered were the onus of the process for the lack of a credible opposition, a weak society, a weak economy, the political monopoly of the ruling party, the potential for military intervention, and a weak democratic culture.[23]

The recommendations are therefore that the newly elected authorities should address the issue of impunity and ensure accountability for serious and systematic violations of human rights and humanitarian law by repairing an effective strategy.[24]

Strengthening and involving civil society, in practice, helps effectively resolve dilemmas. For the UN, it is essential for its proper functioning. These activities for democracy are carried out through its agencies, such as the UNDP,[25] the United Nations Democracy Fund (UNDEF), the Department for Peacekeeping Operations (DPKO), the Department of Political Affairs (DPA), and the OHCHR, among others, which allows the United Nations to be considered as one of the largest providers of global technical cooperation.

These agencies have the fundamental objective of promoting human rights and the development of peace and security. Thus, they can help parliamentarians to strengthen the controls of nations in seeking to achieve balance, allowing democracy to flourish; helping to find ways of making national human rights and judicial systems mechanisms impartial and effective; collaborating to develop political and technical capacities to guarantee access to information and freedom of expression; providing electoral assistance and long-term support to management bodies; promotion and participation of women in political and public life.

In democracies in countries emerging from conflict, OHCHR[26] collaborates with governments and other actors to address the past to rebuild public confidence and restore peace and the rule of law. Focusing on the fight against impunity, it has actively

---

[23] These observations were systematized by Usman Tar in analyzing the challenges of democracy and democratization in Africa (Tar 2010).

[24] Transitional justice, as a conception of justice associated with periods of political change, characterized by legal responses to tackling irregularities committed by repressive regimes, emerges, according to the UN, as an imperative for successful transitions. It will serve as accountability, justice and reconciliation. They may include judicial mechanisms or not, with different levels of involvement, individual accusations, clarification of the truth, institutional reform.

[25] UNDP has already helped more than 130 countries and dedicated over one and a half billion dollars to the promotion of democratic governance; supports one in three parliaments in the world in the process of developing elections; also works to promote partnerships and share ways to develop participation, accountability and effectiveness at all levels, with the goal of building legitimate and development-friendly States.

[26] OHCHR leads the United Nations human rights efforts. The Management Plan for 2014/2017 defined the axis of thematic priorities, among others: strengthening international human rights

supported transitional justice programs in more than twenty countries around the world during the last decade.

This support includes ensuring that human rights and transitional justice considerations are reflected in peace agreements; in participation and implementation of national consultations, including transitional justice mechanisms; in supporting the creation of truth-seeking processes; mechanisms of judicial accountability and reparation programs; and strengthening institutional reform.

The main challenges, according to OHCHR, are to address deepening poverty; threats to human security; violations of individual rights and impediments to the enjoyment of fundamental freedoms; the erosion of the rule of law in contexts of armed conflict; illegal occupation, involving the use of force; the escalation of conflicts; unequal access to justice by disadvantaged groups; and impunity.

In the early days of March 2010, DPA, DPKO, UNDP, and IDEA organized a roundtable[27] in New York to review the role of the United Nations in promoting development, peace, and security. In this meeting, there were four main recommendations[28] regarding substantive problems and procedures for the consolidation of democracy in and after conflict situations.

(a) Policies, practices, and knowledge related to assisting democracy in post-conflict situations evolve very rapidly. It is necessary to draw new lessons and put them into practice to foster a constant and fruitful experience between research, policies and practice;
(b) The democratization of countries affected by conflicts is a multidimensional problem. For the implementation of assistance programs, more strategic and sustainable support for security, policy, and development is needed;
(c) Democracy grows from within and external actors can only support it. It is a long-term process, complex and very context-determined. The United Nations, in its assistance, should draw on both deep local knowledge and solid comparisons;
(d) The UN system should work in collaboration with other stakeholders to provide effective support, which will require an integrated strategic approach.

In this sense, and through the guidelines of the members who composed the Round Table, there is always the possibility of improving the instruments and means, since it is impossible to determine a single project, model, or form of democracy, which, if imposed, already is born doomed to failure or inability to sustain.

---

mechanisms; promoting equality and combating discrimination; combating impunity and accountability; integration of human rights in the economic sphere; expansion of democratic space; alert and protect human rights in situations of conflict, violence and insecurity.

[27] This round table took place at an opportune moment: 10 years after the paradigmatic Brahimi report, in which the difficulties faced by United Nations activities for peacekeeping with the end of the Cold War were considered; 5 years after the creation of the Peacebuilding Commission; and one year after the initiative Novo Horizonte, which was launched by the General Secretary in search of new dimensions in peacekeeping activities. This program was organized around five studies: Afghanistan, Nepal, Timor-Leste, Haiti and West Africa.

[28] These recommendations are available in the book: Tomassoli (2010).

Thus, the great and permanent provocation will be the construction of a democratic ideal that is propelling and capable of providing the development of a nation that has just opened the door to the new challenge: democracy.

4.3 Change of Perspectives on the Role of the UN: The Political-Legal Structuring

The constitution of a country is the legal document that captures the basis of the social contract between the State and the people it is willing to serve.[29]

It can act as a legal foundation that enshrines the nation's social, cultural, economic, and political values and is generally enshrined after the conflict.[30] Whenever this contract is carried out by coercion or force, however, often the result is the eventual collapse of constitutional governance, which, in its most extreme form, leads to conflict or violence.

UN support for "constitution-building processes" in post-conflict scenarios encompasses both its formal and substantive content, reforms of existing constitutions, and the formulation of the process at the operational level.

The UN has been involved in several "constitution-building"[31] processes, including those in Afghanistan, Cambodia, Iraq, Nepal, East Timor, Haiti, among others, learning great lessons from the experiences.

This coordination task among international actors is substantially more complex and difficult than in the electoral field because it lacks a precise organization, especially to avoid wastage and duplication of tasks, mainly in conflicting advices from technical advisors, over-funding, and may lead to an imbalance between the capacities of the State and civil institutions. And the Organization is prepared to facilitate this coordination among the international actors involved in building institutions for democratization.

Among the forms of assistance, one can cite the decision-making processes, including political rights and their strategies; the development of institutional capacities; financial, logistical, and administrative support.

---

[29] United Nations Development Programme (2014).

[30] The UNDP identifies three types of post-conflict situations: self-enforcing cases, in which a winner can be identified, the defeated party can be territorially displaced, and there is a strong consensus in society on the way forward, such as Timor-Leste in 1999 and Ethiopia and Eritrea in 2000; mediated cases, in the brokered cases, the belligerent factions are relatively successful in the negotiations, which usually includes an agreement on the institutional political framework, but the suspicions and tensions do not cease, for example Guatemala in 1996 and Mozambique in 1992; conflict, in which case one side achieves a military victory, but there are no agreements or negotiations to resolve the issues that led to the conflict, for example in Nicaragua in 1979, Burundi in 2005 and Afghanistan in 2003. The level of new State is directly connected to how the conflict has ceased. In cases of self-enforcing cases the response tends to produce clearly more stable results than in conflictual cases (Hoove et al. 2008).

[31] There are many studies involving the topic such as, how O'Connor (2015), Pruitt and Thomas (2008), Benomar (2003), Harris et al. (2001).

It will be the Rule of Law Coordination and Resource Group, chaired by the Assistant General Secretary, with the support of the Rule of Law Unit, the mechanism convened for UN constitutional assistance, to ensure effective mobilization in the combination of competencies of the various departments of the Organization.

As the UNDP has extensive experience in supporting the forging of constitutions around the world, the observation made is that these processes are open and inclusive. For this reason, they tend to produce constitutions that respond to the needs of the people, including the disappeared and marginalized.

In 2009, UN General Secretary Ban Ki-moon released a note providing the principles for UN involvement in the drafting of a constitution, and at the time, stated that the Guidance Note[32] is a living document to be updated from time to time and derives from the lessons learned from the constitutional experiences of previous assistance, with guiding principles.

(a) *Seize the opportunity for peacebuilding in conflict and post-conflict countries*

Considered a key opportunity, it should be understood as the means to support a comprehensive political transition, requiring a coherent and multifaceted approach. This engagement should be evaluated on a case-by-case basis. This means that there must be prior and full knowledge of the national situation and the political complexities, as well as the practical and symbolic implications of its involvement. The requested assistance may range from technical and legal expertise to facilitate negotiations between stakeholders on the structure of the process and on fundamental constitutional principles. It can involve assistance in the creation of education and public consultation campaigns, as well as providing administrative and financial support for the construction of the body of the charter;

(b) *Encourage compliance with international standards*

Thus, the UN should systematically promote compliance with the constitutions with a commitment to the realization of human rights under the norms of international law. In this sense, it must interfere when a draft constitution is not in conformity with these norms, especially regarding the administration of justice, transitional justice, electoral systems, and several other issues having, for this, involving national actors in a dialog and explaining the country's obligations to international law and how these predictions should be met in the charter. These incentives are intended to ensure the rights of groups subject to marginalization and discrimination in the country, including women, children, minorities, indigenous peoples, refugees, stateless persons, displaced persons. One example is the principle of equality between men and women, which should be incorporated into constitutions;

(c) *National ownership*

It means that the UN must recognize that the process of building the constitution is national and sovereign. It must ensure that its success is owned by all and must

[32] The 2009 version is the result of a review, the original of which was prepared in 2006. The framework is derived from lessons learned in previous UN experiences, as already shown in the respective chapter.

be sensitive to the need for counseling, preventing the UN or other international bodies from imposing a foreign constitution. Such advice should carefully observe the local context, recognizing that there is no single model or constitutional process, and should include official actors, political parties, civil society, and the public.

(d) *Support for inclusion, participation, and transparency*

These must also be their efforts, given the comparative experiences and the impact of inclusion/exclusion that participation can promote, including the legitimacy of new documents. This exercise can be transformative, providing a means for people to experience the basics of democratic governance and learn about international principles and norms, thereby raising expectations for engagement in the democratic process. Inclusive and participatory processes are more likely to generate consensus around a desirable constitutional framework. This includes government officials, politicians, religious leaders, and civil society (trade unions, community organizations, social movements, and academic institutions). In this way, the dissemination to all social groups, including children and the support of education campaigns and public consultation are essential mechanisms.

(e) *Mobilize and coordinate a wide range of knowledge*

It means that knowledge must come both from outside and within the UN system. This will ensure best international and comparative practices. It will also contribute to broadening the knowledge of the options of national actors and helping them to explore solutions that are technically sound and possibly conducive to long-term stability. While national authorities should play the role of lead coordinator, there should be an incentive to expand partnerships with other national and international actors, regional organizations, and other networks to assist the coordinator in designing more effectively the structure and competencies of institutions democratic institutions.

(f) *Promoting adequate follow-up after the adoption of the Constitution*

Follow-up may include dissemination and education on the charter approved, development of subsidiary legislation, and the full range of capacity building and institutional development.

The elements that make up the process of refounding a nation at the operational level are numerous and complex.[33] It begins with a high-level negotiation between the fundamental constituents, eventually forging an agreement on how the constitution will be and its adoption.

[33] One of the major difficulties faced by UN agencies, such as the UNDP, is the financial assessment and the administrative and specialized support to be provided. In this sense, operational support, such as the coordination of the participants, is crucial for defining the success of the mission.

The UN, in its experiences, has also used ad hoc[34] approaches, leading to mixed results, and there is a need to develop strategic guidance on how to support national actors in designing and implementing the fundamental charter exercise.

National and transitional authorities can request their assistance[35] by pointing out that, regardless of the request, it requires careful planning and knowledge of the reality of the requesting State, which is an important element in promoting inclusion, participation, and transparency. The assessment and need[36] for building a constitution in a conflict or post-conflict situation can be predicted in a peace agreement or similar. This assistance is limited to negotiation or technical-legal expertise.

Each application is procedurally followed by a sequence that includes the official request; the evaluation; the drawing; the execution; and monitoring. Emphasis is often placed on the ability of national electoral management bodies to implement legitimate elections. This also includes training, the media, political parties, civil society, as well as parliament and the judiciary.

As a relevant segment of support offered by the UN in the process of re-democratization, electoral assistance is a team effort involving several programs, funds, agencies, and departments and is closely regulated by the General Assembly.[37] In addition to the UNDP, DPKO[38] also plays an important operational role in

---

[34] Ad hoc approaches are constituted by informal groups created by States to support the United Nations in this effort and served to establish, among other goals, a coordinated approach in promoting a culture of democracy. Such was the case of the "Friends of the General Secretary for El Salvador", the "Friends of the General Secretary of Guatemala", the "Friends of the General Secretary for Haiti", where the United States and the Organization of American States a joint mission in defense of human and civil rights (Boutros-Ghali 1996).

[35] Assistance may include, but is not limited, depending on the country context, to assistance in negotiating an initial agreement on the structure of the constitution process; strategic assistance in the process of selecting the body that will make up the representative forum; political facilitation on key controversial issues, both material and procedural; providing comparative legal analysis on institutional designs and options for addressing key constitutional areas; advice on the requirements of international treaties (declaration of rights, internal effect of treaties, rules of acquisition and loss of nationality, etc.); advising on the creation of the institutional structure of a secretariat and its development; assistance in the training of drafters to incorporate technical and negotiation skills; assistance in the creation and implementation of civic public training; assistance in creating and implementing a public consultation process (including local groups, questionnaires, village meetings, and synthesis of information collected) to be led by national actors; assistance in implementing measures for ratification, including referendum on the draft constitution; financial assistance, including budgeting, donor coordination, etc.; logistics assistance and administrative support.

[36] As this process is highly political, a "local institutional and context" analysis is strongly recommended. This term refers to the analysis in which the political and institutional factors related to the use of national and external resources on the implementation of the UN programs of political advice are concentrated. It assists in mapping the main stakeholders in the process, which includes the views of parliament, militias, political parties, local, indigenous or religious leaders, civil society groups. For more information, consult United Nations Development Programme (2012).

[37] United Nations (2012).

[38] The DPKO provides policy and executive guidance for UN peacekeeping operations. In direct contact with the Security Council, this department works to integrate the efforts offering guidance and support of military forces, police, demining, among others. Created in 1948 with the first UN

providing security, technical advice, and logistical support to national authorities administering elections in peacekeeping missions.

In many contexts, the United Nations, to ensure the effectiveness of its guidelines, establish coordinated actions in the constitution-making process in view of the fact that many of its agencies have the expertise, such as the OHCHR on human rights; the United Nations Entity for Gender and the Empowerment of Woman, UNHCR (United Nations High Commissioner for Refugees) on refugees, UNICEF (United Nations Children's Fund) on the rights of children in gender equality, UNODC (United Nations Office on Drugs and Crime) on Anti-Corruption Liability.

The United Nations Integrated Mission for Peacebuilding in Sierra Leone Sierra in 2013 (United Nations Integrated Peacebuilding Office in Sierra Leone—UNIPSIL) was designed specifically to recognize the various United Nations agencies with different technical competencies that have integrated the project. It included UN-Woman, OHCHR, UNICEF as well as DPA.

While it should not be considered as a model of a single electoral system, it is important that this means fulfills the obligations and commitments set out in international human rights instruments. It was Resolution A/RES/46/137,[39] which was approved by the General Assembly, which authorized the General Secretary to establish rules to support the coordination and examination of electoral assistance.

Its primary activity is the analysis of petitions concerning the requests, in the presentation of an opinion on the apparent needs, in the collaboration with other agencies of the United Nations system, in the design of assistance projects, and in the practical guarantee of the electoral processes of peace operations maintenance.

In addition, it also provides logistical support and advice to international observer groups, facilitating coordination among countries, maintaining a list of electoral experts, organizing conferences and training courses, advising on the administration of party funds, among others.

In 1991, the General Assembly of the United Nations issued a Resolution establishing the Electoral Assistance Unit to institutionalize the considerable demand for election observation around the world.[40] The UN was the first organization to observe the Korean elections in 1948 and in later decades acquired considerable importance in the period of decolonization by organizing 30 missions between 1956 and 1960.

Operations followed a common pattern. The first step was to determine when and under which circumstances an election, plebiscite, or referendum[41] should be held. This decision was taken, in most cases, by the government in charge of the territory administration, which communicated with the organization, requesting its assistance in the observation and supervision of the process.

---

peace operations: *UN Truce Supervision Organization* (UNTSO) and *UN Military Observer Group in India and Pakistan* (UNMOGIP) (United Nations 2012).

[39] United Nations Organization (1991).

[40] Carrillo (2007).

[41] Boneo et al. (2007).

The first mission of the Trusteeship Council including an electoral component took place in Togo in 1956, hitherto under British administration.[42] Between 1956 and 1960, a peculiar feature of these operations was their size, rarely included more than 30 observers, although in cases of a high degree of distrust or potential conflict.

Between 1989 and 1992, 23 observer missions from a total of 30 applications were attended. The observation is a pioneering mechanism that would allow the creation of several ways for the international community to participate in the processes of democratization in the different countries, without prejudice to their sovereignty and independence, although the impact is directed to two spheres, political and technical.

At the time of the Namibian elections in 1989, which corresponded strongly to the category of "decolonization", scope, scale, and duration became a category. The United Nations Transition Assistance Group (UNTAG) was created to have 8,000 people, including 2000 civil servants, 1,500 police officers, and 4,500 military personnel. The 1,800 UNTAG employees oversaw 380 polling places.[43]

There are three aspects of UNTAG that need to be highlighted: (i) trust in the process—because it relied on a massive public information campaign, using radio, television, and printed materials, as well as direct contact with voters, relevant actors; (ii) it was the first UN electoral mission resulting from a broad political agreement, which served as a parameter for other large operations; (iii) good results, visibility contributed to the creation of a myth that the success of an election observation is directly related to the number of observers.

High-level negotiation among key constituencies can lead to agreement on the charter or its reform. It will be introduced the structure and model for the process, also mentioning who will be involved in the project, how the articles will be selected, how the consensus will be built, how it will be approved, the timeline, and who will be responsible for resolving the conflicts. The development of these capacities and institutional support include, for example, the creation of a constituent assembly, a constitutional review committee, round tables or national conferences, analysis of the final draft of the constitutional charter, etc.

In Zimbabwe, at the request of the government, UNDP assisted the Constitutional Parliamentary Commission in technical expertise, providing a constitutional consultant with regional and international experience in the constitution-making process, who could provide technical and strategic advice proving that this aid is crucial, especially during the constitutional project phase.

Another supportive experience occurred in Kyrgyzstan, where in 2010, in a context of political instability, the UNDP, in cooperation with the European Union, assisted the constitutional reform project that involved both the substantive elements of the charter as well as local awareness. Four working groups were developed on the key sectors of the project: constitutional and State-based foundations, human rights, judiciary, and self-governance. As a result, the charter has been commended for the integration of democratic principles and human rights.

---

[42] Boneo et al. (2007).

[43] Boneo et al. (2007).

In 2011, the National Constituent Assembly of Vietnam called on the United Nations to help bring in international experts and comparative experiences to discuss controversies, including different models of constitutional and government review, as well as human rights provisions.[44]

In Tunisia, support for the constitution-making process was conceived in 2009 at the request of the new Tunisian authorities and was implemented from 2012 to 2015. The UN supported the National Constituent Assembly in three main areas: organizing an open and participative process; institutional capacity building; and the development of mechanisms for constitutional and political dialogs to ensure civil society's contribution to the process.

A "Constitutional Commission" may be established to conduct civic education and public consultation campaigns, as well as to prepare the project. There will be a secretariat or other body to support and implement the committee's decisions, being responsible for logistics. What includes the structure, technological support, equipment, etc.

Essential to the public consultation, to have the points of view and guarantees the inclusion of the population on the project of the constitution. For example, the documentation to be distributed to the population needs to be prepared to contemplate local languages. The process must be followed by a lengthy population dialog that will also feed the forum into the formation of the constitution.

As an example, the process of constitution-making in Kenya was a key pillar in the country's transition to more democratic development. And it was the UNDP that helped spread public awareness about the charter project through town hall meetings, radio and television campaigns, newspapers, and village meetings in various parts of the country. About seven million copies of the project have been distributed. At the end of the process, the charter was approved following a referendum with more than 65% of voters ratifying the document in early August 2010.[45]

In Georgia, UNDP supported the State Constitutional Commission to review the constitution to resolve the political crisis facing the country. The emphasis was on the inclusion of all stakeholders in the process to ensure the broad support and legitimacy of the charter. This included awareness-raising and consultation with the Georgian people, holding round tables and seminars. He also supported Parliament to create an official web page and Facebook so that citizens could access the constitutional project and its amendments and share their own ideas and observations. A specialized consultancy was also provided to include a new chapter in the project concerning self-governance as a constitutional guarantee, which occurred for the first time in the country's history.

In Fiji, to maximize participation in the constitutional development process, UNDP implemented the Community Outreach to Support the Constitutional Development Process Project, which aimed to improve public understanding of why the

---

[44] The UNDP used the advice got in *Interpeace Manual "Constitutional-making and reform: options for the process"*. Interpeace is an independent peacebuilding organization and a strategic partner of the UN (Brant et al. 2011).

[45] United Nations Development Programme (2014).

constitution is important to Fijian life (through workshops) and promoted inclusive and participatory spaces so that people could talk.

The final draft of the constitutional charter, following recommendations from the UN, must also be presented by a representative forum for discussion, thus enabling changes. In addition, for the text approval, a qualified majority quorum in the forum should be required, followed by a referendum. Civic education on the newly approved charter and on how to develop your commandments and strategies for its implementation will be the next step.

4.4 The Foundational Charter: A Pre-requisite to Achieve the Development of Nations

In their seventy-one years of life, and in the pursuit of their goals, although historically recent, the various interventions that led to this have made it possible to weigh the results of their actions, as well as to carry out self-analyzes in the search for improvement of the implementation tools of change.

According to Benomar,[46] it is in the process of drafting a new constitution that there are issues and dilemmas. For example, for him there are not many benefits to uniting the peace term with the making of a charter. Experience has shown that, in this case, public participation is generally minimal. It ends up being conducive only for purposes of conflict resolution. It is extremely important to increase the number of groups participating in the constitution-making process, as the exclusion of key actors may compromise the legitimacy of the outcome, including the durability of the document.

Still aiming at conflict resolution, it has been shown that an initial or provisional power-sharing agreement, guaranteeing the representation of the main parties, is a good thing; the process of negotiation between stakeholders on fundamental constitutional principles is crucial; the extended deliberation between the key groups and the involvement of the participants lays the foundation for a multi-party policy and consultation culture.

One of the main concerns of societies emerging from conflict is the difficulty of making democratic institutions impartial and strong. Often organizations are weak, corrupted by the collapse of the State, and there is no political will for reconciliation coupled with popular mistrust.[47] Bosnia and Herzegovina and Zimbabwe[48] are examples of countries where the combination of the process has provoked profound

---

[46] Jamal Benomar is a special adviser to the General Secretary of the United Nations and since 2011 served as special envoy for the construction of democracy in Yemen (Benomar 2003).

[47] Benomar (2003).

[48] The empirical data supporting these claims have been mapped out in a joint project sponsored by UNDP/BCPR in partnership with the United States Institute of Peace. The following countries were surveyed: Bosnia and Herzegovina, Brazil, Cambodia, Colombia, East Timor, Eritrea, Ethiopia, Fiji, Namibia, Nicaragua, South Africa, Spain, Venezuela and Zimbabwe (Benomar 2003).

disagreements without providing a solid path to political change and guaranteeing the political system.

The purpose of the process is not only to resolve conflict between groups, but also to be inclusive and transparent, and to be successful in managing conflicts and facilitating negotiation, reciprocity, and collaboration.

In this way, it can have a double effect: to contribute significantly to national reconciliation or to further destabilization if the sense of belonging and identity are not intertwined.

In addition, there are issues of extreme relevance that need to be considered, such as the peace agreement and the building of the charter; the internal security of the country; the inclusion of political actors; constituent assemblies or constitutional, appointed, or elected committees; public participation; human rights.

Benomar[49] further states that the constitution is a vital component of conflict resolution and national reconciliation, although not all litigation can be settled through a constitution. For this reason, military and security issues are taken in moments prior to democratization or re-democratization. The end of the armed hostilities and the signing of the peace agreement are preconditions for the beginning of the construction of the fundamental document. Namibia is an example of a country that the agreement was entered before the start of work on the new order.[50]

Another extremely relevant issue that should be considered in the analysis is internal security.[51] It is considered as a key issue, as turbulence can prevent that the process of drawing up an open and transparent charter happens. The experiences of Ethiopia and Cambodia are reflective of this assertion, where political leaders justified the participation of the public in an inadequate way, in view of the population's great fear of vulnerabilities due to violence.

In Ethiopia, there was no national army or police force legally constituted to ensure the necessary security for the elections, which was eventually associated with lack of time, helping to establish the conditions for effective local participation.

In Cambodia, the agreements concluded were supervised by the UN, but the implementation of security, such as disarmament, demobilization, and ceasefire agreements, was not successful. In view of this, the UN assumed the calculated risk to continue with the composition elections of the constituent assembly. As a result, the political violence continued until the elections, during the election and before the interim government. Although they were considered free and fair and the mass participation of the people, the continuation of internal violence was the justification for closing the method.

[49] Benomar (2003).

[50] Benomar (2003).

[51] Benomar (2003).

It is imperative that internal conflict be solved, or that it risks inhibiting meaningful debate and consensus-building among all stakeholders, as well as jeopardizing the durability of the text.

In Nicaragua and Colombia, armed combat did not cease during the procedure of fabricating the founding text and significantly impaired the ability of the parties concerned to reach an agreement on the future of the State.[52]

The constitution contributes to peace and stability when it reflects an acceptable political pact between those who control political and capital power in the post-conflict context.[53] In the case of countries emerging from civil conflicts, the losing party is not always included in the process, as the experience in Cambodia indicates. This issue has been overcome in the context of South Africa, where there have been political parties of questionable moral repute.

This is an extremely delicate but essential issue for the survival of any post-conflict agreement. It is important to increase the number of groups participating in the system. In some situations, it is difficult to foresee a solution, which ends up not guaranteeing all actors some political representation, decision-making power, and permanent territory, as in the case of the Balkans.

On the other hand, this magnification can also bring risks. Accommodating the various interests can lead to a counterproductive and ineffective response, compromising even the stability of the document.

Embedded by experience, when the process is merely a political compromise, it risks producing a short-term agreement that serves merely the interests of the elite over the construction of strong and stable democratic institutions. Fundamental principles and respect for human rights are at risk.

The method of producing a constitution must be inclusive. This form has the power to prevent a counterrevolutionary threat to the new order that emanates and ultimately forms a consensus on fundamental constitutional principles.

This response can be seen in the process of drawing up the South African charter—the sharing of power between key groups, which existed from the early stage of the transition to a democratic government, has effectively contributed to the resolution of conflicts.

52 Benomar (2003).

53 Benomar (2003).

The experiences of Namibia[54] and Spain[55] have also shown great advantages, while Ethiopia,[56] Venezuela[57], and Colombia[58] have finally confirmed the detriment of the exclusion of the main elites.

In the case of Nicaragua, the dominant political force in the country could have imposed a charter, but it did open space to various sectors of society, accommodating several opposition concerns in trying to resolve the conflicts. Even so, the main differences between the actors were not solved, which ended up containing in their texts principles and contradictory ambiguities, in addition to a superficial consensus.[59]

Another major problem to be faced is the formation of the constituent assembly: elected or appointed. The composition of the assembly tends to be an extremely important factor as it becomes the subject of dispute between the key groups. This encompasses the type of chosen institutions to be involved during the process, the time, and sequence of the phases. This context exists mainly to prevent a single group from dominating the process and to allow legitimacy from opening to the public.

Facing the problem from the logic of the formation of the constituent assembly is essential, since if there are elections, these will legitimize the domination of the process by the winner. In this sense, the main foundation can be compromised since the objective is to resolve the struggle between classes and guarantee the future interests of society.

On the other hand, the alternative of developing this same function by appointed commissions does not enjoy the legitimacy of an elected body, but it can contribute to edification by informing and providing equal access to all debates.

Essential to the preparatory work for the establishment of an acceptable institutional order are those that precede the election of members, which may include preparatory campaigns for civic education and opportunities for consultation and debate among those who wish to participate in the process.

---

[54] In Namibia, all stakeholders in 1981 reached agreement on the principles relating to the Constituent Assembly and the Constitution, adopted unanimously in 1989.

[55] In the case of Spain, except for a very small minority, most of all relevant groups chose to participate in the process rather than creating obstacles.

[56] In Ethiopia, opposition leaders rejected the legitimacy of the Constitutional Commission and its project, out of resentment of exclusion from the transition agenda. In addition, the Commission worked "behind closed doors", which eventually contributed to the exclusion of minority groups. Another issue was the lack of dialog between groups of important and controversial issues regarding race, self-determination and the form of government.

[57] In Venezuela, only one group was part of the constitutional process to facilitate takeover and control of the State. In this sense, all possibilities for inclusion were wasted. As a result, the main concerns of the people with important issues such as decentralization and party reform have not been addressed. The political system still needs significant reforms.

[58] The production of the Colombian letter failed to achieve peace, mainly due to the absence of two rebel groups at the negotiating table.

[59] Benomar (2003).

Namibia[60] and South Africa[61] are experiences of considerable preparatory work, thus preventing a single group from determining the outcome of the constituent process. On the other hand, Bosnia and Herzegovina offers a great example of a country where the charter was forged in a short space of time, since the emphasis was on the ceasefire, which did not reflect the agreement of the parties concerned on the nature of the State and the political system and the common future. Their disagreements and positions of power remain rooted and consequently the charter may not have the capacity to guarantee the longevity of the current political system.

It is undeniable that committees should have independence and be able to consider long-term interests. Combining an elected constituent assembly with a nominated commission and a referendum may represent a resolution of the problem.

The means of producing a document that will be determined by the nation contributes significantly to the development of its democratic culture. It may lose its legitimacy when it fails to find civic education, political participation and activism, and respect for civil and human rights. Standards cannot be imposed by elites and international bodies and should reflect an agreement within the population on how to live together. This allows accommodating the constitutional identity of the subjects and the claim of a document that is proper, representing a sense of belonging.

Although international law does not specifically define the policies and processes required to construct a charter, an international norm that requires popular participation is emerging. This standard provides for the involvement of the public and civil society in the debate. Most countries that have been involved in the process of composing a new institutional model in several different ways over the past twenty years have tried to incorporate the public, such as South Africa, Namibia, and Eritrea. In South Africa, the work was open and transparent, via broadcast and media publications of all debates, and counted on almost two million requests from the population, whether by e-mail, meetings, surveys, or contributions over the Internet. In Namibia, information was transmitted by political parties and by the radio system, which contributed to inform essential questions.

Eritrea is a great example of public opening of the process. It included a civic education phase consisting of a series of seminars, held at village level by more than four hundred specially trained instructors. The second phase consisted of a public consultation on proposals made by the constitutional commission. In the third, the

---

[60] In Namibia, substantial and long-term discussions among all actors resulted in an agreement where there would be an election to compose the Assembly, which would adopt the Constitution of Independence. A constitutional commission analyzed the draft constitution before being submitted to the Assembly. The constitutional debate in Namibia lasted for a long time, about 15 years, which eventually invaded the political landscape and effectively influenced political developments. This included strengthening political parties. In 1982, an agreement was reached that guided the future of the letter, being decided that "Namibia will be a unitary, sovereign and democratic State".

[61] In South Africa, a provisional constitution preceded the 1996 letter. This was born out of intense negotiations between the parties, which eventually established principles governing the election of a Constituent Assembly through a system of proportional representation. The path taken by South Africans was the result of various political pacts that established informal institutions of power sharing. The Record of Understanding of November 1992 formed the core of the 1993 Provisional Letter.

commission received comments on the design of regional assemblies, local and civil society members and organizations, as well as on an individual basis.

The Colombian procedure also deserves to be highlighted, since the government has created more than 1,500 work groups throughout the country to receive proposals from different social groups, including positions of academics, lawyers, workers, farmers, among others.

On the other hand, Cambodia, Ethiopia, East Timor, and Fiji, whose popular participation has been limited, both because of the secrecy of the negotiations and because of the insufficient time devoted to public deliberations. In these cases, the charters suffer from a lack of legitimacy.

According to the UN, when a society commits itself to a fundamental charter it cannot abandon its obligations under international law and must remain faithful to the common principles of humanity. Most of the post-conflict constitutions adopted over the past 10–15 years have been deeply influenced by the centrality of human rights and the universal principles of international law.

A great example is the Timorese Charter, which was inspired by international law, since all civil and political rights and many of the economic, social, and cultural rights were included. The Constitution of Nicaragua also recognized the importance of these rights, including in its provisions the Universal Declaration of Human Rights, the International Covenant on Economic and Social Rights, among others.

References

Benomar, J. (2003). *Constitution-making and peace building: Lessons learned from the constitution-making processes of post-conflict countries*. United Nations Development Programme. Retrieved Mar 9, 2013, from http://www.unrol.org/doc.aspx?n=Constitution+making+and+peace+building+Report_Jamal+Benomar.doc

Boneo, H., Carrillo, M., & Valverde, R. (2007). La observación internacional y nacional de las elecciones. In D. Nohlen, D. Zovatto, J. Orozco, & J. Thompson (Eds.), *Tratado de Derecho Electoral comparado de América Latina*, 1077 (2nd ed.). Fondo de Cultura Económica. Instituto Interamericano de Derechos Humanos, Universidad de Heidelberg, International IDEA, Tribunal Electoral del Poder Judicial de la Federación, Instituto Federal Electoral.

Boutros-Ghali, B. (1996). *An agenda for democratization* (Vol. 1). UN.

Brant, M., et al. (2011). Constitution-making and reform: Options for the process (Interpeace).

Carrillo, M. (2007). Cooperación Internacional. In D. Nohlen, D. Zovatto, J. Orozco, & J. Thompson (Eds.), *Tratado de Derecho Electoral comparado de América Latina* (Vol. 86) (2nd ed.). Fondo de Cultura Económica, Instituto Interamericano de Derechos Humanos, Universidad de Heidelberg, International IDEA, Tribunal Electoral del Poder Judicial de la Federación, Instituto Federal Electoral.

Harris, P., Reilly, B., & Zovatto, D. (2001). Democracia constituição y conflictos profundamente arraigados: opciones para la negociación vii. Estocolmo: International Institute for Democracy and Electoral Assistance.

Hoove, L. T., Scholtbach, A. P., & Maul-Phillips, J. (2008). *Democracy and political party assistance in post-conflict societies* (p. 6). Netherlands Institute for Multiparty Democracy, NIMD Knowledge Centre.

O'Connor, V. (2015). Mapping the justice system and legal framework in a conflict-affected country. International Network to Promote the Rule of Law, 4-41. Retrieved Nov 04m, 2015, from http:/ /ssrn.com/abstract=2665652

Pruitt, B., & Thomas, P. (2008). *Diálogo democrático um manual para practicantes*. Agencia Canadiense de Desarrollo Internacional (ACDI), Instituto Internacional para la Democracia constituição la Asistencia Electoral (IDEA), Secretaría General de la OEA (SG/OEA), Programa de las Naciones Unidas para el Desarrollo (PNUD).

Tar, U. A. (2010). The challenges of democracy and democratization in Africa and the Middle East. *Information, Society and Justice* 81–94. Retrieved Jun 13, 2014, from http://eprints.londonmet.ac.uk/100/1/InformationSocietyAndJustice_v3n2_p81-94.pdf

Tomassoli, M. (2010). *Democracia, paz y seguridad: el rol de las Naciones Unidas*. Institute for Democracy and Electoral Assistence, UN, PNUD.

United Nations. (2012a). *Global issues, democracy, democracy and elections*. http://www.un.org/en/globalissues/democracy/elections.shtml

United Nations. (2012b). *Global issues, democracy, democracy and United Nations*. http://www.un.org/en/globalissues/democracy/democracy_and_un.shtml

United Nations. (2012c). *What we do, maintain international peace and security, peacekeeping, about us*. Department of Peacekeeping Operations. http://www.un.org/en/peacekeeping/about/dpko

United Nations Development Programme. (2012). *Democratic governance, institutional and context analysis guidance note* (New York). Retrieved Aug 23, 2013, from http://www.undp.org/content/undp/en/home/librarypage/democraticgovernance/oslo_governance_centre/Institutional_and_Context_Analysis_Guidance_Note.html

United Nations Development Programme. (2014). *UNPD guidance note on constitution-making support 5* (New York). Retrieved Mar 23, 2015, from http://www.undp.org/content/undp/en/home/librarypage/democraticgovernance/parliamentary_development/GuidanceNote_ConstitutionMakingSupport.html

United Nations Organization. (1991). *General assembly. Increasing the effectiveness of the principles of periodic and genuine elections*. Resolution A/RES/46/137. Retrieved Jun 26, 2013, from http://www.un.org/documents/ga/res/46/a46r137.htm

United Nations Organization. (1993). *General assembly. Increasing the effectiveness of the principles of periodic and genuine elections*. Resolution A/RES/48/131. Retrieved Jun 26, 2013, from http://www.un.org/documents/ga/res/48/a48r131.htm

United Nations Organization. (1996a). *General assembly. Support from the United Nations system for the efforts of governments to promote and consolidate new or restored democracies*. Resolution A/51/512. Retrieved Jun 26, 2013, from http://www.un.org/en/ga/search/view_doc.asp?symbol=A/51/512&referer=http://www.un.org/en/sc/documents/search.shtml&Lang=S

United Nations Organization. (1996b). *General assembly. Support from the United Nations system for the efforts of governments to promote and consolidate new or restored democracies*. Resolution A/51/761. Retrieved Jun 26, 2013, from http://www.un.org/en/ga/search/view_doc.asp?symbol=A/51/761&referer=http://www.un.org/en/sc/documents/search.shtml&Lang=S

United Nations Organization. (2002a). *General assembly. Studies on the common challenges of States in their efforts to ensure democracy, the rule of law and human rights*. Resolution A/HRC/22/29. Retrieved Jun 26, 2013, from http://www.ohchr.org/Documents/HRBodies/HRCouncil/RegularSession/Session22/A.HRC.22.29_English.pdf

United Nations Organization. (2002b). *General meeting. Studies on the common challenges of States in their efforts to ensure democracy, the rule of law and human rights*. Resolution A/HRC/22/29. Retrieved Jun 26, 2013, from http://www.ohchr.org/Documents/HRBodies/HRCouncil/RegularSession/Session22/A.HRC.22.29_English.pdf

United Nations Organization. (2002c). *General meeting. Studies on the common challenges of states in their efforts to ensure democracy, the rule of law and human rights*. Resolution A/HRC/22/29. Retrieved Jun 26, 2013, from http://www.ohchr.org/Documents/HRBo

do Valle, V. R. L. (2011). Direito fundamental à boa administração e governança, 133 (Fórum).

Chapter 5
A Constitution-Making Analysis from the Un Intervention: The Difficulties of Materialization of the Constitutionalism of Transition and Transformation

5.1 Constitution-Making

In this scenario, according to Teitel,[1] democratization in the periods of change is aimed at the construction of the political order, being fundamentally constitutive of the perception that involves the study of the nature of the constitutionalism employed.

According to Widner,[2] during the last forty years, more than 200 new constitutions have appeared in countries that presented internal violence. This experience, which began to incorporate foreign actors, presupposes significant questions about the concept of constitutionalism employed and its ability to guide the process of institutional restructuring.

In this sense, does the role that the UN intends to develop enable the emergence of a merely symbolic constitutionalism or a transitional and transformational constitutionalism?

In the case of a nation needy of strong democratic traditions, this international intervention can prove to be extremely important, helping to shape the process of constitutionalization of a new democratic order, giving the institutional framework economic and political support for the very sustenance and implementation of new values or on the contrary, provoking new and successive social destabilization. It will be the materialization of the constitutionalism of transition and transformation that will deflagrate this progressive ideal.

According to Barros,[3] transitional change occurred because of five different contexts: (i) an important wave occurred as part of the post-World War II decolonization process, whose emphasis revolved around the creation of new sovereign States. The choice of procedure was partially influenced by domestic factors, such as the complexity and diversity of society; (ii) another influence was associated with

[1] Teitel (2003, 70).

[2] Widner (2008, 1513).

[3] Workshop on Constitution Building Processes (2007, 5).

C. B. Gouvêa and P. H. V. B. Castelo Branco, *UN Interventions and Democratization*, Societies and Political Orders in Transition,
https://doi.org/10.1007/978-3-031-32715-5_5

democratization, initially in Latin America and part of Asia and later in Africa. The intention was to deepen democracy; (iii) the collapse of communism presented a third wave in the political context. The end of the Soviet empire brought a change of regime to the relatively strong States in Central Europe and the Baltic countries; (iv) in other States, sometimes related to the collapse of communism, sometimes related to the democratization that followed the fall of the Berlin Wall, as in parts of Africa. These constitutions had to face institutional crises, in addition to regime change; (v) and the drafting of a post-conflict charter that has attracted significant attention, since it is partly about the reconstruction of a political community as well as about State structures.

The causes, forms, and rhythm of these different tendencies varied considerably, but they shared a characteristic, simultaneous, dominant movement towards more liberal and often more democratic governance, known as a global democratic trend that thanks to Samuel Huntington[4] to be widely known as the third wave of democracy.

Most of these new political systems, in addition to democratic institutions, have a form of active judicial review. Constitutional courts have emerged as the translators of these provisions to guide constitutional living. This traffic has been intense and reflects what may be called the "supposedly universal speech".[5]

These demonstrations eventually created constitutional charters with similar patterns from a liberal matrix, which provoked a reflection on their real "power relationship".[6] This means an openness to participation, considering its architectural design and development.

According to Richie,[7] it must be organically connected to develop the concept of "constitutional belonging," relative to the level of investment a people must have with a document that is the legal and political basis of the Nation-State in which they live.

A simplistic but powerful view cannot be forgotten: the constitutions neither originate nor operate in a vacuum. Its importation cannot be described or explained independently of the social, political, and economic forces, national and international.

The UN[8] believes that democracy is consolidated over time and its maintenance is a time consuming and continuous exercise demanding a constant investment, and democratization refers to the crystallization of a new system. Chapter 4 gave us an account of how the international body acts in the consolidation of democracy through political-legal structuring in the processes of building a constitution that is connected to three distinct phases: the pre-constituent; the constituent and the post-constituent.

---

[4] Huntington (1991, 17).

[5] Hirschl (2013, 1–12).

[6] In the same sense, Sburg et al. (2010, 1–11) (A letter will be maintained only if it makes sense to "those who live under its dictates," therefore an essential quality for its self-execution), Richie (2014a, 308). (It must be elaborated locally, hence it must be knowledgeable about the economic, political, and sociological heritage, being considered organic).

[7] Richie (2014a, 308).

[8] United Nations Organization (2002).

5.2 Intervention in the Pre-constituent Phase

For purposes of consideration, a pre-constitutional intervention will be defined in which UN assistance is connected to three specific stages: support for electoral campaigns; intervention in educational campaigns, and popular participation.

5.2.1 *Support for Election Campaigns*

International cooperation[9] in electoral matters focuses on the aspect of representative democracy, which refers to democratic access to power.[10] In view of the waves of democratization, since the 1970s, as mentioned in Chap. 4, this process was more directed towards the promotion of human development and ended up provoking the opening of political systems and the expansion of regimes of liberties.[11]

In this sense, there was a broadening of electoral matters to develop institutions, procedures, strategies, models, programs, and centers of intellectual production that are aimed at supporting and strengthening the international community to support this process, duly recognized by the constitutionalism of transition.

Post-conflict democratic assistance is, by its very nature, a dynamic process and at the same time a boiling cauldron. Operating in hostile environments with limited infrastructure and significant pressure, it is convenient to illustrate the positive role of the UN in the pre-constituency phase towards governance.[12] According to Carrilo,[13]

---

[9] In June 2014, the Libyan Constitutional Assembly commissioned a study funded by the "United Nations Development Program Libyan Mission," which compared 18 countries and their constitutional construction processes to assist their own constitutional drafting process, which covered Distinctive methods of process design. This study has been the main source of orientation for constitutional assemblies in their analogical reasoning, presenting itself as a comparative and carefully nuanced case study (Toler, 2014, 1260–1286). All studies developed by international organizations and entities are diagnosed and cataloged from the experiences of post-conflict countries, so defining "constitutional success" is also a methodological challenge. These comparisons will also guide the empirical examples presented throughout the chapter, especially Afghanistan, Bosnia, Iraq, Kenya, and Nepal. Countries were mentioned since UN interference was considered strong among the quantitative elements on a weak, moderate and strong range of variation. To access the complete table, consult: http://media.wix.com/ugd/fa311e_cc038eafa08d459abbd6b57e462e8337.xls?dn=%22UNDPLCC%20Comparison%20Chart%201APR2014.xls%22. Accessed on: Dec 11, 2014.

[10] Carrillo (2007, 84).

[11] According to the UNDP, from 1973 to 2003, 93 countries moved to democracy; in the 1970s there were 08 countries; in the 1980s, 23 countries and between 1990 and 2003 were 62 countries. Of the 191 member countries of the United Nations, 140 of them had democratic elections. This analysis represents the data collected in 2007 year (United Nations Development Program, 2002).

[12] Lapping (2009, 14).

[13] Carrillo (2007, 88).

this is a valuable help[14] to meet the needs of countries in transition by building, improving, and strengthening their electoral systems and bodies.

In most countries involved in the re-democratization, process there was a citizen and political claim that electoral processes were involved in fraud and irregularities and that they altered the popular will.[15] It should be noted that credibility in the outcome of elections, as well as the improvement of electoral systems, depends directly on a combination of factors, including internal political conditions, country culture, and the degree of professionalization of political-electoral institutions.[16]

Although there has been UN intervention, there are cases where the consolidation of democracy has progressed slowly, as in the case of Nicaragua, while in others there is a clear setback, as in Haiti.[17] According to Hampson,[18] one interesting suggestion to avoid regression would be to pair elections with ways of power sharing. Stability among political factions can be established by dividing power between coalition forces.

International assistance to political parties focuses on individual and system-wide support, whose aim is to strengthen representative democracy,[19] that pursues functions with the purpose of: developing coherent government policies and programs, acting as a coordinator of interests; connection with the needs of social demands and consolidation of the same, the function of articulating interests; the quest to select and train candidates to hold positions in government and in the legislature; the supervision and control of governmental actions.

Conflicting elections, for the most part, act as a catalyst for the development of parties and other organizations that are mainly and often the only vehicle to help local elites gain access to the ruling power.[20] Unless there is some way of compensation, those who lose at the polls can have a strong incentive to take up arms again, and refrain from the use of force to reach their political goals.[21]

---

[14] In the elections that took place in South Africa in 1994, UN participation was clearly aimed at reducing the level of violence; the same occurred in the Haitian elections in 1991 (Boneo et al., 2007, 1077); Their presence in Haiti has greatly helped to curb domestic violence and facilitate the way to deal with differences, which included technical elections, as well as security and protection of citizenship, greatly reducing the spread of political violence. Initially, the forces were focused on the organization to replace the holders of power and guarantee clean, transparent and reliable elections that clearly reflected the popular will as a neutral mediator able to guarantee impartiality. The work was evolving and the degree of action was broadened beyond the day of the election, to consider also the preparatory acts and subsequent to the electoral day (Boneo et al., 2007, 1103).

[15] Carrillo (2007, 100).

[16] Carrillo (2007, 102).

[17] Boneo et al. (2007, 1105).

[18] Osler (1997, 710).

[19] Catón (2007, 6–7).

[20] Reilly (2004, 4).

[21] In Chile, the promulgation of the 1980 Charter, without popular participation, under the mantle of the dictatorship and after a fraudulent plebiscite, ended up fueling the conflict even more, mainly because it promoted the segregation of other parties. It is the pre-constitution factors that can shape a better response to the conformation of dissent already constituted. In Cambodia, for example, the

The process of democratization is not uniform and linear, and it is not enough to solely and exclusively serve the electoral system to solve governance problems. International experience itself has shown that it is necessary to integrate into the cooperation and plan the strengthening of the system in the promotion of civic education and popular participation.

Representative democracy helps us solve many issues, but it will always be in permanent deficit if it is not followed by competing actions that tend to improve and enrich parties and governance.[22]

Those countries that have demonstrated their ability to renew, over time, their alliances, both institutional and opening the democratic space, as well as the methods that are projected in a broad spectrum—ranging from the organization, through civic education and even, the generation of democratic and technical doctrine on electoral observation[23]—have great tendencies to gradually achieve democratic development.

The UN's choices are made based on the crucial issues surrounding the electoral system, power-sharing structures, and the transformation of rebel forces into political parties. These choices have far-reaching consequences for the scope and pace of democratic transition.[24]

However, it is necessary to stick to the weaknesses that, at first sight, may seem contradictory: the lack of systemic methodology and insufficient contextualization.[25] As for the first, it means that there is no general framework to deal with what is supposed to mean assistance to political parties and how programs should be implemented. As for the second, it refers to the way service providers use their strengths, that is, they tend to repeat the same solutions in all contexts or simply replicate the experiences of other countries.

This weakness may come from the composition of the assistance since it is traditionally made up of Western consultants. Although well informed about how a consolidated democracy works, they have never experienced a democratic transition and are less able to appreciate the dynamics and subtleties involved in the real process of democratization.[26]

According to Lappin,[27] the speech especially brought by the United States in support of democracy has been approached as a way of national security and protection of Western States. In this sense, this product ends up being valued by the Western look instead of being a process that values the identity of those in need of international support.

---

parties recognized from the outset that a coalition government was needed to appease groups and advance the process of national reconciliation.

[22] Carrillo (2007, 107).

[23] Boneo et al. (2007, 1105).

[24] Hoove et al. (2008, 9).

[25] Catón (2007, 19).

[26] Lapping (2009, 17).

[27] Lapping (2009, 17).

Lappin goes on to argue[28] that any democracy assistance project can undoubtedly be considered paternalistic in that it implies a transfer of knowledge to those who do not have the basic understanding or capacity to achieve the development itself.

This situation is aggravated because the solutions offered have little relation with the realities experienced by those who seek to rebuild society. This challenge will be softened by creating a social space where these perspectives and contrasts can meet and where actors can recognize their interdependence and negotiate a peaceful and mutually shared future.

A good exit was found by Michel and Cofone,[29] supporting a referendum qualified to enforce the charter bill. If the foundation is to include all social groups in this process because they tend to directly influence the stability and legitimacy of the charter, then it is reasonable to consider that particular attention should be paid to them at this stage of choice. The rules of voting in the constitutional set should make sure that these groups can exert some influence on the result and the rules of the qualified majority can directly achieve popular participation.

The "two-thirds" rule in promoting consensus has been widespread for constituent assemblies, for example in Egypt, Tunisia, and Libya. However, this demand should also be achieved through popular referendum ratification.

The qualified majority rule aims to hear everyone who is part of the procedure and this inclusion is able to validate the constitutional identity of the subject, hence connects it to a responsive response.

The choice[30] of the type of electoral system will depend on the specific situation of the country concerned, and should cover its political culture, its history in representative democracy, the size of parliament, knowledge of the electorate, and the quality of its political organizations and leadership, and not be a "one-size-fits-all" approach, generally considered the best remedy for all post-conflict scenarios.[31]

The electoral system in a divided society should not only promote proportional representation, but mainly must provide incentives for political parties to avoid partisan fragmentation and lack of governance.

The UN intervention in support of institutional development and promotion in electoral campaigns demonstrates that the use of its expertise helps to improve and strengthen electoral systems and bodies. And, as an impartial body to participate in the process, it ultimately gives credibility to the electoral process.

These practices developed by the UN can be translated as "active stimulation" of the local community, strengthening the civic virtue and the growth of solidarity by betting directly on the postulates required by a nation in transition.

---

[28] Lapping (2009, 23).

[29] Michael & Cofone (2015, 1–23).

[30] According to Reynolds and others, its development will depend to a large extent on other structures inside and outside the constitution (Reynolds et al., 2006).

[31] Hoove et al. (2008, 11).

5.2.2 Intervention in Educational Campaigns and Popular Participation

The most successful constituencies of comparative studies were those involving significant popular participation mechanisms. This participation must be preceded by impartial civic intervention, according to Toler.[32] Colón-Rios[33] had already warned us that to satisfy democratic legitimacy, the process of constitutional creation must allow the greatest possible participation of those who will be subject to it.

The goal is to help the public to participate and to know what their constitutional choices are. Starting transformations in relation to the political culture of a society is one of the most difficult aspects of any democratic transition. It requires substantial changes in behavior as well as expectations. The use of standards requires long-term strategies, involving large segments of society with extensive education and sensitivity campaigns, as well as dialogue and consensus building. The main purpose of this activity is to increase democratic participation, particularly for women, the poor, indigenous groups, and other underrepresented segments of society. It includes awareness-raising actions to highlight the rights and responsibilities of citizens inherent in the society to be built.[34]

These intangible building aspects of democracy are often neglected. There is much uncertainty about the impact of different governance structures because it requires a complex interaction between the various institutions of a particular historical environment.

Although it cannot be considered as an element of constitutional success, the constitutions of Norway, South Africa, and Kenya are strong in popular participation in the consultations held internally regarding the constitutional content.[35]

In South Africa, an independent electoral commission has developed a plan that has been divided into several sectors, such as educating the population about the special nature of the elections for constituent assemblies; the call for popular participation in different dialects; and the fight against illiteracy.

In Cambodia, UNTAC (United Nations Transitional Authority in Cambodia) teamed up with the Human Rights Task Force, civil servants, monks, judges, and NGOs to develop constitutional literature through mass communication efforts. This eventually mobilized 4.6 million Cambodians to vote in the elections and especially inspired women of the Buddhist clergy to get involved in the process of writing.

Public comments cannot become meaningful if they are not produced in formats that can be easily incorporated by writers, either due to volume or due to nature. In Iceland, being relatively smaller than South Africa, the process proved to be more useful and more homogeneous.

---

[32] Toler (2014, 1272).

[33] Cólon-Rios (2015, 1–11).

[34] Reilly (2004, 8).

[35] Toler (2014, 1273).

Successful participation presents the public with real choices.[36] In Morocco, the public received advertising from the monarchy rather than information presenting constitutional choices. In Iraq, the information was less biased, but failed to focus on important issues, which ended up preventing the public from affecting the outcome of these matters. The lack of precision tends to preclude widespread popular adherence.

These problems are also directly contaminated when the time for consultations tends to be eminently short, as in Afghanistan, Iraq, and East Timor.

The impact of participation is also greatly impaired by political maneuvers.[37] In Kenya, the legislator rewrote the constitution by canceling a great portion of the popular remarks. In Eritrea, the consultation process was widely praised for its various phases, although the President who refused to implement the charter and hold new elections frustrated it.

One of the best ways to ensure public education is a transparent process and good record keeping that can be shared with the public, which has been considered essential for constitutional success. In Eritrea, whose UN intervention was considered moderate, public mass meetings were held; all recorded, and were held in 157 different locations across the country. In Kenya, in 2005, although the constitutional committee meetings were not opened, public reports on long deliberations were produced and the charter incorporated the results of a wide campaign.

An alternative is the inspiration that transitional constitutionalism is capable of highlighting, the elaboration of the participatory constitution, which can provide a forum for the negotiation of open solutions, involving adversarial or controversial issues, resulting in an expansion and democratic formation of the population for, gradually, achieve a process of healing and reconciliation and to forge a consensus view on the future of the State.

This popular inclusion reflects a measure of success, since it can influence durability, reduction of violence, and political awareness. Its purpose is to bring together as many groups as possible to broaden the dialogue and to shape constitutional dissent. The shared and open environment, through public hearings, local, regional, and sector conferences, or requests to express their opinions in research, make a big difference in the sense of integrating, which has been diminished. In hostile environments, most of the time, communication channels are limited or dominated by a particular group.

In this line, one can think of participation that encompasses the unity and stability of society, tolerating and valuing the plurality of conceptions, and characteristics of a free democratic culture, with potentially conflicting assets and values. The unity of society and the fidelity of the citizen-people to the common institutions are not since everyone adheres to the same conception of good, but in the fact of publicly accepting a political conception of justice, admitted as a way of governing the basic structure of society.[38]

---

[36] Toler (2014, 1274).

[37] Toler (2014, 1275).

[38] Gouvêa (2015).

5.3 Intervention in the Constituent Phase

5.3.1 The Contribution in the Design of the Constituent Process and the Enunciation of the Constitutional Content

The involvement of the United Nations in the constituent phase can be perceived from premises established by the body itself, as already described in Chap. 4, which may vary from technical-legal knowledge to the structure of the process and fundamental constitutional principles.

These practices invest in different methods that include both the incentive of compliance with the norms of international standards in the national charters for the realization of human rights as well as the participation in the constituent assemblies as political actors. According to the UN, this aid will also contribute to broadening the knowledge of national actors and helping them to explore solutions that are technically solid and possibly consistent with long-term stability.

All constitutions considered successful included local specialists in the design of their process. Mapped by Toler,[39] such was the case in Norway, Poland, and South Africa, where the assemblies were constituted by national jurists. In the South African experience, the international influence was only consulted after the presentation of the first project.

Too much international influence can be detrimental to a constitutional process because the outcome may be mismatched with local needs. The Afghan charter was effectively rewritten by international interests, producing a document with little local interest.[40]

Haiti, in February 2004, once again became an unstable country after at least 10 years of nation-wide reconstruction efforts from international intervention; Liberia has had at least two rounds of international intervention since the UN oversaw the 1997 elections; there is daily violence in Iraq and there is ongoing instability in Afghanistan; Kosovo remained under the umbrella of the United Nations administration for a long time, with an uncertain future and continuing conflict chains.[41]

According to Samuels,[42] there is no shortage of theories for the failure to construct a constitution in post-conflict settings. Some focus on the operational limitations and unintended negative consequences of international aid, while others focus on the institutional gap.

On average, at least 50% of the emerging States of conflict return to the initial situation. According to Collier and Hoeffler,[43] civil war is such a profound experience

---

[39] Toler (2014, 1279).

[40] Toler (2014, 1280).

[41] Samuels (2006, 663–682).

[42] Samuels (2006, 663–682).

[43] Collier & Hoeffler (2004).

for a society that other subsequent events are not likely to be firmly established, such as elections, constituent assemblies, and referendums. The authors' research revealed that, after the end of the conflict, in the 21 countries investigated during the period 1965–1999, the predicted risk for new insurgencies rose by 38.6%. If stabilization is maintained, the risk gradually decreases.

The intervention of the international community ends up grafting devices that directly influence the key issues of the charter and its development.[44] There may be affectation of content, agenda, choice of forum, and a variety of other aspects.

The choice of process and its terms may end up valuing the international system, with special attention to international conventions. What can be concluded, according to Barros,[45] is that agreements are concluded by experts who generally understand the immediate political context but who cannot understand the long-term implications of the constitutional provisions that they advocate.

There is no way to measure the complexity of these processes and the wide variety of factors that influence their results.[46] The most representative and inclusive building processes were those that favored free and fair elections, greater political equality, social justice provisions, protection of human rights, and strong mechanisms of accountability.

For Barros,[47] a charter written in the context of high levels of violence and insecurity tends to make work much more difficult, since conducting electoral deliberations or projects ends up exacerbating political passions and makes both exercises extremely difficult to achieve success.

There are several risks and consequences associated with writing an official document in conflict resolution, which may include: the possibility of adverse factions wanting to consecrate their power; the emergence of new political interests in order to claim a seat on the negotiating table; the exclusion of groups that will be excluded from the negotiations, usually minority; exclusion of non-combatants from the process; the feeling of lack of belonging of the local community, in view of the composition of the negotiators; the domination of international mediators.

The legal constitution should not seek to build the State in an abstract and theoretical way, where there is no force to be aroused. This—which stems from the nature of things—cannot be a mere document to lend direction to it; if important cultural, social, political, and economic laws are ignored, it would lack the essential germ of its life force.[48] According to Hesse,[49] the document becomes an active force to

[44] Workshop on Constitution Building Processes (2007, 18).

[45] Workshop on Constitution Building Processes (2007, 16–18).

[46] The Institute for Democracy and Electoral Assistance has already carried out several studies on the construction of constitutions in transactional periods. MCool (2004), Mohamoud (2005), Momtes & Viál (2005), Marulanda (2004), Garrison (2005, 12), Cottrell & Ghai (2004a, 2004b), Brett & Delgado (2004), Mezei (2005), Schneier (2005), Simpkins (2004), Ankut (2005). All the cases studied are available on the IDEA International page http://www.idea.int/cbp/. Accessed on Feb 2012.

[47] Workshop on Constitution Building Processes (2007, 5).

[48] Hesse (1991, 4).

[49] Hesse (1991, 4).

become present in the general consciousness, particularly in the main responsible for the constitutional order, not only the will of power, but also that of the constitution. It should not be based on a unilateral structure if it is to prove its strength in a world in the process of permanent political-social change.

To think about the contribution of the UN in the constituent process, one must measure the size of its action and how this will be perceived in the final draft of a fundamental charter. The combination of forces—understood here as an open process of participation, coupled with local needs and the UN acting as a "consultative" body—would be able to overcome some structural and substantial problems, since it focuses on non-claimed forces in a previously established model, but built by the inner hands.

5.3.2 *The Composition of the Constituent Assembly: Looking for Constitutional Legitimacy*

Constitutional theory has a valuable contribution to the way in which constitutions and their mechanisms are elaborated.[50] In this sense, creating constitutions involves making choices within certain constraints. In most cases, such choices are collective and are the work of a constituent assembly. This composition, most of the time, is formed by local political actors and by society forces.[51]

This promotion was developed in different stages and that for Hippel[52] meant demilitarization, denazification, or re-education of an entire population. The priority has been to restrain communist advances and not to implement democratic reforms. The promotion of democracy is based on the hypothesis that they rarely wage war against each other, and therefore a growth in the number of democratic States would imply a more secure and peaceful world.

The conditions under which a country enters the constitution creation process have been identified and the following consideration will be to understand the internal dynamics of such a process.[53] Traditionally, two methods involve the creation of the text, which has been done by constitutional assemblies specially constituted for this purpose or by legislatures that are proposing a substitution constitution or, more narrowly, by constitutional amendments. The second involves the interpretation of texts that have been carried out by specialized constitutional courts or generalist courts.[54]

The model of constitutional construction by a constitutional assembly that Schmitt, according to Arato,[55] considers fully democratic involves: the dissolution

[50] Elster (2009, 9), Arato (1997, 5–51).

[51] Arato (1997, 5).

[52] Von Hippel (2003, 21).

[53] Elster (2009, 18).

[54] Tushnet (2015, 1189).

[55] Arato (1997, 5–51).

of all powers previously constituted; a popularly elected or acclaimed assembly with full powers; a provisional government based entirely on this assembly; a constitution led to a national and popular referendum; the dissolution of the constituent assembly after the ratification of the constitution, which establishes in due time the constituted government.

Elster's[56] considerations are that constituent assemblies are seldom self-created, since they generally have two external creators. On the one hand, there is an institution or individual that decides to convene the assembly and on the other hand, there is the institutional mechanism that selects the representatives. In this context, the author argues that there are upstream and downstream constraints. The superiors are imposed before it begins to deliberate, that is, they determine or condition the participation in constituent assemblies. The lower ones must be accepted by means of a process, by the necessity of ratification of the produced document, which ends up conferring more legitimacy to its proposition.

In Germany, the Allied powers also reserved for themselves the right to approve the constitution before it was passed for approval by popular referendum. In addition, in the face of this perception, Elster[57] informs that the division between self-imposed or inferior superior controls is somewhat arbitrary. Typically, lower controls are imposed by the higher authority.

The relationship between the assembly and its creators can be summed up in two opposing statements: "let him who establishes the king watch over the king" versus "let the king watch whoever lays him down."

And experimentally Elster[58] suggests the following recommendations: elections for constituent assemblies must follow the proportional system to the detriment of the majority; must be unicameral and not bicameral; the role of experts should be kept to a minimum because solutions tend to be more stable if dictated by policy to the detriment of technical considerations; one should work with a time limit so that no group can use postponement tactics to achieve its goals; should not be effective immediately after its adoption to reduce the impact of short time and party motives.

From the countries in which UN intervention was considered strong, the average length of the charter was relatively short,[59] as in Afghanistan, in 2 years and 1 month; Bosnia in 06 months, Iraq in 01 year and 07 months, and Kenya in 01 year and 08 months. The constitutional drafting committee for Afghanistan was composed of nine members selected by the UN and later the committee was enlarged to thirty-five members mainly politicians and relevant experts.

---

[56] Elster (2009, 18–21).

[57] Elster (2009, 18–21).

[58] Elster (2009, 39–40).

[59] Research conducted by IDEA International has stated on several occasions that reconciliation is a long-term process and there is no immediate reconciliation. Take time and take your own time. Your pace can not be imposed and should be local. The role played by international actors should be to provide support and supervision of local programs, providing advice, expertise and training, providing material resources (Instituto Internacional para la Democracia Y La Asistencia Electoral (2003).

Delegates to the peace agreements drafted the Bosnian charter and the Assistant Secretary of the United States, Richard Holbrooke, and American mediators and experts represented the members of the "contact group".

There is a broad consensus that the participation of external actors in the constituent process should be reduced. In this sense, there is no concern with form, that is, the formalistic facade of the method of building the constitution, but who is part of the process.

Being part of the constituent process with the expertise of legal and technical knowledge—which includes the structure and fundamental principles—does not necessarily mean being part of the process as a political actor. An external force with a political capacity for interference can contaminate the choices and empty the performance of the local community and social forces. Even because a constitutional text only makes sense if it knows the plurality of its sources.

5.3.3 Substantive Democracy Thesis

Feldman[60] argues that the "constitutionalism imposed" here understood in its material and substantial form, eventually shapes the conflict between the principles of equality and autonomy. Advocates of equality, often-international actors, are pushing for a constitutional guarantee that expressly triumphs over any other device. For democratic theory, the conflict between autonomy and equality cannot be easily resolved or explained.

Souza Santos[61] alerts us to the tension between the universal and the foundational. It is said to be universal what valid independent of context is at any time and place and is representative because of its breadth. The foundational is something that has a transcendental importance because it is unique. It represents a specific identity that has memory, history, and roots, and its unique and specific character can be as powerful a force as the universality and generality of the universal. Any of these values, universal or fundamental, presents today as one that has ultimate legitimacy, although both end up producing exclusions. And it is these values that now constitute the source of tension between the principle of equality and the principle of recognition of difference.

What we consider universal today is the foundational of the West transformed into global. For Souza Santos,[62] it is a "globalized localism". Over the past five centuries, Western economic, political, military, and cultural hegemony has been able to convert what was, or is supposed to be, unique and specific to this region of the world into something general. It is the product of the historical transformation of the Western Eurocentric foundation through the process of globalization of colonialism and capitalism.

---

[60] Vol. 37, Feldman (2004/2005, 857).

[61] Santos (2014, 37).

[62] Santos (2014, 38–39).

The universal conception of what equality requires takes different forms in different societies, because its evolution, culture, and history is what ultimately determines the meaning of its laws and policies.[63] It is this command that allows, for example, the construction of policies such as compulsory maternity leave in the United States and not compulsory in France and Sweden. A universal right has different signs in the universe that is influenced by its own constitutional identity and constitutional vision.

The role of carrying values and norms and this is the vector advocated by its members, that is, the reception of these principles on the ground according to Rich and Newman[64] "tends to be more successful if the agents are disinterested in the results." Anyone wishing to adopt it should automatically incorporate this principle and be considered a democracy.[65]

The United Nations has played a role in the coercive promotion of human rights as well as more functional technical assistance, as in Somalia, Haiti, and East Timor.[66] According to Rich,[67] one of the main reasons for adherence to human rights is to ensure that minimum substantive rights are respected in newly democratized nations. The unrestrained imposition of these rights may directly conflict with the principles of self-determination or national autonomy.

The culture and ideology of these organizations are committed to universal vision and this highly symbolic nature of membership reflects a trend of global models.[68] Three historical perspectives may confirm this trend, according to Beck, Drori, and Meyer[69]: the language of human rights may be a product of the regime's most common character and history among democracies, States, and modernization, and of those countries seeking reconciliation after episodes authoritarian and oppressive; the adoption of international norms may reflect formal or informal links of direct between the Nation-State and the international system; and the national framework reflects the global environment of human rights at the time of adoption of the charter particularly for the emerging and peripheral States, more exposed to the world order.

Many treaties and other global instruments establish a matrix that has the primary purpose of dissemination. Most constitutions, especially in conflict countries, present a Universalist understanding of human rights. Many principles end up not being consistent with national culture, although this language is a product of democracy and a modern liberal view of citizenship embodied in "democratic" regimes. This status may be more pronounced in post-conflict nations, as the institutionalization of provisions also serves as a blocking clause against authoritarian opponents.

---

[63] Hellman (2012, 1844).

[64] Rich & Newman (2004, 9).

[65] Vol. 37, Feldman (2004/2005, 865).

[66] Rich & Newman (2004, 11).

[67] Rich & Newman (2004, 11–13).

[68] Beck et al. (2012, 1–30).

[69] Beck et al. (2012, 1–30).

In addition, the language reflects the connection with the world community. The multilateral character of international organizations, such as the UN and the World Bank, operates in accordance with international human rights standards.[70]

This statement is the result of a research developed by Beck, Drori, and Meyer,[71] who analyzed 189 charters, tracing the references referring to human rights and reaching the conclusion that about 60% of them make at least one mention. Countries with stories of torment and influenced by UN intervention such as Bosnia, East Timor, Haiti, El Salvador, Uganda, and Guatemala, tend to classify more broadly and abstractly the terms of this language in their constitutions.

It is Feldman's assertion that this adherence to human rights defenders is a real victory, but it can also represent an unbridled internalization or domestication of international law regimes in nations without traditions.

It is Feldman's[72] assertion that this adherence to human rights defenders is a real victory, but it can also represent an unbridled internalization or domestication of international law regimes in nations without traditions.

Gargarella[73] announces that the growing weight of international norms in charters ends up adding a complexity of meanings to the local community. Norms often refer to inaccurate content, and there is no clear way to carry out its interpretation mainly in newly democratized countries.

The authority of international bodies with some degree of legitimacy is not denied at all, especially when the intention is to reverse the framework of instability experienced by non-democratic regimes. But if there is no clear way to carry out its interpretation, most laws and international rules are rarely enforced, but generally obeyed.[74]

For Koh,[75] if the goal is a better application of general, global rules, obedience must be voluntary and its fulfillment cannot be coerced—nations, perceiving that a rule "is fair," are more inclined to respect it.

This can occur with the interference of international actors in the process of construction of the new order. In these interactions, it is possible to discuss with local elites interpretative statements of the world norm that would be appropriate to the concrete situation. In doing so, the actors do not simply seek to coerce the other party, but rather to integrate it into the normative system; with the aim of making the community identify this interpretation as part of its set of values. There would be a perfect alignment between the moral, political, and legal dimensions of human rights, that is, a global consensus on the import of these rights.

---

[70] Beck et al. (2012, 1–30).

[71] For access to the document, consult Beck et al. (2012, 1–30).

[72] Vol. 37, Feldman (2004/2005, 867).

[73] Gargarella (2015, 36).

[74] Koh (1997, 2604).

[75] Koh (1997, 2645).

According to Rosenfeld[76] in such a scenario, the transition to political and legal domains would be easy and seamless, and democratic integration by a globally unified and politically indivisible subject would be purely formal and apparently superficial.

Ensuring respect for human rights in the nations is a global trend that is fundamental, whether for the maintenance of the nation—survival—; this is to ensure the minimum protection of the human being.

Its incorporation into constitutional charters is a necessity since it cannot be agreed with its systemic violation and will effectively contribute to human, social, and political development. However, this process must be normative, dynamic, and constitutive. Benhabib[77] associates these rights with the one of "self-government" that is exerted through suitable political channels, since its defense are limits of the exercise of the public power and therefore it needs the civic-republican vision that is formed by the exercise that comes from the public autonomy of citizens.

5.4 Intervention in the Post-constituent Phase

5.4.1 Constitutional Development

The constitutions of Germany and Japan were strongly influenced by the United Nations. The Japanese charter may remain the best example we have of an imposed constitution, implemented in an autocratic way by the American military. According to Hippel[78]:

> The goal of the United States towards Japan is to establish a peaceful and responsive government that respects the rights of other States and supports the interests of the United States as reflected in the ideas and principles of the Charter of the United Nations. The United States wants this government to conform to the highest possible degree to the principles of democratic self-government, but it is not the responsibility of the allied powers to impose on Japan any form of government not supported by the freely expressed will of the people.

Democratic reforms in Japan were implemented relatively autocratically by the US military. The general idea was the change of political and economic institutions. The US government, for this, focused on an extensive program of re-education of the masses—and such a program proved to be very successful because the Japanese had high regard for education.[79]

According to the presidential policy, the Japanese people will be encouraged to develop a desire for individual freedoms and to respect fundamental human rights, particularly freedom of religion, assembly, expression, and the press. Although they

---

[76] Rosenfeld (2012, 1937–1970).

[77] Benhabib (2011, 1889–1906).

[78] Von Hippel (2003, 29).

[79] Von Hippel (2003, 29).

had formulated the first draft constitution, it was heavily influenced by MacArthur—Supreme Commander of the Allied Powers—and his team, much more than in Germany.

Democratization in Germany began at the lowest community level and was worked in an orderly manner to the top, including the formation of political parties. The democratic reforms, externally influenced and controlled by the American military, permeated every segment of German society, to the point that most Germans today believe that their country is firmly democratic.[80]

According to Hippel,[81] despite the support of the public will for the success of the allies in the democratization of Germany and Japan, even more crucial were the people's respect for education, high levels of literacy, and the advanced stages of industrialization together with the commitment of allied forces to administer broad political and educational economic reforms that affected entire populations and most government institutions.

Today's prosperous democracies in Germany and Japan attest to the success of external nation-building efforts; however, three significant factors facilitated this process: the unconditional defeat after World War II gave the Allies[82]—the former Union of Soviet Socialist Republics, today Russia, the United States, England, France, and China carte-blanche to do as they wished; the level of development and education in the two countries and the serious commitment on the part of allies to create democratic States in both countries.[83]

Foreign interventions in nations considered "undemocratic" have come about because of a combination of factors, including the increase in refugee flows that hit developed countries, the media spotlight that illuminated the plight of crowds, the continuing daring of sordid governments and increasing sanctions, where all of this caused the "do something" effect and induced the beginning and application of the building component of the nation.[84]"

This fact demonstrates how difficult it has been to imitate these models—such as Japanese and German—especially in situations where the underlying political culture, inherited institutional conditions, and consensus conditions are significantly different.[85]

Feldman[86] argues that this intervention imposed from the outside can produce constitutional results preferred by international actors. This practice was called by the author as "imposed constitutionalism".

---

[80] Von Hippel (2003, 28).

[81] Von Hippel (2003, 28).

[82] The UN's powers are also based on the Security Council, which is composed of the five permanent members with the right to veto. What prevailed after the Second World War was its willingness to maintain the status quo, with the intention of ensuring that no further questioning of the international order would surface (Conceição, 2009, 1–7).

[83] Von Hippel (2003, 25).

[84] Von Hippel (2003, 39).

[85] Arato (1997, 5–51).

[86] Vol. 37, Feldman (2004/2005, 856).

An imposed constitution is not covered with the guarantee that it serves the best interests of the people or expresses their national identity. In this way, a new charter must be drawn up locally to gain legitimacy, since for him there is a serious tension between the views of the local elites involved and the international community.

This is because it is rare to find a nation conformed to embrace formal constitutional equality from the propagation of the matrix of democracy that international actors, including the UN, tend to propose. The road to any democracy is idiosyncratically beset by a series of specific national political and cultural concerns.[87]

To conjecture the success or failure of a charter in reconstruction scenarios of the political community becomes a challenge, for some of the results can materialize only after a considerable period, while others may appear quickly.[88]

Some factors may influence the positive response, such as adaptability and economic development. The economic development of the nation acts directly in its capacity of sustentation. A growing economy facilitates compromise and acceptance of imposed terms, and has sometimes proved to be a motivating factor that leads one to believe in the possibility of achieving development. Economic geography and the constitution are closely linked, as the distribution of a country's resources between its regions motivates discussions of revenue sharing and other devices to divide incomes. The income level of a country, its Gross Domestic Product (GDP), also shapes its profile.

For Barros,[89] adaptability can influence this response because it ends up representing the senses to accommodate political, social, and economic change. According to Ginsburg and others,[90] This characteristic ends up making the card more resilient, since its flexibility represents the capacity to adjust to the evolution of circumstances, which can be achieved through formal (amendments) or informal (interpretations that update comprehension of the text among the relevant actors), continuing to provide a framework for the resolution of disputes and the definition of public policies to promote development.

This flexibility, according to Vilhena,[91] can be called "constitutional resilience", which accommodates incentives and pressures, preserving their function and their identity in different environments. It can assimilate changes of course determined by consistent political consensus without losing its identity, which ends up making its reform feasible for adaptation to new situations, while preventing the basic elements of the constitutional pact from being abandoned.

In addition, this resilience contributes to ensuring the stability of the charter and the gradual realization of long-term constitutional promises.

---

[87] Rich and Newman (2004, 4).

[88] Workshop on Constitution Building Processes (2007, 6).

[89] Workshop on Constitution Building Processes (2007, 6–10).

[90] Ginsburg et al. (2010, 7).

[91] Vieira (2013, 23–24).

5.4.2 Constitutional Effectiveness

A modern constitution is a document that can be written by anyone with specialized knowledge in constitutional theory and major international initiatives have enshrined this presumption, undermining the connection between the people of a new State and the document governing society.[92]

This view ends up treating the identity of a State as permanent, contrary to local interests, which are social products of learning, knowledge, cultural practices, and ideologies built. Still in this thought, Koh[93] asks a constructivist critical question, leaving it unanswered: to what extent does conformity with international law itself help to constitute the identity of a law-abiding, and therefore liberal, State?

These risks trigger problems that are systemic. By putting into the charter provisions that at least local elites have no intention of observing as government, editors or those who have put pressure on them may have weakened the potential capacity of constitutional government.[94]

According to Richie,[95] the way a charter is written and who commands the writing process is as important as the outcome of the document and must relate to the society it intends to guide. Tushnet[96] has already stated that the normative recommendations made by specialists on what should be included or how the elaboration process should be is largely useless, since what determines essentially the immense local political considerations and, therefore, there is the possibility of being more successful.

There is also a problem of the great deficit of citizens in political life, either because of low participation or because of lack of access to institutions. In Carothers's words,[97] the "irresponsible pluralism syndrome" defines this situation well. In countries whose political life is marked by this contingency situation, despite having an interesting and significant amount of political freedom, regular elections, and alternating power between genuine and different political groupings, democracy remains superficial and troubled.[98]

The political elites that command the nation are perceived as corrupt, with no interest in promoting the State, increasingly discrediting the population. Countries with this syndrome have increasingly limited political space, preventing some contestations by groups and oppositions through their institutions. Even if people are aware

---

92 Richie (2014b, 308).

93 Koh (1997, 2650).

94 Vol. 37, Feldman (2004/2005, 872).

95 Richie (2014b, 311).

96 Tushnet (2008, 1473–1495).

97 Carothers (2002, 5–21).

98 The paradox that arises stems from the fact that the task of drafting a constitution usually emerges under conditions that are adverse to the proper elaboration of the text. Because it is written for an indefinite future, the letters should be adopted in ideally calm and trouble-free conditions (Elster, 2009, 38).

of the terms of the agreement, this is not enough to fill the gap since little willingness to resolve disputes through established channels—"constitutions without constitutionalism" is demonstrated.

It is not denied that the success or failure of a charter is built from its temporal experience and the other source of legitimacy derives from the performance it intends to achieve, which includes both "democracy", that is, inclusion in self-government as well as their capacity to respond to the promotion of development.

There is no denying the difficulty that the United Nations faces in transposing into reality the categories of constitutionalism of transition and transformation. Feldman[99] does not deny that the support of international actors can have social and transformational constitutional effects. The main argument against an "imposed constitution" and even against those intended to ensure egalitarianism will depend on how democratic constitutionalism, as a structure of government, will be designed to work in the long term, given that the charter is only a part of a successful agreement.

In most cases progress can be achieved when local conditions are favorable, that is, when there is a convergence of forces both within the community and internationally to coalesce around a democratic future.[100]

In short, and not intending to "empty the elements"[101] that can positively influence the construction of a constitution, success for Widner[102] may have other dimensions, such as the choice of terms in the document. This means that the nature of the conflict, the political context, or the period are important issues and must be considered.[103]

According to Arato,[104] it is necessary to go beyond using a model or even a specific organizational form to evaluate efforts in constitutional politics. One should overcome the liberal tendency to focus, in the case of constitutions, only on the substantive result. In addition, one way of doing so is to find principles that help us to form a perspective with institutional solutions and help us achieve legitimacy in the history of constitutionalism.

Does the method by which a constitution is made matter? According to Arato,[105] the method itself can be considered an epiphenomenon, a formalistic facade, either for the activity of the specialists or for the self-expression of an unlimited sovereign power.

The challenge of dealing with this complexity can be perceived in three distinct dimensions: (i) social, where actors have diverse perspectives and interests. Experts

---

[99] Vol. 37, Feldman (2004/2005, 882).

[100] Rich & Newman (2004, 15).

[101] It is not intended to exhaust the complex and systemic problems found for the forging of a constitution, nor to establish pre-developed mechanisms. The focus is the presentation of a possibility based on the view of the democratic constitutionalism that will enable, in newly democratized countries, to influence a dialogical conformation and that allows the fortification of institutions and democracy.

[102] Vol. 49, Widner (2008, 1515).

[103] Workshop on Constitution Building Processes (2007, 12).

[104] Arato (1997, 5–51).

[105] Arato (1997, 5–51).

and authorities cannot address such situations, if not only through the direct commitment of the actors or stakeholders; (ii) dynamics—cause and effect are distant in time and space. The causes are not obvious, cannot be easily determined, and cannot be treated by considering the system as a whole; (iii) generative—the future is unknown and indeterminate. Such situations cannot be determined by applying lessons or general rules.

The international legitimacy of the UN should be emphasized in promoting its role as the vector of ideas and ideals, since there is no "authority of the Western constitutions".

5.5 Un Intervention Through a Practical Perspective

Personal experiences[106] are then presented to those directly or indirectly involved in UN operations and missions, one of whose objectives has been to consolidate democracy. With the main objective of verifying the role played by the UN, concerning political-legal intervention in the constitution-making processes, especially about the implementation of the infrastructure of this modality, the interviews also contributed to the challenges of materializing the ideals sought by the UN.

The experiences of the interviewees fell into the following categories: (a) participation as a member of an office division or department; (b) participation as a member of Staff, Joint Operations Center, or similar, in Group, Mission, or Peace Operation; (c) other types of participation, including experiences as part of missions not directly under the command of the UN, but in multinational post-conflict missions endorsed or in direct coordination with the adjacent or overlapping missions of the United Nations.

The military interviewed participated in several missions, encompassing different periods and varied countries, giving the collection of data a considerable variety.[107]

To specify the individual approaches and preserving the identity of the participants, the presentation will be according to the following codes: Brazilian military 1 (MBR1), Brazilian military 2 (MBR2), Brazilian military 3 (MBR3), Brazilian military four (MBR4), five Brazilian military (MBR5) and American military (MA).

[106] The form used to design the interviews was semi-structured, combining open and closed questions, thus allowing the participant to have the possibility to discuss the proposed topic. According to Boni & Lent (2005, 75), the main advantage of combining these two techniques is that they always produce a better sample of the population of interest. One can highlight the interview as a data collection technique, that is, a method of social interaction between two people, in which one of them, the interviewer, has the objective of obtaining information about objective and subjective data on the part of the other (Haguette, 1997, 86). Allowing to contribute to the debate with elements drawn directly from the reality of the facts. It was possible to interview six military personnel, including five Brazilians and one North American.

[107] From the responses, missions from 1996 to 2015 can be observed, including a variety of countries such as Angola, Sudan, Central African Republic, Argentina, Syria, Haiti, Egypt, and Croatia.

It should be mentioned that the responses given by the participants do not represent the official positioning of any organization. For example, according to MA, your comments are personal and incomplete, and should only be used in conjunction with other probative field research data and data from other participants, thus being considered an academic colleague and educator.

The various functions assumed by MA can be broken down as follows: from 1986 to 1989, in West Berlin, comprising the Occupation Army, in order to secure the Potsdam Agreement (1945); from 1991 to 1992, in Sinai, Egypt, as part of Peacekeeping and Multinational Force & Observers (MFO), in the implementation of observation, reporting and verification components of Camp David Accord (1978); from 2001 to 2002, in Tuzla, Bosnia, and Herzegovina, with responsibility for maintaining peace, forming the Stabilization Force in Bosnia and Herzegovina (SFOR), and the implementation of Dayton-Paris Agreements (1995); from 2004 to 2005 in Sarajevo, Bosnia, and Herzegovina, participated in the support of SFOR, the European Union Force (EUFOR) and the North Atlantic Treaty Organization (NATO); in 2006, in Bosnia and Herzegovina, Croatia and Serbia, in support of NATO and EUFOR headquarters.

MBR5 joined the United Nations Angola Verification Mission III (UNAVEM III) in 1996, serving as commanding platoon commander of the Brazilian Peace Force Battalion (BRABAT). The main objective of the mission, which was divided into three phases, was to maintain order in Angola. According to the military, there were other international organizations involved, such as Médecins Sans Frontières and Red Cross, and there was no articulation among the agencies, since they acted independently.

MBR3 participated as a military observer and officer of the General Staff in 1997 in Angola; served as an instructor at the Argentine Center for Joint Training for Peace Operations (CAECOPAZ) from 2006 to 2008; he served as DPKO Training Officer and Head of Support to Member States in the United States from 2009 to 2013; in Syria in 2012, served as Head of Military Training at the Mission Training Center.

The objectives of UNAVEM III and the United Nations Observer Mission in Angola (MONUA), among others, were to promote the process of national reconciliation and achieve the conditions of the ceasefire for sustainable peace in its structure political components, human rights, humanitarian coordination, military, police, and administrative support. It is observed that, among its phases, the following stand out: national reconciliation; the formation of new armed forces and national police; the delivery of municipalities in the hands of the National Union for the Total Independence of Angola (UNITA); the integration of UNITA as a political party into the national process; the signing of the peace agreement; the promotion of periodic elections.

As is the case today in the current multidimensional missions, there were multiple international agencies involved, in addition to UN agencies, such as international and national NGOs. Unlike the current situation, the mandate of the mission did not include robust actions, protection of civilians, and incorporation of gender issues. Here, the integrated actions did not exist yet. The different agencies worked in an organized way, but not in cooperation. There was a doubling of efforts in certain areas, but very small. Both OHCHR and UNDP were already organized in clusters to avoid duplication of effort and better meet priorities.

The United Nations Mission in Syria (UNSMIS) also aimed to implement the peace plan for a ceasefire and the signing of a definitive agreement. In its organizational structure, there were departments of political affairs, human rights, military components, and administrative support.

Its phases were divided into consolidation and verification of the ceasefire, identification of actors and promotion of political dialogue, and the search for a lasting peace agreement through the Six Point Plan of the envoy Kofi Annan. It also informs us that the environment was very dangerous and the mission had many difficulties in establishing and supporting civilian, UN, and international organizations. Some organizations have tried a landing in Damascus, but few have done so, including UN agencies, and thus the conditions for organizing and establishing work programs have not been formed.

MBR2 participated in the United Nations Mission in Sudan (UNMIS) in 2005 and 2006 as a military observer and Acting Staff Officer. The main objective of his mission was to help maintain the peace agreement signed between the government of Sudan and the leadership of the guerrilla movement and, as a second objective, assisted in conducting the plebiscite held in 2011, when the population can thus choose democratically between remaining as a single country or dividing it into two nations.

MBR4, between 2009 and 2010, served as deputy of the BRABAT Intelligence Section, with the main attributions being the assessment of risk areas, signal analysis, organic safety, and the survey of adverse force activities. The United Nations Stabilization Mission in Haiti (MINUSTAH) had as its main objective to maintain a safe and stable environment in Haiti.

In 2014 and 2015, MBR1 participated as a Staff Officer—the United Nations Multidimensional Integrated Stabilization Mission in the Central African Republic (MINUSCA), with personnel control, evacuation of wounded/dead, coordination of ceremonies, reconciliation of armed groups and security briefings with NGOs and humanitarian agencies. Its structure was multidimensional, including more than 1,200 people, among them other international organizations in different phases: security establishment, stabilization, consolidation, and transition. It also included other international organizations involved in the operation. According to MBR1, the main objective of the mission in which it participated was the protection of civilians, especially women, and children.

As a result of their experiences, most of the military reported that there is no democratic matrix (constitution) implemented by the UN, and MBR4 reported only that this model exists. In MA's view, the Potsdam Agreement in Berlin would have been supplemented by the constitutions of the German Democratic Republic and the Federal Republic of Germany. Already the Israeli, Egyptian, and Saudi constitutions would have supplemented the Camp David Accords. Bosnia and Herzegovina would be sufficiently grounded in a sustainable constitution.

In Chap. 4, it was shown that the main UN document for the drafting of a constitution is the Guidance Note, which maintains in its first guideline that to support a political transition one must have prior and full knowledge of the local situation. According to the Brazilian interviewees, they objectively stated that they had prior and full knowledge of the internal situation and the political complexities related to the country where the mission in which they participated took place, which ends up endorsing the UN guiding principles. According to MA, this prior knowledge happened "within reasonable limits," further stating that missions over six months focused on preparation, which was as intense as its implementation.

Knowing that the impact of inclusion/exclusion is even capable of influencing the legitimacy of the new document, we highlight the response obtained from MA when asked if it participated in the process of electoral campaigns, civic education, public consultation, or contribution to the design of the constituent process. For the said interviewee, the mission was responsible for ensuring peace, stability, and freedom of movement during the process.

About inclusion, social participation, and transparency in the process of construction of the new constitution, only MA reported, objectively, that there had been such support. The other interviewees reported that it was not possible to make such an observation, due to different situations.

Inclusive and participatory processes are more likely to generate consensus around the desirable constitutional framework. According to MBR3, who participated in several missions, in UNAVEM III/MONUA and UNSMIS, there were effective discussions for the formation of consensus and consolidation of the political process with a view to sustainable peace.

Knowledge about the best practices of constitutional living for the UN must occur both from the outside, that is, by the eyes of foreign actors, as well as from within the State. In this sense, the use of experts for "counseling" is a common practice for the UN.

According to MBR3, UNAVEM III/MONUA had high-level DPA representatives with extensive experience in conflict resolution prevention; political actors from countries with a conflicting interest in collective or bilateral consultations (Angola, Great Lakes region, USA, Russia, and South Africa). Already in the UNSMIS mission, there was the Arab League, in addition to the representatives of the Security Council.

In the MA experience, the external experts were represented by the Allied Kommandatura Council (Berlin); by the Director of the Multinational Force & Observers (Egypt/Israel) and team; by OHCHR; by the Organization for Security and Cooperation in Europe; by the Institute for Peace of the United States; by UNHCR; by the European Union; by NATO; and EUFOR.

The incentive to comply with norms of international standards, as perceived by the UN vision—developed in items 3.2, 3.3, and 3.4, and criticized in Section 4.3.2—was pointed out in the MA experiment. OHCHR and the OSCE have used Election Process Observers to enforce this role.

Once the responses of the pre-constituent and constituent phases were drawn, the open questions in items 20–25 of the questionnaire were exposed so that the interviewees could express their affective and evaluative aspects.

Asked if there was any implementation of democracy in the country where he participated, MBR2 reported that although he had only experienced the initial phase of the mission, only the fact that the Sudanese people have had the opportunity to participate in the plebiscite, which allowed the dismemberment of part of its territory, demonstrated the role of the UN in supporting a democratic initiative. Subsequently, with the creation of South Sudan, presidential elections were held, with the support of the UN, allowing the new country to adopt the model of democratic governance.

In the words of MBR4, there was support from his organization in national elections, where many direct representatives of the people were elected. The participation of the population in the powers is evident, although modest.

From the perspective of MBR3, this practice occurred in part. In his words, the efforts expended by the UN were intense, but they were stumbled and were minimized due to the international and regional politics of the moment. Angola was a typical case in the post-Cold War context conflict and where there was influence of that period. In Syria, the high interests at stake, still obviously present, have posed serious obstacles to democratization platforms. A parallel between the two cases can be traced in the sense that there are two strong governments, with the same Head of State retaining power for many years, in a relativized democracy with little political plurality. External actors politically supported by relevant international community follow-up have been hampered by the lack of consensus and inaction by the Security Council on some occasions.

In MA's view, this question encountered three developments: the implementation of democracy in German constitutional unification, which was favored by a pre-existing structure; there were no Israeli and Egyptian political regimes that were affected by corruption; and was partly in Bosnia and Herzegovina, since the evolution of its constitution is too slow to develop in a sustainable way and achieve integration in the EU.

To understand the problems arising from the process of implementation of democracy, already considered difficult and complex, interviewees expressed opinions that coincided with the comments provided in items 4.3.2 and 4.4.2.

In Syria, according to MBR3, this process has faced difficulties in the cultural aspects of the population, in view of not exactly affecting the Western democracy model and issues of international political interest in the highly important geopolitical region of the Middle East.

MA pointed to two countries, which reflected these impasses: Egypt, due to a criminal nationalist military oligarchy; and Bosnia, by virtue of a criminal transnational oligarchy linked to Serbia/Russia and Iran.

What was intended in the later question was to show the opposite of the previously questioned—in which nation was considered easier the process of implementation of democracy and its motives. MA pointed to Germany. According to him, the war ceased with the hopelessly defeated German people and the war criminals condemned. People were exhausted by war and fascism. The democratic process had significant support, including from the Marshal Plan and the occupying forces for 11 years. Even though there was an imposition, it was the education of the German people that allowed this edification.

This statement had already been set out in 4.4.1, concluding that despite UN support, even more, crucial were people's respect for education, high levels of literacy, and advanced stages of industrialization coupled with the commitment of the Allied Forces to reform. Although the constitutional charter was taxing, these peculiarities made it possible for the nation to develop independently.

Almost unanimously, the interviewees objectively stated that in their opinion the UN's support in the process of building a constitution has been effective, enabling it to conform, political stability, and the extinction of violence. MBR2 stressed that the UN only "assists" the host country.

For a democratic system to be effectively implemented, there must be real participation and interest from the local population. MBR3 stated that, apart from the missions it participated in, it could cite other cases such as Cambodia, East Timor, and some Central American countries.

Based on the interviewees' experience, it was asked whether people who leave conflict would really want and need democracy. MBR2 stated that in most situations democracy was desired by a large part of the population. For MA this answer is positive with respect to the German example, for three conditions: the population had surrendered without hope of military rebirth; the existence of educated people who could, on their own, imagine good and more democratic freedoms; solid and sustained investment in nation building, as well as counseling and the march against corruption.

Contributing to the construction of constitutional legitimacy and effectiveness, through their experiences, the interviewees described how the implantation of democracy (constitution) should be in scenarios of deep social needs. The proposals demonstrate the relationship of the empirical data with the theoretical conception already mentioned, and it shows, in synthesis, which are the main recommendations that the interviewees make before the problems pre, post, and constituent:

(a) *Cessation of the conflict*. UN missions are often deployed in countries marked by great political instability. In the case of Sudan, the existence of several ethnic groups, with distinct cultural characteristics, contributed to the imbalance that led the country to a protracted civil war. The cessation of hostilities/conflicts is a fundamental condition for the beginning of this process. It must be accompanied by a process of disarmament, demobilization, reintegration, and reinsertion of former combatants of armed.

(b) *Unrestricted permanence in power*. In Sudan, President Omar al-Bashir remains for more than 25 years in power. After the signing of the peace agreement in 2005, the country experienced the second process of presidential elections, but with little transparency and direct influence of the current government. Recently, following a change in the Sudanese Constitution, the governors of the 18 States were appointed by the President instead of being elected. The change was widely criticized for concentrating more power in the hands of al-Bashir, showing that there is no consolidated democracy in the country. The elected authority to preside over the country must represent the intent of most of the people, so that its government is considered legitimate and can maintain the power.

(c) *Democratic matrix*. In regions where democracy does not flourish, effort must be understood as a venture of many years and no model should serve exactly. One must consider the culture, the moment, and the stage of development that the nation finds, and not impose "universal" models on the nation that is probably not able to fulfill it.
(d) *Facilitation of negotiations*. The democratic process requires solid plans that are the product of the political consensus of the main national actors and presupposes the stabilization and security of the environment throughout the period of democracy.
(e) *Accomplishment of lawful elections*. That is, they express the real will of the people. At this point lies the difficulty, because, depending on the country (sometimes tribal culture), the people have no access to any kind of information, nor what the word democracy is. In this way, Multidimensional Missions (Military, Humanitarian, Electoral, Police, Health, etc.) are fundamental for the establishment of an environment that favors the maturation of society and the future elaboration of the Constitution.
(f) *Open and inclusive political participation*. The lack of participation of minority groups in the political and economic processes of the country was a decisive factor for the outbreak of the conflict in South Sudan. With emancipation, presidential elections were established, aiming to give equal opportunity to the representatives of the different ethnic groups. Today, however, the country is experiencing a politically troubled moment, due to the dissatisfaction of the ethnic groups that are not part of the current government. It is essential that there is participation of all segments of the population. The construction of political dialogue will determine the best democratic outfit for the nation.
(g) *Investment in education*. Strong investment in basic public education (availability of resources, training of teachers, construction of schools of good standard, literacy and continuity plan, school motivation plan, temporary hiring of experienced foreign teachers, continuous flow of resources for the activity, motivational plan for teachers, school dropout control plan). Implantation in the school system of matters related to civic awareness and notions of democracy, and law, among others that allow to form a generation of citizens aware of their rights, how the State works, and how the country can grow and reduce inequalities.
(h) *Adequacy of the constitution to the local community*. Establishment of a basic constitution, with the appropriate adjustments to the reality of the target country.
(i) *Social development*. Long and multinational campaigns of support and commitment to the promotion of constitutional and social development.
(j) *Building the institutional structure*. Establishment of State authority at all levels (Municipal, State, and Federal). Institutions such as Congress, judiciary, Armed Forces, and public security, must take an active position, providing sufficient political stability to the country. In this context, the UN has an important role in

assisting host countries in the articulation, reform, or even construction of these institutions.

In short, the ideals formulated by the UN, as described in Chap. 4, incorporate the elements that characterize the constitutionalism of transition and transformation, demonstrating the extreme difficulty of materializing these categories, thus generating a potentially illegitimate fundamental charter.

References

Ankut, P. Y. (2005). *The role of constitution-building processes in democratization: Rwanda case study*. Intl IDEA.

Arato, A. (1997). *Construção constitucional e teorias da democracia*. Lua Nova: Revista de Cultura e Política. Retrieved August 24, 2012, from http://www.scielo.br/pdf/ln/n42/a02n42.pdf

Beck, C. J., Drori, G. S., & Meyer, J. W. (2012). World influences on human rights language in constitutions: a cross-national study. *International Sociology*.

Benhabib, S. (2011). On Michel Rosenfeld's the identity of the constitutional subject. *Cardozo Law Review* (2011). Retrieved June 23, 2014, from http://cardozolawreview.com/content/33-5/Benhabib.33-5.pdf

Boneo, H., Carrillo, M., & Valverde, R. (2007). La observación internacional y nacional de las elecciones. In D. Nohlen, D. Zovatto, J. Orozco, & J. Thompson (Eds.), *Tratado de Derecho Electoral comparado de América Latina* (2nd ed.). Fondo de Cultura Económica, Instituto Interamericano de Derechos Humanos, Universidad de Heidelberg, International IDEA, Tribunal Electoral del Poder Judicial de la Federación, Instituto Federal Electoral.

Boni, V., & Quaresma, S. J. (2005, January–July). Aprendendo a entrevistas: como fazer entrevistas em Ciências Sociais. *Electronic Journal of Post Graduates in Political Sociology*, UFSC. Retrieved May 13, 2015, from www.emtese.ufsc.br

Brett, R., & Delgado, A. (2004). *The role of constitution-building processes in democratization: Guatemala case study*. Intl IDEA.

Carothers, T. (2002). The end of the transition paradigm. *Journal of Democracy*. Retrieved March 20th, 2014, from http://www.journalofdemocracy.org/articles-files/gratis/Carothers-13-1.pdf

Carrillo, M. (2007). *Cooperación Internacional*, Dieter Nohlen, Daniel Zovatto, Jesús Orozco, José Thompson, Tratado de Derecho Electoral comparado de América Latina (2nd ed.). Fondo de Cultura Económica, Instituto Interamericano de Derechos Humanos, Universidad de Heidelberg, International IDEA, Tribunal Electoral del Poder Judicial de la Federación, Instituto Federal Electoral.

Catón, M. (2007). *Effective party assistance: Stronger parties for better democracy*. International IDEA.

Collier, P., & Hoeffler, A. (2004, March). *The challenge of reducing the global incidence of civil war*. Copenhagen Consensus Challenger Paper. Centre for the Study of African Economies, Department of Economics, Oxford University. Retrieved November 25, 2014, from http://www.copenhagenconsensus.com/sites/default/files/CP%2B%2BConflicts%2BFINISHED.pdf

Cólon-Rios, J. (2015, December). Apuntes sobre legitimidad democrática y asambleas constituyentes. *Revista Argentina de Teoría Jurídica*. Retrieved January 8, 2016, from http://www.utdt.edu/ver_contenido.php?id_contenido=11169&id_item_menu=5858

Conceição, J. A. (2009). *Conselho de Segurança da ONU e sua imprescindível reforma*. Diálogo e Interação. Retrieved April 20, 2014, from http://www.faccrei.edu.br/gc/anexos/diartigos27.pdf

Cottrell, J., & Ghai, Y. (2004a). *The role of constitution-building processes in democratization: Fiji case study*. Intl IDEA.

Cottrell, J., & Ghai, Y. (2004b). *The role of constitution-building processes in democratization: Kenya case study.* Intl IDEA.
Elster, J. (2009). Forças e mecanismos no processo de elaboração da constituição. In: A. C. A. Bigonha & L. Moreira (Eds.), *Limites do controle de constitucionalidade.* Lumen Juris.
Feldman, N. (2004/2005). Imposed constitutionalism. *Connecticut Law Review.*
Gargarella, R. (2015). *La sala de máquinas de la Constitución: dos siglos de constitucionalismo en América Latina (1810–2010).* Katz Editores.
Garrisonm, R. (2005). *The role of constitution-building processes in democratization: case study East Timor.* Institute for Democracy and Electoral Assistance. Retrieved April 13, 2014, from http://www.idea.int/conflict/cbp
Gouvêa, C. B. (2015). *O direito fundamental à saúde, um olhar para além do reconhecimento: construindo à efetividade que opera em favor da democracia e do desenho institucional.* Gomes & Oliveira.
Haguette, T. M. F. (1997). *Metodologias qualitativas na Sociologia* (5th ed.) Vozes.
Hellman, D. (2014). *Comments on Michel Rosenfeld's the identity of the constitutional subject: Selfhood, citizenship, culture, and community.* Cardozo Law School Legal Studies Research Paper. Retrieved October 24, 2014, from http://cardozolawreview.com/content/33-5/Hellman.33-5.pdf
Hesse, K. (1991). *A força normativa da constituição.* Sérgio Antônio Fabris.
Hirschl, R. (2013). From comparative constitutional law to comparative constitutional studies. *International Journal Constitutional Law.*
Hoove, L. T., Scholtbach, A. P., & Maul-Phillips, J. (2008). *Democracy and political party assistance in post-conflict societies.* Netherlands Institute for Multiparty Democracy, NIMD Knowledge Centre.
Huntington, S. P. (1991). *The Third Wave: Democratization in the late twentieth century.* Norman and London, University of Oklahoma Press.
Instituto Internacional para la Democracia Y La Asistencia Electoral. (2003). *Reconciliacíon luego de conflictos violentos: resumen de políticas.* Retrieved November 5, 2015, from http://www.idea.int/publications/reconciliation/upload/policy_summary_esp.pdf
Koh, H. H. (1997). Why do nations obey international law? *The Yale Law Journal.* Retrieved May 13th, 2014, from http://digitalcommons.law.yale.edu/cgi/viewcontent.cgi?article=2897&context=fss_papers
Lapping, R. (2009, July). What democracy? Exploring the absent centre of post-conflict democracy. *Assistance Journal of Peace Conflict and Development.* Retrieved August 5, 2015, from www.peacestudiesjournal.org.uk
Marulanda, I. (2004). *The role of constitution-building processes in democratization: Colombia case study.* Intl IDEA.
MCool, C. (2004). *The role of constitution-building processes in democratization: Afghanistan case study.* Intl IDEA
Mezei, A. (2005). *The role of constitution-building processes in democratization: Hungary case study.* Intl IDEA.
Michael, S., & Cofone, I. N. (2015, May 15). *Fixing popular participation in constitution-making.* Rotterdam Institute of Law and Economics, Erasmus University Rotterdam. http://ssrn.com/abstract=2580849
Mohamoud, A. A. (2005). *The role of constitution-building processes in democratization: Bahrain case study.* Intl IDEA.
Momtes, J. E., & Viál, T. (2005). *The role of constitution—Building processes in democratization: Chile case study.* Intl IDEA.
Osler, F. (1997). Hampson, Can peacebuilding work. *Cornell International Journal.* Retrieved April 20, 2015, from http://scholarship.law.cornell.edu/cilj/vol30/iss3/5
Reilly, B. (2014). *Electoral assistance and post-conflict peacebuilding: What lessons have been learned?* Asia Pacific School of Economics and Government Australian National University.

Retrieved March, 2014, from http://aceproject.org/ero-en/topics/elections-security/Reilly-2505.pdf
Reynolds, A., Reilly, B., & Ellis, A. (2006). *Diseño de sistemas electorales: el nuevo manual de IDEA Internacional*. IDEA Internacional.
Rich, R., & Newman, E. (2004). Approaching democratization policy. In E. Newman & R. Rich (Eds.), *The UN role in promoting democracy: Between ideals and reality*. United Nations University Press.
Richie, D. (2014a). Constitutional belonging. In F. D. Asensi & D. G. de Paula (Eds.), *Tratado de direito constitucional: constituição, política e sociedade*. Elsevier.
Richie, D. (2014b). Pertencimento constitucional (Vol. I). In: F. D. Asensi, De Paula, & D. G. de Paula (Eds.), *Tratado de direito constitucional: constituição, política e sociedade*. Elsevier.
Rosenfeld, M. (2012). The constitutional subject, its other, and the perplexing quest for an identity of its own: a replay to my critics. *Cardozo Law Review*. Retrieved June 23, 2014, from http://papers.ssrn.com/sol3/papers.cfm?abstract_id=2021356
Samuels, K. (2006). Post-conflict peace-building and constitution-making. *Chicago Journal of International Law*. Retrieved January 17, 2014, from http://chicagounbound.uchicago.edu/cgi/viewcontent.cgi?article=1476&context=cjil
Santos, B. S. (2014). *Derechos humanos, democracia y desarrollo*. Centro de Estudios de Derecho, Justicia y Sociedad, Dejusticia.
Sburg, T., Melton, J., & Elkins, Z. (2010, January). *This endurance of national constitutions*. University of Chicago Law & Economics Working, Paper N° 511. Retrieved March 20, 2014, from http://papers.ssrn.com/sol3/papers.cfm?abstract_id=1536925
Schneier, E. (2005). *The role of constitution-building processes in democratization: Indonesia case study*. Intl IDEA.
Simpkins, J. (2004). *The role of constitution-building processes in democratization: Nigeria case study (external perspective)*. Intl IDEA.
Teitel, R. G. (2003). Transitional justice genealogy. *Harvard Human Rights Journal*. Retrieved December 11, 2012, from http://www.law.harvard.edu/students/orgs/hrj/iss16/teitel.pdf
Toler, L. U. (2014). Mapping the constitutional process. *Cambridge Journal of International and Comparative Law*. Retrieved August 18, 2015, from http://cjicl.org.uk/archive/
Tushnet, M. (2008). Some skepticism about normative constitutional advice. *William & Mary Law Review*. Retrieved June 19, 2014, from http://scholarship.law.wm.edu/cgi/viewcontent.cgi?article=1149&context=wmlr
Tushnet, M. (2015) Novos mecanismos institucionais para a criação do direito constitucional. *Quaestio Iuris*. Retrieved February 15, 2016, from http://www.e-publicacoes.uerj.br/index.php/quaestioiuris/article/view/16915
United Nations Development Program. (2002). *Human Development Report 2002: Deepening democracy in a fragmented world*. Trinova.
United Nations Organization. (2002, 17 December). *General assembly*. Studies on the common challenges of States in their efforts to ensure democracy, the rule of law and human rights, Resolution A/HRC/22/29. Retrieved June 26, 2013, from http://www.ohchr.org/Documents/HRBodies/HRCouncil/RegularSession/Session22/A.HRC.22.29_English.pdf
Vieira, O. V. (2013). Do compromisso maximizador ao constitucionalismo resiliente. In O. V. Vieira et al. (Eds.), *Resiliência constitucional: compromisso maximizador, consensualismo político e desenvolvimento gradual*. Direito Getúlio Vargas.
von Hippel, K. (2003). *Democracia pela força*. Biblioteca do Exército Brasileiro.
Widner, J. (2008). Constitution writing in post-conflict settings: an overview. *William & Mary Law Review*.
Workshop on Constitution Building Processes. (2007). *Workshop report*. Bobst Center for Peace & Justice, Princeton University, International IDEA, Nova Jersey (New Jersey).

Chapter 6
Hybrid Constituent Power as a Subcategory of the Original Constituent Power

6.1 Conception of Hybrid Constituent Power

> La historia, será la encarregado dedelegitimize o legitimar la incursión de otros países com el objetivo "de democratizarlos".
>
> Román Lazcano

Contemporary doctrine bets on the people as a subject of the constituent power that inaugurates a whole new era of political ideas. In this way, the nation's "people", for theory, remains the basis of all political happening, the source of every force that manifests itself, never subordinated. Therefore, the constituent power of the people is supreme, original, and endowed with sovereignty and with the capacity for decision in the last institution.

However, the formation of some states, especially nations plagued by civil war, has revealed major fissures for the theory of original constituent power. The constituent power represented exclusively by the "people" is relegated to the second category, as major powers are intervening in the construction of constitutions, imposing agreements and, in certain cases, continue to decisively influence the functioning of such constitutional orders.[1]

In this sense, should we accept as constituents not only the people, but also an assembly of political powers that participate in political formation both inside and outside the borders of the nation?

The original constituent power has suffered these "fissures" since the decolonization where major powers and international organizations are intervening in *the processes of constitution-making* in nations, such as in Afghanistan, Cambodia, Timor-Leste, Bosnia and Herzegovina, Nepal, Haiti, and Kosovo, among many others. In these cases, it was not the "people" who used their constituent power to establish their respective constitutional orders. On the contrary, external actors

[1] Oklopcic (2012).

C. B. Gouvêa and P. H. V. B. Castelo Branco, *UN Interventions and Democratization*, Societies and Political Orders in Transition,
https://doi.org/10.1007/978-3-031-32715-5_6

using political power and the interpretation of norms of international law created the possibility that the populations captured within these orders would be recognized as "people".

Some authors, such as Simpson,[2] have acknowledged that these phenomena of creating new states such as Kosovo and Bosnia and Herzegovina are examples of a founding constitutional moment, where great powers break with the "international legal framework", finding normative foundations to justify intervention, such as maintaining international collective security, self-defense, and the protection of human rights, to rebuild or intervene in the states. It is the self-imposed restriction generated by arguments of great powers that wards off any simplistic notion of popular sovereignty, self-determination, or sovereign equality. And this is the final agency of the legality or legitimacy of the intervention.

But why does the theory of constituent power remain reluctant to include a kind of external constituent powers as part of its constitutional categorization?[3]

For Oklopcic, the "external constituent" power is inevitably intertwined with an unprecedented involvement of external powers in imposing a new political topography.

The Dayton Peace Agreement of 1995 created Bosnia and Herzegovina as a state of three politically organized constituent peoples in an almost federal consociation consisting of two constituent units. The Constitution of Bosnia, provided for in Annex IV to the Agreement, determined and enthralled this condition on behalf of its "three constituent peoples". And this situation, in fact, remains only in the Agreement witnessed by the major foreign powers such as the United States, Britain, France, Germany, Russia, and the UN. The external constituent power has been materialized.

In announcing these axioms, these great powers not only determined who the "peoples" will be by delimiting the borders, but also established a range of options of the fundamental status based on the Western theory of democracy for these peoples. In Bosnia and Herzegovina, Cambodia, Timor-Leste, and Afghanistan, the great powers determined the identity of the "people" or the "peoples" when they detained the territory and spatial aspect of the constitutional order.

The constitutive involvement of the hybrid constituent power operationalized in Bosnia and Herzegovina continued after the formal establishment of the constitution. The Office of the High Representative of the United Nations was created to implement the civil aspects of the Agreement and its textual mandate was relatively modest, according to Oklopcic[4]: monitor, maintain contacts, promote cooperation, coordinate activities, respect autonomy, and provide guidance, among others. The constitutive examples that will be the object of case studies, as described in the following items, show that prominent countries have determined what and who the people are, especially in Bosnia and Herzegovina.

The idea of internationalization of the constituent power, that is, in the conception of research as "hybrid constituent power", representing the approach of the influence

[2] Simpson (2004).

[3] Oklopcic (2012).

[4] Oklopcic (2012).

of international law on the normative content of constitutional law from the intensification of international relations, was presented by Helène Tourard,[5] later by Nicolas Maziau[6] and Luis Cláudio Coni.[7]

According to Tourard,[8] this idea goes beyond the context of the relations between the state and international law, that is, it is architected beyond the problematic relationship between international law and domestic law.[9] It is, in fact, the approaches that involve the issue of relations between Constitutional and International Law in a less abstract perspective, considering the reality of political phenomena and international relations. For Coni,[10] this concept reflects that the "internationalization of law" corresponds to the influence of international law on the formation and content of normative species of a given state legal system, meaning the concrete impact on constitutional norms.

Thus, the hybrid constituent power means that the rules that must order the activities of citizens are not produced only by the national legislature, which creates a problem of legitimacy as to the normative bodies corresponding to an increasing degree of penetration of international law into constitutional law.

According to Maziau,[11] the internationalization of the constituent power is a general product of the evolution of society and of the relationship between the state and the idea of sovereignty, a kind of framework resulting from the de facto situation.[12] This constituent power infiltrated or under the tutelage of international law leads to a system of horizontal convergence of values.[13]

According to Coni's specialized study, what can be extracted from the view of the doctrine is the fact that it represents, effectively, a reorganization, a kind of displacement in relation to the traditional categories of Constitutional Law, with loss of autonomy of the state legal order. This can be understood as the direct influence of international law on the production of internal norms, the recipients of which are now suffering the effects of a political choice which has also been made outside state borders.

Thus, two situations deserve to be highlighted to the author[14]: the deterioration and consequent deterritorialization of certain state powers by the transfer of a portion of sovereignty to supranational bodies, or from the intervention of peacekeeping missions,[15] in a work of restructuring and reconstruction of the state through *experts*.

[5] Tourard (2000).

[6] Maziau (2002).

[7] Coni (2006).

[8] Tourard (2000).

[9] Coni (2006, p. 68).

[10] Coni (2006, p. 70).

[11] Maziau (2002).

[12] Maziau (2002).

[13] Coni (2006, p. 70).

[14] Coni (2006, pp. 71–75).

[15] In the case of UN interventions in the process of building constitutions, this measure is determined via resolution by the Security Council.

It can be mentioned that the hybrid constituent power causes a shift from the institutional balance of the state because international norms interfere in the formation of internal material or procedural norms, affecting state structures, namely: political organization and the distribution of competencies.

The "international community"[16] is a collective term that refers to the wide range of countries and other international actors that can influence, directly or indirectly, in a process of building a constitution in the constituent phase. This community is not homogeneous and does not represent a single policy or point of view.

To Brant et. al., there are some types of international actors that can make up this category in any post-conflict context: (i) international, regional, and multilateral organizations such as the United Nations, the European Union, the League of Arab States, and the South Pacific Forum. They can initiate or sometimes lead the process of building a constitution by providing political legitimacy through their resolutions. They can also implement missions to support the process, provide special representatives, or financially support the State; (ii) international agencies such as the United Nations Development Programme, the United Nations Development Fund for Women, the United Nations Children's Fund, the United Nations High Commissioner for Human Rights or international financial institutions, which can provide knowledge, make donations or provide assistance programs; (iii) individual countries,[17] which may have a direct interest in the process and provide diplomatic support or skills such as technical assistance or resources; and (iv) International Organizations may provide resources and knowledge or implement programs related to the process of building a constitution.

Historically, countries that wanted to create their constitutions have done so. Currently, any developing country that wants to create or revise its constitution can request the support of the international community. However, with the acceptance of funds or foreign advisors to assist the transition process, it can often represent "pressures to serve particular interests on the part of the international community". This support can occur for a variety of reasons: promoting democracy, encouraging international standards, preventing terrorism, and improving national and institutional security.

Sometimes these interests coincide with those of the creators of the constitution, and, at other times, they will conflict with them. For example, the international community may try to keep references to Sharia law outside an Islamic constitution because it believes that such a law is in human rights.

The international community has put substantial pressure on outcomes in many constituent processes—especially in Bosnia and Herzegovina and Iraq. The United Nations has also played a key role, often in partnership with other key players, in countries such as Afghanistan, Cambodia, Namibia, and Timor-Leste. In other contexts, such as Peru and Sudan, regional associations have taken the lead in

[16] Brant et al. (2011, p. 175).

[17] Such how in Australia, through Of *Australian Agency for International Development*; in Kingdom United, hair *Department for international Development*; or us States United especially through of the *Office of Transition Initiatives of the United States Agency for International Development*.

peace negotiation and in the formation of the constitutional process.[18] The United States, Afghanistan, and Iraq have significantly shaped the process and influenced the content of the constitutions.[19] These practices represent the embodiment of hybrid constituent power.

These roles are assumed mainly in post-conflict situations or armed conflicts, where the absence of an effective state ultimately results in UN-led transitional administrations, authorized by resolutions via the Security Council, or situations in which a much more powerful country, with strategic interests in the area, plays a political leadership role in the transition or becomes a power of military occupation, for example, as *occurred in the constitution-making process of* Namibia (1990), Peru (1992), Cambodia (1993), Bosnia and Herzegovina (1995), Eritrea (1997) Timor-Leste (2002), Democratic Republic of Congo (2004), Afghanistan (2004), Iraq (2005), Somalia (2009), and Egypt (2012).

In many of the constituent processes in which international actors have exercised a high degree of control, common problems have been experienced, as in the case where the influence of the international community tends to undermine national appropriation in the process of building a constitution. Constituent Assemblies must contain local experts in the design of their process—if the feeling of belonging and identity are not interconnected, a new destabilization can be triggered.[20]

The imposition of short deadlines for the forge of the constitution also represents a problem for the constituent phase, and these times can be guided for various reasons: security issues, mission cost, and political imperatives. Calendars are almost always less than 90 days to debate, draft, and adopt a constitution. Such agendas often reflect the high cost of international funding for this purpose and the desire to deliver a new constitution to the nation to begin a new transitional cycle.

In late 2001, a group of Timorese civil society actors[21] sent a letter to the United Nations Security Council, demonstrating that a hastily made constitution may represent a rhetorical document.

> A Constitution is a complex document embodying fundamental choices about the type of country an independent East Timor will be. This Constitution must be a living document, which reflects how the East Timorese as a people see themselves, report to each other, and finally, after many centuries, govern themselves.
>
> For this to happen, the East Timorese people have to be provided with the information on the choices that have to be made, information on what a Constitution is, and information on the options available to them on the fundamental issues. They will then need time to

---

[18] Brant et al. (2011, pp. 176–177).

[19] Brant et al. (2011, p. 176).

[20] Gouvêa (2016).

[21] One of the main tasks of the *United Nations Transitional Administration In fashion East Timor* (UNTAET) was to prepare timor-leste's independence and facilitate the drafting of a constitution. The calendar was formally approved by the National Council and implied the process of constitutional development for the country and its future regime. It was established that the Constituent Assembly would draft a draft constitution after 90 days of its election. (Gouvêa, Carina Barbosa (*Un interventions in the process of constitution-making in states in political transition*: the role of the United Nations in the rescue of the democratic order. Curitiba: Juruá, 2016, p. 179).

consider and debate so that they are able to form opinions, time to hold discussions to seek consensus where opinions are divided, and finally time to officially record their views. None of this can happen in three months.

All the legitimate constitutional processes that have taken place in recent years [in other countries] were carried out over a period of three to four years. The public consultation process for the South African Constitution lasted for three years. A three-month process would rob the East Timorese of their right to contribute to the future of their country and it will alienate them from the very document that should voice their aspirations.

(Brant et al. 2011, p. 323).

In a post-conflict environment, where many national actors may have moved internally, a constituent process rushed by the international community often will lead technical consultants to take control of the constituent process. In Somalia, in 2010, the UN imposed a deadline of 60 days for unseasonalist constitutional commissioners to deliver a draft constitution, resulting in a strong dependence on foreign experts to meet the deadline.

In Timor-Leste, in 2002, international actors oversaw directing and drafting the work of secretariat of the Constituent Assembly rather than empowering and supporting the national actor to accomplish this task.

A hasty process will also limit the quantity and quality of training and/or training that will be intended for local actors to ensure that they perform their tasks effectively.

These statements were corroborated by the research, who listed a series of other issues that need to be better defined and appropriate to the context of the intervention and that become key questions for discussion in the constituent phase: the imposition of a western democratic matrix; open and inclusive political participation (Namibia, Timor-Leste, and Cambodia); adequacy of the constitution to the community and local ethnic groups; and building the institutional structure, among others.

The *constitution-making process in* the constituent phase can represent an opportunity to undertake a deliberative and democratic process that can promote conflict resolution, national reconciliation, the participation of vulnerable groups, and distinct ethnic groups. The problems to be faced with post-armed conflict societies are highly sensitive and, if their solutions are unduly hasty, it can lead to greater polarization of society, rather than achieving its main goal of promoting peace and social and economic development.

The method for producing a constitution must be inclusive. This formula has the power to prevent a counterrevolutionary threat to the new order and ends up forming consensus on fundamental constitutional principles. Several constituent processes that were led by the local population were recognized as contributions to conflict resolution and peacebuilding (South Africa and Uganda). This type of broad openness to popular participation—consultation and dialogue—has not yet been seen in processes conducted or strongly influenced by the international community.[22]

For Brant et al., the international community often states that popular participation in transitions to democracy is critical, mainly because the imposition of the agendas of the international organizations involved is mostly tight. A hasty process will also

[22] Brant et al. (2011, p. 324).

limit the amount of capacity development or training available that can be given to local actors to ensure that they perform their tasks more effectively with the previous elections and constituent assemblies. On the other hand, if there is an effective civic education, these same people can be used to lead to the education of voters in the future.

If the international community intervenes by negotiating or mediating the conflict, it will usually do so with local political elites and leading opposition groups. These negotiations, for the most part, take place before the composition of the Constituent Assembly.

High-level negotiations with local constituents could lead to an agreement on the constitution and its reform. The structure and model for the process will be considered, mentioning who will be involved in the project; how the articles and chapters of the new constitution will be selected; how consensus will be built; how the new constitution will be approved; how will the schedule; and who will be responsible for mediating the possible conflicts that will arise during the process. The development of these capacities and the support of the international community include, for example, the creation of a constituent national assembly, a constitutional review *committee, round tables or national* conferences, the analysis of the final draft constitution, etc.

According to Brant et al., the constituent process in a divided society must promote national unity, consensus building, reconciliation, and a sense of shared national unity. And in this sense, these objectives are only achieved through an inclusive process. The contribution of a wider range of actors can improve perspectives and processes, co-adjuvanating to a national consensus on the new paths to follow.

Several resolutions issued by the UN Security Council call for the conduct of this path, such as Resolution 1325 of 2000,[23] where the international community recognized that women's participation is fundamental to achieving and maintaining peace. They are proven agents of change and can do much more if they can speak out, so this resolution required women to participate in peacebuilding. And there is no doubt that the constituent process can become a major catalyst for this construction if it includes the general population and not just the local political elites.

An extreme example occurred in Bosnia and Herzegovina, where the Dayton Agreement and the constitution negotiated by the United States completely excluded popular participation. The nation was not consulted on the content discussed on what would make up the constitution or received any opportunity to reflect on the letter contained in the peace agreement. The focus was to end the civil war and secure an agreement between the warring factions, no room for the development of a constitutional culture or to challenge the legitimacy of the agreement.

About international constitutional assistance in the constituent phase, it generally focuses on technical aspects rather than focusing on driving on the dynamics of how to structure the process to better seize opportunities to build peace. Most countries that, in the last 20 years, have engaged in processes of composition of a new institutional

[23] United Nation (2000), Resolution S/RES/1325 (2000).

model in several different ways have tried to incorporate the public, such as South Africa,[24] Namibia[25], and Eritrea.[26]

As mentioned, on Zimbabwe, at the request of the government, UNDP assisted the Constitutional Parliamentary Commission in technical knowledge, providing a constitutional consultant with regional and international experience in the *constitution-making process*, who was able to provide technical and strategic advice, proving to be crucial this aid, especially during the phase of the constitutional project.

Another supportive experience, already described, occurred in 2010 in Kyrgyzstan, where, in a context of political instability, the UNDP, in cooperation with the European Union, assisted the draft constitutional reform that involved both the substantive elements of the letter, as well as local awareness. Four working groups were developed on the key sectors of the project: constitutional and state institutions, human rights, judiciary, and self-governance. As a result, the letter has been for the integration of democratic principles and human rights.

On the opposite way, Cambodia, Ethiopia, Timor-Leste, and Fiji, whose popular participation was limited, either due to the secrecy of the negotiations or due to insufficient time devoted to public deliberations.

In the research developed by Brant et al.[27] they eventually revealed that, in general, assistance focused on the drafting and content of the constitution, rather than creating the conditions for broad population participation, civil society involvement, dialogues, and deliberations of the fundamental issues of the new constitution.

In many cases, the main effort of the international community was to hire a constitutional law professor, often western and with no experience in a post-conflict environment, to advise national actors. This approach can help to stimulate the imposition of a liberal western constitutional structure rather than supporting national actors in the construction of designs that are more adaptable to the context.

As already reported, in 2011, Vietnam's National Constituent Assembly asked the United Nations to help bring in international experts and comparative experiences to dialogue about the controversies, including different models of constitutional and government review, as well as human rights provisions.

In Tunisia, support for the *constitution-making process was* conceived in 2009 at the request of the new Tunisian authorities and was implemented from 2012 to 2015. The UN supported the National Constituent Assembly in three main areas:

---

[24] In South Africa, the work was opened and transparent, via publication and transmission in the media of all debates, recounting almost two million interferences of the population: by e-mail, meetings, surveys, and contributions over the Internet.

[25] In Namibia, the information was transmitted by the political parties and by the radio system, which contributed to the dissemination of the essential issues that would be incorporated into the constitution.

[26] In Eritrea, a phase of education was included which consisted of a series of seminars held at village level by more than four hundred specially trained instructors. The second phase consisted of a public consultation on the proposals prepared by the constitutional commission. In the third phase, the committee received comments on the draft regional, local, and civil society assemblies and other organizations, as well as individually.

[27] Brant et al. (2011).

strengthening institutional capacities and developing mechanisms for constitutional and political dialogues to ensure the contribution of civil society in the process.

The international community tends to emphasize the use of elected political actors to form the constituent assembly, and representative democracy tends to be the most legitimate to design the new constitution. The composition of the assembly tends to be an extremely important factor, as it becomes the object of dispute between the key groups. This includes the process, time, and sequence of phases and this context exists to prevent a single group from dominating the process and to allow legitimacy from openness to the public.

However, particularly in the first post-conflict elections, the parties can be nascent and based on ethnic affiliation or united with populist leaders or personalities. This model ultimately prevents marginalized groups during the conflict or even in society, such as women, young people, minorities, from having access to participation in the drafting of a new constitution. In this way, this type of election may not lead to the creation of a legitimate body.

In Timor-Leste, the Transition Administrator Sérgio Vieira de Melo argued that the only way to build a constitution that reflected the country's independence and became legitimate was for it to be debated, drafted, and adopted by an elected Constituent Assembly. Civil society itself and other local leaders called for an independent and elected assembly to create the new constitution.

And this process, within the context in question and for the experts, was the most appropriate. However, as expected, a single party dominated the seats for the composition of the assembly—the Revolutionary Front of Independent Timor (FRETILIN) composed of a 55-seat bench of 88—and this domination meant that Timor-Leste missed the opportunity to promote an inclusive process and encourage a wider set of stakeholders to seek consensus for the drafting of the new magna carta. The constitution fruit of the assembly was seen by the opposition as the result of a single party and this could once again incite violence.

In Afghanistan, in 2004, a constitutional commission developed a draft of the constitution and was an *elected national assembly, the Constitutional Loya Jirga, which* considered the project and had the responsibility for deciding and adopting the new constitution. The UN advised that special *seats in constitutional Loya Jirga* should be reserved for marginalized groups, which eventually included women and other minorities, directly impacting the final version of the constitution and giving these groups greater constitutional rights.

Facing the problem from the logic of the formation of the constituent assembly is essential, since, if there are elections, they end up legitimizing the domination of the process by the winner. Here, the main foundation can be compromised, considering that the goal is to resolve the struggle between the classes and ensure the future interests of society. On the other way, the appointed committees do not enjoy the legitimacy of an elected body, from the theoretical point of view, but can contribute to the construction of the constitution project, informing and providing equal access to all.

For the UN, promoting proper monitoring after the adoption of a constitution is part of the *constitution-making process*. This follow-up may include dissemination and education on the approved charter, the development of subsidiary legislation, and the full range of institutional training and development. To give life to the constitution, one must pay attention to how it will be implemented after it is adopted. Funding, resources, and assistance that must be provided to emancipate the constitutional person will be necessary to encourage the development of a constitutional culture.[28]

According to Brant et al., where the international community played a dominant role in the process of building the constitution, there is little evidence of continued support for implementation.

In South Africa, a wide range of political awareness was designed to engage rural and mass media campaigns to provide these people with minimal knowledge of the new constitution. The final step was the distribution of seven million copies of the constitution in all eleven official languages. All these activities were coordinated by a secretariat created by the constituent assembly that ceased to operate once the constitution was adopted.

The constitution of the Republic of Ghana, of 1992, providing for a civic education commission to create and maintain the development of a constitutional culture. Unfortunately, in Brant's conception; et al., most of these provisions have limited effect, since governments give low priority to these measures, investing few resources in their implementation.

There are at least two aspects to the implementation of the constitution: one is internal and involves issues such as document coherence, institutional responsibility and cooperation, issues related to the transition and the progressive introduction of new social and economic rules and rights; and the other is external, involving people's empowerment, internalization of constitutional values and quality of leadership.

There are at least two perspectives of external support that need to be considered. The most obvious is that the people of the country in question must be the last guardian of the constitution and to play this role people need to be encouraged to understand the larger charter and their rights. And this incentive should involve all civil society—with or without national representation, non-governmental organizations, which can be recognized by the state to also perform this task.

---

[28] The concept of constitutional culture, proposed by Siegel, is the result of dialogue and formal and formal interactions of the fundamental text (Valle et al. 2016, p.15). These meanings include, among other things, the willingness of ordinary citizens to recognize and accept that they are governed by a written document that create government institutions and set limits to what this government can do; the settled belief that the governance charter is created by the population; the recognition that the letter is not timeless, but that the population may alter or even revoke it in certain circumstances; the understanding that until the letter is modified, we are constricted by it and call to agree with its effects, even if we are free to disagree with them (Mazzone 2005, pp. 671–69). Towards Mazonne, constitutional culture also includes the understanding that a constitution unifies a population beyond the immediate sphere of acquaintances, so that these people, elsewhere, are equally governed by this written document and that, despite our differences, is something we have in common. This locution is no stranger to the doctrinal universe; however, it has usually been associated with a sociological concept, which comprises a unilateral perception between citizen and constitution, welcoming its cogent character, and at the same time instituting a collective unity of coexistence. This conception is interrelated with other concepts equally present, such as that of constitutional feeling (see Verdú 1994, p. 27) and constitutional identity (see Rosenfeld 2003, pp. 22–23). (Valle et al. 2016, pp. 15–16).

The second aspect of the support concerns the role developed by the international community, which, since the end of the 1980s, has had a significant participation in many processes of building a fundamental charter and, often, remains involved in supporting its implementation in various ways. This generally extends beyond the risk to establish laws and operate institutions with the primary objective of safeguarding the integrity of the new constitution. Of course, there is always a need to balance the power of such support—too much international influence on sensitive domestic affairs can be maladjusted or inoperable for the development of a constitutional culture.

In 2005, a report was commissioned to participants with high-level experiences in these processes on "constitutional technical assistance in post-conflict UN countries"[29] and they concluded that, while the UN provided various forms of assistance, there was an alternation of positive and negative results[30] and recommended that assistants receive more theoretical guidance and that a central agency be established to be responsible for coordination of UN constitutional assistance.

The *Rule of Law Coordination and Resource Group* (RoLCRG), chaired by the UN Deputy Secretary-General, with the *support of the Rule of Law Unit*, is the mechanism convened for the constitutional assistance of the United Nations and aims to ensure effective mobilization in the combination of the necessary skills residing in the various UN departments, with the following responsibilities: ensure the coherence and development of UN policies; document the experiences of the United Nations; build institutional capacity and record lessons learned; mobilize and coordinate efforts between the various UN departments and agencies providing constitutional advice; and lead an advisory process to further develop the UN policy on constitutional assistance.

In 2009, Ban Ki-moon released a *Guidance Note*,[31] which represents the guiding principles for the United Nations involvement in *constitution-making processes.* Segundo Brant; et al., until 2011, however, the RoLCRG has not yet been able to build its capacity to implement this mandate in an integral way. In any case, the researchers believe that the guidance notes constitute a significant step for the international community to understand the importance of the *constitution-making* process and its general principles.

Finally, among the experiences of hybrid constituent power, from the UN interventions already consummated, some lessons can already be demarcated through

[29] Brant (2005).

[30] For more information, see Gouvêa, Carina Barbosa (*Un interventions in the process of constitution-making in states in political transition*: the role of the United Nations in the rescue of the democratic order. Curitiba: Juruá, 2016; Brant (2005).

[31] The *Guidance Note* it is an indication of intentions with six guiding principles: seize the opportunity for peacebuilding in conflict and post-conflict countries; promote compliance with international standards; recognize that the constitution it is a "sovereign national process" and that to be successful this procedure must be owned and nationally leadership; support ways of building an inclusive, participatory and transparent constitution; provide, where necessary, a wide range of knowledge, both outside and within the UNITED NATIONS system; and promote appropriate monitoring after the adoption of the constitution.

the practical perspective, by those who were directly or *indirectly involved in peacebuilding operations,* in which one of the objectives was to consolidate democracy.

Observing, primarily for the purposes of delimitation of the object from the chapter, the constituent phase and contribution to the construction of the legitimacy, and effectiveness of the constitution, some guidelines can be delineated for the improvement and legitimacy of the hybrid constituent power:

a. The constituent process is sovereign, political, and social.
b. It should be necessary to promote genuine public participation, inclusion, and attribute ownership of the constitutional project to the nation.
c. The imposition of conditions by the UN, such as compressed agendas that meet only the interests of international actors, most often makes the constituent process impossible to be open and inclusive.
d. When asked to provide constituent assistance, the political nature of the conflict—ethnic, opposition, minorities—should be understood, the existing institutional design as well as the logistical needs of resources, in order to ensure that aid is needed from a human and humanitarian point of view, as well as to promote democratic principles, not marginalizing national actors, thus providing coordinated support with UN agencies to avoid problems such as duplication of effort and waste of resources.
e. Not to finance or support constituent movements where the established conditions do not lead to a participatory process, demonstrating not to involve the public or allow their vocalizations, either through social movements or through an independent media. For example, a constituent national assembly that places only leaders of a single party or political faction, or even conducted by manifestly authoritarian government. The UN may end up activating the use of abusive constitutionalism, reinforcing the illegitimacy of a process that has largely excluded popular participation and is manipulated by some elites.
f. When providing advice on how to form, elect, or structure the constituent national assembly, one should consider which mechanism—including, but not limited to, elections—will lead to a more genuine constituent process with a plurality of representatives capable of portraying national vocalizations. The mode of appointment, co-optation, and election of delegates should be transparent and, where possible, participatory.
g. The "principle of national property", established by the UN and which is also a pillar of the theory of original constituent power, requires not only those national actors lead the process, but also that civil society and the public, including immigrants and displaced persons, be given opportunities for them to speak out. And this requires that engagement be planned at each stage of the process, even during the initial phases, such as those performed through *round tables.*
h. International actors shall provide advice or assistance in such a way as not to marginalize or exclude local actors through their involvement in the constituent process and agendas should be adapted to local needs so that the process can

move forward, ensuring that the nation itself prepares to perform its functions effectively.

i. The extent of the capacity of local actors, through specific studies, to implement or rebuild "democracy", must be evaluated before formalizing the constituent assistance through the technicians or counselors determined by the UN. These studies should be part of the planning for the development of civic education and local training, when requested.

j. The constituent consultants, when indicating the options on the structures of the new institutional design, should consider the incorporation of the theory of separation of powers, in order to contemplate the four essential nuclei: independence, harmony, political freedom, and cooperation between the powers; the model of state, centralized or federalism, which best suits local needs, and that does not favor hyper-presidentialism[32] or other anomalies arising from the arbitrary use of the functions of the powers; and the study of constitutionalism, favoring the development of a constitutional identity and culture so that the development of institutional, social, and economic capacities can be aligned with the guarantees of human and fundamental rights that will compose the nuclei of the new constitution.

6.2 Empirical Experiences of Hybrid Constituent Power[33]

As the UN has been increasingly called to mediate the transition from war to peace, the constitutions for this international body provide a unique opportunity to encourage a process that promotes reconciliation, development, and consensus for the country's future. In this sense, the process of creating a constitution, that is, the way the original constituent power is materialized, is as important as the content of the constitutional charter, either to legitimize the new constitutional order or to create a sustainable peace.[34]

The case studies presented below will provide a brief overview of the role of UN constitutional assistance in the constituent phase in four case studies: Cambodia,

---

[32] For more information, see Kings (1988, pp. 57–90), Penfold (2010), Bologna et al. (2015, pp. 115–140), Pulido (2015), Carvalho (2017, pp. 399–411), Rose Ackerman and Desierto (2017).

[33] This chapter focuses exclusively on the description of the UN's intervention in the *constitution-making* constituent phase of the states described. The subject of this analysis will not be the chronological conduct of internal conflict and the *Peacekeeper* developed by the UN.

[34] The conflict prevention and peacekeeping are being touted as one of the highest global priorities for the United Nations System. The adoption of simultaneous Resolutions of the Security Council and the General Assembly—S/RES/2282 (2016)—are incentives to renew attention in these areas. Thus, to understand that there are three pillars that underpin the Charter of the United Nations—development; peace and security; and human rights—priorities and are at the top of the agendas to improve the effectiveness and coordination of the UN System. In this way, the rule of law and human rights continue to be recognized as key areas where the contribution of the entire organization can increase the possibility of transformational change through rational and coherent analysis, planning and provision of high-quality care (United Nations and the Rule of Law (2017).

Bosnia and Herzegovina, Timor-Leste, and Afghanistan.[35] Thus, deference will be given: the overview of the legal framework; the description of the process, considering the degree of inclusion, transparency, and participation of the local population; focus and forms of intervention.

Case studies will allow us to understand whether in these processes there was a matrix in how the intervention, in the constituent phase, occurred or if the approaches were *guided by* ad hoc *processes depending* on the choices of UN leaders in the field.

The mandates of *the peacekeeping and peacebuilding* operations covered by these studies incorporate complex operations that involved the escalation of tasks that were performed, sometimes simultaneously. In other words, security must be maintained, human and humanitarian rights protected, humanitarian crises avoided, and the development of the economy and dialogic policy promoted. For UN leaders in the field, all these issues are priorities.

In this perspective, the constituent phase of the *constitution-making process is* only one element within this of these herculean efforts. Thus, the fact is that the decisions taken by UN leaders in the field were also conditioned by a range of competitive demands which unfolded in real time. Improvisation, for Brant, is often a necessary virtue.

It is also noteable that many missions, especially those carried out before 2006, were carried out without a basis of guiding principles, doctrine, and guidance, such as the current *Guidance Note.* A good example is Resolution A/RES/46/137[36] which established the rules to support the coordination and examination of UN electoral assistance, such as design and implementation of electoral processes, operational strategies for electoral components for peacekeeping, list of electoral experts who can provide technical assistance in the short term, etc. This Resolution serves as an institutional memory of the UN in the electoral field.

Another important step signed by the UN Electoral Assistance Division (DIE) was to establish co-operations with institutions that conduct research in these areas and are not directly linked to the UN to create a much broader set of resources and knowledge.

The case studies presented do not represent a definitive answer to what the broad set of UN experiences in the field of the original constituent phase meant. However, the examples set out point to some gaps in which it is possible to analyze the compatibility of these interventions with classical theory and, from there, build propositional elements, either for the construction of new semantic nuclei that will make up the old theory or to attribute reflections that lead the UN experience in relation to this matter to a more legitimate and democratic path, thus contributing to the recent democracies "not dying" or suffering from the so-called use of abusive constitutionalism.

---

[35] Empirical analyses were extracted from research conducted by Brant (2005, 2011); Gouvêa (2016); Keil (2012, pp. 205-218), Chandler (2000), Hippel (2003); Marks (2010, pp. 207–244).

[36] United Nations (1991).

6.2.1 *Cambodia*

The Paris Peace Agreement was signed on October 23, 1991 with the aim of ending the civil war between Cambodian government forces, on the one side, and the Khmer Rouge and other factions of the Cambodian National Resistance, on the other. The civil war began with the Vietnamese invasion in 1789.

This Agreement refers to a comprehensive political resolution of the Cambodian conflict and provided a legal framework for the drafting process. All parties to the conflict are present in the negotiations that took place between 1989 and 1991.[37]

The Agreement allowed the creation of a United Nations Transitional Authority to prepare a new constitution and the return of the monarchy in Cambodia, restoring the power of Prince Norodom Sihanuk[38] and led to the implementation of the first UN peacekeeping mission called *the United Nations Transition Authority in Cambodia* (UNTAC) post-Cold War. This was the first occasion in the history of the UN that a mission took over as government of a state with civilian and military components and with such an extensive and complex mandate.

The Agreement also created the Supreme National Council (CNS) as the only legitimate body and source of authority, and that, during the transition period, would enshrine three pillars: sovereignty, independence, and Cambodian unity. These members of the Council were responsible for holding the free and fair elections that would be organized and conducted by the UN, through its specialized agencies, for the formation of a new and genuine government. It also predicted that the CNS would delegate all necessary powers to ensure the implementation of the Agreement.

It was agreed that the UN would oversee the government, administrative structures, facilitate the cease-fire, disempower competing factions, maintain law and order, assist in the repatriation of refugees and displaced persons, and promote human rights.

For the Agreement, under Article 12, the Cambodian people would have the right to determine their own political future through a free and fair election through a constituent assembly that would draft and approve a new constitution and become a legislative assembly. These elections would be held under the auspices of the UN in a neutral political environment, with full respect for Cambodia's national sovereignty.

There was also, in the Agreement, the provision on the basic principles relating to human rights and fundamental freedoms, as well as respect for the status of neutrality among the opposing factions that the new Cambodian constitution would incorporate.

Some provisions drew attention: the CNS should offer advice to UNTAC, which will comply with the Agreement provided there was consensus among CNS members and provided that this council was in harmony with the objectives of the Agreement; if there was no consensus among CNS members, President Sihanouk would have the right to take the decision on the assistance that would be offered to UNTAC, and should take into account the views expressed by the CNS, so UNTAC would deliver the opinion only if it were consistent with the objectives of the Agreement;

---

[37] For more information, see Ratner (1993, pp. 1–41).

[38] Valenzuela (1991).

if the President was not, for any reason, in a position to take the decision, his power would be transferred to the Transitional Authority and the latter should take the final decision, taking into account the grounds stated by the CNS.

However, the Agreement provided that in all cases, the Transitional Authority would determine whether the advice or action of the CNS was consistent with the Agreement. In this sense, he would attend all meetings of the CNS and any subsidy body that will be created.

The UNTAC was also responsible for organizing and conducting the election and was able, in accordance with its liberality, to consult the CNS on the organization and conduct of the electoral process.[39]

According to the Agreement, the National Constituent Assembly would be composed of 120 members and the constitution should be adopted after 90 days of its composition. This election would be held throughout Cambodia in a provincial structure and in accordance with the proportional representation system, based on the list of candidates submitted by the political parties. Refugees and displaced persons would have the same rights, freedoms, and opportunities to participate in the electoral process.

The 120 seats were distributed as follows:

58 seats for *front Uni National pour un Cambodge Indépendant (FUNCINPEC);*
51 seats for the *Cambodian People's Party* (CPP);
10 seats for the *Buddhist Liberal Democratic Party* (BLDP); and
01 seat for the *Mouvement pour la Liberation Nationale du Kampuchea* (MOLINAKA).

The *Khmer People's Revolutionary Party* (KPRP), a key faction in the conflict, was not involved in drafting the constitution. The Assembly also did not have a mechanism for representing or contributing to a broader set of *stakeholders in* the process, such as young people, women, and minorities, so it was not inclusive in this regard.

Women were poorly represented in political parties, featuring only five percent of all candidates. In this way, the UN has failed to put all the adverse factions on the same table.

The Agreement did not provide for popular participation in the process of drafting the constitution and nor mechanisms by which the population would be consulted. The trend towards more participatory processes carried out for the UN had not yet taken root, according to Brant.

Political parties could be formed by any group of 5,000 registered voters and party platforms should be in line with the principles and objectives of the Agreement on a global political solution.

Thus, party affiliation would be required to run for election to the constituent assembly. The UNTAC would be responsible for registering the parties and candidates and confirming whether they met the criteria established for qualification and participation in the elections. The adhesion a Code of Conduct established by UNTAC

---

[39] For more information see Cambodian Information Center (1991).

and in consultation with the CNS would also be a selection criterion. The constitution, according to the Agreement, would be adopted by a two-thirds majority of the members of the constituent assembly.

Assembly members would become the new legislators in the political transition. On the one hand, this bionic insertion allowed the transition to have a shorter route. However, this procedure may represent a conflict of interest. If not, let us see given that the members of the constituent assembly projected their own powers as future members of the legislature, this could represent that, in practice, the legislature resulting from the constituent process would become addicted.

The principles for Cambodia's constitution were also the objects of the Agreement. In this way, the bill should already recognize that the constitution would be the supreme law and that it could only be amended by legislative authorization and referendum.

For the UN, Cambodia's tragic history called for special measures to ensure the protection of human rights. Thus, the constitution should contain a declaration of fundamental rights, including rights to life, personal freedom, security, freedom of movement, religion, association, assembly (including political parties and trade unions), due process, equality before the law, protection against arbitrary imprisonment, property, without racial discrimination, among others—that is, consistent with the provisions of the Universal Declaration of Human Rights.

Moreover, the constitution should incorporate the following dictates: that Cambodia would be a sovereign, independent, and neutral nation; that it would follow a system of liberal democracy based on pluralism; would provide periodic and genuine elections; the right to vote and to be elected by universal and equal suffrage; and the existence of an independent judiciary empowered to enforce the rights provided for in the constitution.

Although the parties agreed with these sets of constitutional principles there was no review mechanism to verify whether the final constitution fully incorporated these principles.

The Cambodian constitutional process, as defined by the Paris Agreement, had three main phases: the elections to the constituent assembly; the drafting of the constitution; and the adoption of the constitution. In this way, the Agreement did not include a civic education campaign on constitutional issues or public consultations. Currently, UN missions incorporate these elements (South Africa, Rwanda, Afghanistan) and consider them essential to the legitimacy of the constitutions. But in 1993, the focus of the international community and political elite was focused on the outcome of the constitution to create the development of democratic governance.

The schedule was set as:

April 1993—political campaign;
May 1993—holding of elections for the composition of the constituent assembly;
June 1993—opening of the work of the constituent assembly; and
September 1993—promulgation of the new constitution.

On May 29, 1993, the Yasushi Akashi Transitional Authority declared that the elections to form the constituent assembly were free and fair. At the time, the UN mission was declared a success.

A coalition of 14 members of civil society, entitled *Ponleu Khmer*, formed to encourage popular participation in the drafting of the new constitution. However, as the process did not incorporate mechanisms for this participation to be vocalized and the process of construction of the charter was so short, the coalition struggled to understand the basic issues to which constitutionalism referred to that would be implemented in the new political system. Thus, they hurried to translate other constitutions; share their research with civil society; and meet with as many close communities as possible to discuss constitutional issues and consult them on their aspirations for the future constitution.

The coalition shared the results of its consultations with the constituent assembly and suggested some human rights provisions. According to Brant, in an interview with *the creator of Ponleu Kmer*, the suggested materials were not considered, and expectations were frustrated by the lack of transparency in the constituent process. Feeling out of the process, he wrote a letter to the Transitional Authority, stating that he had the right to know about the articles and provisions that would be positive in the constitution in an open and inclusive manner, since the population also had the right to owe about what they think is inappropriate or that should not be provided for the constitutional life project that will follow from their institution.

The response of the Transitional Authority immediately stated that the people had a democratic right to pressure the members of the constituent assembly and political parties on any matter referred to in the constitution but emphasizes that it was the responsibility of the Assembly to build and adopt the constitution.

From the outset, the issues discussed in the constituent assembly were highly secret, as well as the rules of operation that were also voted on in secret—all without debate and without public record of this internal vote.

In June 1993, the Assembly appointed a committee to draft the constitution with 12 members thus distributed: six members of FUNCINPEC, five of the CPP, and one of BLDP.[40] This committee prepared the draft of the constitution that was kept secret from the other 108 members of the Assembly itself, and this secrecy was provided for in the internal rules adopted.

For Marks,[41] the secrecy of the process made it possible for the most influential political leaders to resort to either of the two previous constitutions (1947 and 1989) and to have their own political interests, rather than allowing the entire assembly to draw on the various models and principles introduced during the transition period.

In the second week of September, the writing committee launched its project, while FUNCINPEC made its monarchical project available.

The Assembly eventually examined the text designed by FUNCINPEC, as edited by Sihanouk, for 5 days and adopted it on September 21, 1993, by a vote of 113 to 5 votes, with 2 abstentions.

The central objective of the Agreement to establish a legitimate governmental authority and a new constitutional order through the elections has deteriorated along the way. The control of political factions in the absolute domain of the Constituent

[40] Marks (2010, pp. 207–244).

[41] Marks (2010, pp. 207–244).

Assembly eventually weakened the sense of constitutional belonging by the population. For Marks, the UN could have exercised more influence so that both the spirit of democracy and the principles of the Agreement were respected, giving some opportunity for public participation in the process.

The way the letter was written led to a path of dominance of a single party that directly influenced constitutional content. In this sense, the UN sinned by not exercising sufficient control and was very sensitive in the negative sense to the question of the sovereignty of the constituent assembly.

According to Brant, a former UNTAC official explained that the planning and management of the process after the election was disastrous because it did not focus on how the new National Constituent Assembly would complete the task of adopting the constitution. The real objective of the mission was political transition and not simply to follow the outcome of the elections.

UNTAC's role in the global transition was defined in the Secretary-General's Report of February 19, 1992,[42] adopted by the Security Council on February 28, 1992. The Report set out detailed guidelines for the seven components of the mission but did not specify any role for UNTAC in the constituent process[43] and thus did not support the population or assist in the design and management of the process.

After the elections for the composition of the Constituent Assembly, the Transitional Authority, representative of the Secretary-General of the United Nations, considered that it was sovereign and that, therefore, UNTAC would not interfere in its deliberations. The mission and the Agreement provided that UNTAC could offer technical assistance or advisors who were not formally accredited to the Assembly of their own free will. Therefore, these assistants had limited access to her. The Assembly had little constitutional expertise within its ranks.

UNTAC members had no offices near or in the Constituent Assembly to help Cambodians move forward with the process. Thus, they prepared alternative drafts of the new Constitution, but did not know how or if the drafts would be used.

Another problem plotted by Brant's research was that UNTAC did not plan the resources that would be needed to assist the Constituent Assembly, and thus members did not have access to facilities with resources for research, library, or technical experts. The concentration of UNTAC resources was to promote the elections, but not the process of drafting of a constitution. This lack of planning eventually resulted in missed opportunities to establish a basis for democratic institutions and practices.

When the Constituent Assembly became the new Cambodian Legislature, it continued to lack resources to improve members' ability to draft and debate new legislation that would be implemented based on constitutional guidelines.

UNTAC's role was, in fact, to exercise its authority to ensure the implementation of the Paris Agreement. The paths that followed the elections were materialized by Sihanouk, who organized an agreement with the parties to form a coalition agreement outside the structure of the Agreement. According to Brant, Sihanouk also restricted

[42] Report of the Secretary-General on Cambodia, containing his proposed implementation plan for UNTAC, S/23613 of February 19, 1992.

[43] Marks (2010, pp. 207–244).

UNTAC's influence in the work of the constituent, hiring a legal expert to prepare a draft constitution for a constitutional monarchy.

In this sense, the Transitional Authority and the international community were concerned about the nature of the project since it was being elaborated in the dark and there was little influence on the outcome of the project. The opening of the path came through Sihanouk, which allowed UNTAC to draw up the human rights standards that would be coupled to the constitution, given that these provisions represented one of the major concerns of the international community and the UN.

The promulgation of the constitution on September 21, 1993 and the formal establishment of the Royal Government of Cambodia ended the UNTAC mandate, as signed in the Paris Agreement.

Cambodia has once again collapsed. Many key elements of the Agreement were not implemented, and the government declined 4 years after the elections.

Although the independent party had won the elections, the Cambodian People's Party, which represented the Cambodian People's Front, retained the dominant military power, and was firmly rooted at all levels of government and much of Cambodia, not willing to accepting the new election result and threatening to trigger a new civil war. Prince Sihanouk mediatized dissent and rearranged a new power-sharing resulting in two co-prime ministers for the universe of Cambodian governability.

The important variable that can be seen in the context in which UNTAC participated was: whether the purpose of the mission was to transform Cambodia into a multi-party political system and into a liberal democracy within 18 months, it clearly did not succeed. However, if it is considered that the purpose of the mission was to appease the exercise of power by introducing the language of democracy and human rights to Cambodian civil society, fostering the creation of a relatively free country, pressuring, and taking steps towards a democratic basis for a legitimate government, it can be considered that the mission has been partially successful.[44]

The lack of regulations of the constitutional provision eventually lead to a coup d'état in 1997 and the 1998 elections failed, indicating that the mission's declaration of success was premature.[45]

The adoption of the Cambodian constitution of 1993 was characterized as a defining event in the implementation of the Paris Agreement's commitment to establish a liberal democracy based on pluralism. The UN has decommissioned a contingent of more than 2,000 military and civilian personnel and spent more than two million dollars to assist Cambodia in the transition period, the end of which was defined as the adoption of the constitution and the establishment of the first government in accordance with it.[46] Without the constitution, for Marks, the UN would have failed in an essential aspect of its mission.

But, considering this experience, to what extent has the process of drafting the constitution in the constituent phase, from the intervention of the UN, contributed

[44] Brant (2005, p. 22).

[45] Brant (2005, p. 22).

[46] Marks (2010, pp. 207–244).

to national reconciliation and the restoration of foundations for the development of a stable and peaceful civil society?

The constitutions in which the UN intervened in the constituent phase can be characterized as "top-down" intervention elements. In UN peacekeeping and post-conflict missions, the most visible operations, from their conduct, relate to the political and military arrangements carried out between the warring factions and a "strong-level intervention" by the international community.

Support for civil society, human rights, and democratic participation is already in the pillars that *underpin the UN constitution-making and constitution-change procedures* that should be conducted as a "bottom-up" movement because they are focused on efforts to drive the process through local actors. This interaction can be a contribution to social transformation through what can be called "democratic strengthening",[47] meaning efforts to increase citizens' ability to participate effectively in society and government.

The UN intervention process at these levels constitutes the hybrid constituent power and can be understood as that established by an elite. On the other hand, it may have as its characteristic a "democratic empowerment". The massive participation in the election of the Constituent Assembleia and the constituent reinforces this empowerment.

In other words, national dialogue and peacebuilding receive a necessary, temporary impetus in the military and political aspects of this "top-down" intervention. On the other hand, ensuring the stability of the constitution and the new division of political power will depend on the development of the nation's democratic capabilities. In the case of Cambodia, the process of drafting the constitution was dominated by the power struggle between the political factions. And in this sense, for Marks,[48] it is necessary to carefully monitor how social development and the application of the constitution will fill the "empowerment" gap created by the process of politicization of factions in the constituent process.

It should be emphasized that, for Marks, the question that remains open is whether the forge of a more democratic and transparent constitution could have provided a more democratic outcome? Could the process itself have served as a capacity building that would strengthen the role of civil society and the general population in the country's political destiny?

Cambodia has not yet fully emerged from the civil war and its democratic foundations are fragile, but the 1993 constitution, for all purposes, cemented this foundation.[49]

---

[47] Marks (2010, pp. 207–244).

[48] Marks (2010, pp. 207–244).

[49] Marks (2010, pp. 207–244).

6.2.2 Bosnia and Herzegovina

> "the cure for the evils of democracy is more democracy"; to which should now be added, "and less internationally imposed democratization".
>
> David Chandler

Bosnia and Herzegovina, established in 1995 from the direct intervention of the UN, has undergone a remarkable process of change. It was dysfunctional and internal obstruction fruit of the ethno-civil war eventually resulted in a lack of political progress. In this sense, Keil[50] points out, important reforms have been carried out to recover the economy, rebuild the country's infrastructure, and bring together society fragmented by years of civil war.

However, the political elites refused to meet again and there was no progress in the construction of the post-war, entre 1995 and 1997, leading the UN to edit numerous resolutions.[51] The UN High Representative was allowed to impose legislation[52] and remove officials who were obstructing the materialization of the Peace Agreement. In this sense, the High Representative became judge and administrator at the same time.

The Dayton Peace Agreement,[53] signed in Paris, on December 14, 1995, incorporated 10 articles, 11 annexes, and 102 maps. The peace talks in Dayton excluded the leaders of Bosnian Serbs (Karadzic and Mladic), who participated only behind the scenes.[54] The Agreement maintained the division between the Croatian-Bosniac federation and the Srpska Republic within a unified state, with Sarajevo being the state capital.

On the one hand, several important reforms have been implemented, such as new state symbols, a new currency, army reform, and constitutional changes of federal entities.

---

[50] Keil (2012).

[51] As an example, UN Security Council Resolution 1034 (1995) on violations of international humanitarian law and human rights in the territory of former Yugoslavia; UN Security Council Resolution 1035 (1995) on the establishment of a UN police force to be known as the International Police Task Force and a UN Civilian Office for the implementation of the Peace Accord; UN Security Council Resolution 1047 (1996) on the appointment of the prosecutor of the International Tribunal in the Territory of the former Yugoslavia since 1991 and the International Court of Rwanda; UN Security Council Resolution 1074 (1996) on the termination of measures imposed by resolutions related to the former Yugoslavia following the elections held in Bosnia and Herzegovina in accordance with the Peace Agreement; among others. For access to all available documents, please refer to the *Office of The High Representative*, available in http://www.ohr.int/?cat=236. Accessed November 24, 2017.

[52] Criminal, electoral, judicial organization, human rights, public institutions, citizenship, financing of the Constitution, police and defense organizations. For more information, see the *Office of The High Representative*, available at http Do www.ohr.int/?page_id=1302 Access on November 24, 2017.

[53] United Nations (2014).

[54] Hippel (2003).

For Keil,[55] in general terms, four periods of reform can be identified: in the first period, ranging from 1995 to 1998, the UN focused on peacebuilding. Troops from the North Atlantic Treaty Organization (NATO) were the main actors and local political elites focused on demilitarization and adjusted to the country's new circumstances. For the author, neither the High Representative nor the local elites have demonstrated any willingness to implement the civil aspects of the Agreement and contribute to its reconstruction. However, the period triggers an important point, and no large-scale violence broke out after 1995.

The Dayton Agreement allowed the Bosnian Serbs and Croats, respectively, access to Serbia and Croatia, and the maintenance of separate armies. He confirmed the right of return for refugees—or compensation in case they do not return—and their right to vote in the original places of their residence.

Annex IV to the Agreement was responsible for structuring the constitutional provisions of Bosnia and Herzegovina, thus its preamble preached respect for dignity, freedom, and human equality by devoting the rights of peace, justice, tolerance, and reconciliation with its inspirations defined in the following terms:

- Convinced that the institutions of a democratic government and fair procedures are more appropriate to establish peaceful relations within a pluralistic society.
- Desirous of promoting general well-being and economic growth through the protection of private property and the promotion of a market economy.
- Guided by the purposes and principles of the Charter of the United Nations.
- Committed to maintaining sovereignty, territorial integrity, and political independence in accordance with international law.
- Inspired by the Universal Declaration of Human Rights, the International Covenants on Civil and Political Rights and Social and Cultural Economic Rights and the Declaration on the Rights of Persons belonging to national or ethnic, religious, and linguistic minorities, as well as by other human rights instruments.
- Recalling the basic principles agreed at Geneva on September 8, 1995 and in New York on September 26, 1995.
- Bosnians, Croats, and Serbs, as constituent peoples (along with others) and citizens of Bosnia and Herzegovina, have established this constitution.

The constitution previously established in the Agreement, which currently maintains the same structure, was divided into 12 articles:

I. Bosnia and Herzegovina, which defined: continuity of the State; democratic principles; composition of the State; movement of goods, capital, services, and persons; its capital; symbols; citizenship.
II. Human Rights and Fundamental Freedoms, which defined: human rights; international standards; the enumeration of rights; the prohibition of discrimination; refugees and displaced persons; their implementation; international agreements; and international cooperation.

[55] Keil (2012, pp. 205–218, p. 215).

III. Attributions of institutions and entities related to them, which defined: their attributions; attributions of entities; the law and attributions of entities and institutions; their coordination; and other attributions.
IV. Legislative Assembly, which defined: the chamber of peoples; the chamber of deputies; its procedure; its attributions.
V. Presidency which defined: election and mandate; its procedure; their duties; councils of ministers; standing committee.
VI. Constitutional Court, which defined: its composition; procedure; jurisdiction; and decisions.
VII. Central Bank.
VIII. Public Treasury.
IX. General Provisions.
X. Reform.
XI. Transitional provisions.
XII. Entry into force.

The timetable established by the Agreement determined that, after its entry into force, elections would be held after 6 months, providing for a postponement, if necessary, for a maximum of 3 months.

The provisional electoral commission, established after the Agreement, would be responsible for approving electoral rules and regulations relating to the registration of independent parties and candidates; determining the conditions necessary for active and passive eligibility; defining the role of national and international election observers; defining the guarantees for an open and impartial election campaign; and carrying out confirmation, publication, and certification of definitive election results.

In 1996, the new state held its first elections, with the participation of two-thirds of the electorate, with Izetbegovic obtaining most of the votes, which put him in the head of state in international terms.

The second period runs from 1998 to 2003, where the High Representative was assigned to coordinate and monitor the civil aspects of implementation, including the rehabilitation and return of refugees, the promotion of elections, monitoring of human rights, demobilization, facilitating dialogue between the parties that are contenders, and reporting the progress of the UN and other international organizations and governments. In this period the High Representative instituted reforms that contributed to the restructuring of the State. Political institutions at the state level have been reformed and have become more influential. For example, there was the removal of ethnic homogeneity as a fundamental constitutional principle in federative entities. Changes in customs and tax duties caused the central state to receive its own independent income.

The Dayton Agreement has strengthened ethnic divisions. The Bosnian war transformed the territory into an ethnically mixed republic with three essentially homogeneous territorial units, with small minorities, each with its own army. According to Caplan,[56] it eventually "entrenched the ethnic divisions that were, after all, responsible for the conflict". By separating the groups, it may be difficult, if not impossible,

[56] Caplan (2005), p. 231.

to convince the three parties that they can live in a multi-ethnic (con)federation after 4 years of fighting against such a solution, albeit within their self-established borders.

There was also a strong refusal by local elites to collaborate with the UN representative, such as the Bosnian-Croatian leadership who refused and challenged international authority and the state. On the other hand, Biljana Plavšic, former President of the Serbian Republic of Bosnia, has shown willingness to work together with the international body.

Reforms to allow the free movement of the economy and its recovery as well as the millions of dollars in aid showed signs of success. The refugees eventually went back to their former homes and the political elites began to cooperate with the international community.

Between 1999 and 2000, democratic governments began to lead the states of Croatia and Serbia and support for secessionist tendencies of the Croats and Bosnian Serbs disappeared. After the Kosovo war in 1999, the European Union (EU) began to become active in the region and offer "support" as a long-term political solution. The reforms focused on reinstalling state structures and providing the central level with more authority and competence. The construction tool was federalism and skill adjustments between states can be seen as an example of this.

Between 2002 and 2006, there is the third period, which can be defined by the connection between state construction and Europeanization. The EU has become increasingly involved and the OFFICE of the UN High Representative has been combined with that of the Special Representative of the European Union. The reforms implemented by the High Representative only took place after discussions with local elites who agreed on the foundations of the reform.

The defense forces were placed under a central command and the new ministries were created to demonstrate the growing importance of the state level. The economy grew by 5% a year and the post-war recovery generated some wealth. However, a consensus on the nature of the state was still lacking. This period ended when a constitutional reform package failed to secure a two-third majority in the House of Representatives.

The final phase may be dated from 2006, considered a phase of permanent crisis, in which the different local elites blocked themselves and their representatives became more radical in their rhetoric and the UN became less focused on national development. The EU eventually became more involved in local problems and tried to manage the reform process. For Keil,[57] progress has not been touted since 2006.

In this way, the UN decided that the elites of the state should take control of their state and that there would no longer be the possibility of reform via international imposition. The EU's "soft" power has focused on cross-compliance as the main tool to motivate local elites to implement important reforms.

For Keil, even with such reservations, success was very limited, because the elites were still very divided on fundamental issues of a material order. While Bosnians preferred more centralization and change in relation to liberal (representative) democracy, Serbs and Croats demanded a new manifestation of the strict system of power.

---

[57] Keil (2012, pp. 205–218, p. 217).

This meant that the Croats demanded a new political entity so that The Croats and Serbs could exercise the right of veto in the decisions of the central government. The state continued to be contested and Bosnian Serbs threatened secession several times.

Bosnia and Herzegovina has become a federal country in a way that is not singular form. Federalism and the constitution were imposed by the UN through the Dayton Agreement as a conflict resolution mechanism to end violence and ensure the establishment of various institutions and levels of governance, consisting of two entities, the Federation of Bosnia and Herzegovina and the Srpska Republic. Since 1995, the system has undergone a series of changes to strengthen the central institutions of the state.

However, more than a quarter of a century later, the country remains divided and living together with a possible division of the autonomous Bosnian Serb. The autonomous federative entities work each on their own and the bloated bureaucratic apparatus ends up further stifling the functioning of the shared state structure.

According to Keil, what Bosnia and Herzegovina need is a consensus on what the state is. To this do so, the political elites of all large groups must find and forge a commitment to define the state and reform institutions to ensure efficient decision-making and the protection of the vital interests of the groups. For the author, the EU could encourage these discussions and countries such as Belgium, Canada, and Switzerland could offer important lessons in terms of management and diversity.[58]

What the UN or the EU cannot do is build or adjust the State of Bosnia and Herzegovina through direct intervention, even though these actors have successfully succeeded in ensuring security and peace.

The impetus behind democratization may be in the needs of international institutional actors to legitimize new forms of cooperation and their role as an international regulator. The democratization process in Bosnia and Herzegovina has been used as a matrix for the reshaping of international institutions post-Cold War. For Chandler, "democratization" provides a perfect way for international progress and cooperation because there is no end point.

Negotiations and solutions were excluded from local elites, and from the outset, a foreign policy agenda was imposed. The logic of democratization and its exercise cannot be given to Bosnian institutions, mainly due to the lack of security on the ground, which eventually became a vicious circle.[59] In this way, elected representatives eventually became superfluous for the implementation of development policies.[60]

Instead of strengthening the central institutions of the new State, facilitating commitment and negotiation, the process removed the capacity-building policies of the State and entities. And this is a situation that the UN needs to increase, that is, to give more levels of autonomy, more autonomy to local elites. Thus, gradually,

[58] Keil (2012 pp. 205–218, p.218).

[59] Chandler (2000, p. 193).

[60] Chandler (2000, p. 196).

there would be less dependence and concern about the withdrawal of the international community from the state.

It is concluded that the experience of hybrid constituent power and democratization by the UN did not bring a character of unity, bond, identity to the Bosnian people; the UN's extended mandates[61] have undermined the main political parties; and no unitary political basis was created, except to the extent of the imposition carried out by the international community; and there was little indication that the established strategy contributed to the development of mechanisms that facilitated interethnic political cohesion.

[61] How example: Resolution 1088 (1996) of December 12, 1996, the Security Council gave UNMIBH additional responsibilities relating to the investigation of allegations of human rights abuses by police officers or other law enforcement officials of the various authorities of Bosnia and Herzegovina. This decision was taken in accordance with the Conclusions of the Peace Implementation Conference, held in London on December 4–5, 1996; Resolution 1103 (1997) of March 31, 1997, the Security Council endorsed the Secretary-General's recommendations relating to international policing in Brcko. This resolution followed the decision of February 14, 1997 by the arbitral tribunal on the disputed portion of the Inter-Entity Boundary Line in the Brcko area. The Council decided to increase the strength of UNMIBH by 186 civilian police personnel, taking into account the fact that the arbitration award called for the monitoring, restructuring, and retraining of the police in the Brcko area with an intensity far beyond that in other parts of the country; Resolution 1107 (1997) of May 16, 1997, the Security Council decided to increase the strength of UNMIBH by 120 civilian police personnel. This decision was based on the Secretary-General's assessment that in order to carry out, in a satisfactory manner, the additional and existing tasks relating to human rights investigation, monitoring of the local police, strengthening of police training, police restructuring, and the development of guidelines for democratic principles, IPTF would have to move from a police force with primarily generalist functions to one with a substantial number of police experts in specialized fields. However, it would remain necessary for IPTF to maintain a sufficient monitoring presence throughout the country to provide an oversight of field activities to prevent violations of international standards of human rights and democratic policing. It would also be necessary for IPTF to continue to monitor key locations, the resettlement areas of the zone of separation, and other areas where substantial tensions still existed; Resolution 1144 (1997) of December 19, 1997, the Security Council decided that UNMIBH, in the framework of the current mandate, should be entrusted with the following additional tasks: (a) the creation of specialized IPTF training units to address key public security issues, such as refugee returns; organized crime, drugs, corruption and terrorism, and public security crisis management (including crowd control) as well as training in the detection of financial crime and smuggling; and (b) cooperation with the Council of Europe and OSCE, under the coordination of the High Representative, in a program of judicial and legal reforms, including assessment and monitoring of the court system, development and training of legal professionals and restructuring of institutions within the judicial system; Resolution 1168 (1998) of May 21, 1998, the Security Council authorized a further increase in the strength of UNMIBH by 30 civilian police personnel to carry out new intensive programs for the local police in a number of specialized fields; Resolution 1184 (1998) of July 16, 1998, the Security Council approved the establishment by UNMIBH of a program to monitor and assess the court system in Bosnia and Herzegovina, as part of an overall program of legal reform under the overall coordination of the High Representative. This program became known as the Judicial System Assessment Program (JSAP); Among Other of the Advice from Safety, how S/RES/1423 (2002), S/RES/1184 (1998), S/RES/1168 (1998); S/RES/1144 (1997); S/RES/1107 (1997); S/RES/1103 (1997); S/RES/1088 (1996); S/RES/1035 (1995).

6.2.3 East Timor

The first UN mission in East Timor, *the United Nations Mission in East Timor* (UNAMET), was established on June 11, 1999. Its main objective was to organize a popular consultation, scheduled for August 8, 1999, to verify whether the Timorese accepted the proposed constitutional framework: special autonomy for Timor within the Republic of Indonesia or the rejection of this autonomy, in accordance with the general agreement.

After the election results, where 78% supported independence, Indonesian militias launched a new campaign of terror and more than 1,000 people were killed, hundreds of people displaced and 60% of the country's infrastructure were attacked and destroyed.

Almost 10 years after the UN intervention in East Timor, when stability was restored, a new mission *called United Nations Transitional Administration in East Timo (UNTAET)*[62] considered transitional administration was established through Resolution 1272, overseeing the Brazilian Sérgio Vieira de Mello, invested with legislative, executive, and judicial powers in East Timor.

This mission, established in 2000, also aimed to establish a new constitution for Timor. The elections to form the Constituent Assembly were held under the mantle of UNTAET in 2001.

The Security Council did not specify in the Resolution how the authority should be transferred to the Timorese government. This plan would be developed from the election of the National Constituent Assembly that would draft the first independent constitution of Timor.

According to Resolution 2001/2, the 75 national seats would be contested via proportional election. The Assembly should adopt the constitution within 90 days, and which would serve as an interim legislature, and could become the future legislature of Timor, if there was provision in the constitution. The constitution would be adopted by a vote of a two-thirds majority of the members of the Assembly.

The official schedule predicted that:

June and July 2001—national council hearings.
August 2001—elections to make up the constituent national assembly.
September 2001—approval by the national constituent assembly of the constitution.
March 2002: adoption of the new constitution.

The broad structure for Timor's constituent process was like that of Cambodia. Similar to UNTAEC's electoral education program, UNTAET's civic education campaign did not cover constitutional issues. These were discussed during the hearings that were conducted a month before the elections.

The UN Political Department was asked to advise on possible structuring for the process of building a constitution. The Department produced a report on the pros and cons, which was forwarded to the National Council. According to Brant, the work

---

[62] Research conducted by Gouvêa (2016, pp. 177–178).

showed a strong willingness to nose an elected body that would make all decisions regarding the new constitution. The report did not note that other countries used a two-level structure: a constitutional commission to prepare the project and a National Assembly to adopt it, like the structures in Eritrea, Ethiopia, Nicaragua, and Fiji.

An independent commission, as already mentioned, tends to distance itself from the political agenda and can allow a greater diversity of views, better opportunities for consensus building—from the view of experts and greater public participation. The structure also allows an elected body to take over and discuss the final project, thus ensuring the legitimacy of the process and the participation of adverse factions.

The timetable for the forge of the Timorese Charter was designed by UNTAET and approved by the National Advisory Council. This Council was created to increase the capacity to advise the Administrator. The Council was composed of 36 members composed of Timorese members and chaired by Xanana Gusmão, leader of the opposition party of the Revolutionary Front of Independent Timor-Leste (FRETILIN). This appointment was made by the UN Transitional Administrator, who kept under his power the final decisions regarding the agreed commitments.

Timor's leaders were pressuring the Administrator for a transfer of power to an elected and unnamed Timorese body. The National Advisory Council had neither the autonomy nor functions of a nascent legislative council.

On the other hand, according to Gouvêa,[63] many civil society organizations argued that more time was needed for civic education and consultation about elections, the role of the Assembly and the very draft constitution for the election to be significant.

Being at the transitional moment, there should be special attention to the composition of the advisory council, which also did not enjoy the legitimacy of an elected body, and too much international influence was detrimental to the constitutional process.

It is the national authorities that must play a role as principal coordinator and, in the case of Timor, the Transitional Authority has retained power over all final decisions relating to the charter's commitments.

It was Regulation 2001/2[64] which gave legislative powers to the Assembly, providing for the establishment of a specialized committee with powers of approval of the Regulation, and the powers of the Transitional Administrator relating to the veto remain unchanged.

A group of international observers for Timor summed up their concerns[65] in a series of notes. An initial problem is that the whole process was very hasty, eventually favoring the interests of the UN and established political organizations rather than Timorese interests.

The elections to make up the Assembly were held in 2001 and led to the adoption of the Constitution the following year. According to Gouvêa,[66] any human rights

---

[63] Gouvêa (2016).

[64] Ferreira (2000–2006), Simião (2007b, p. 154).

[65] Brant (2005).

[66] Gouvêa (2016, p. 179).

guarantee provided for in the project could be stillborn if the process is not subsidized by the principles of democratic participation broadly.

Civic education came too late, and UNTAET did not consult the Timorese about the project, leaving little time for this critical part of the democratic process. On the day of the elections for the composition of the National Constituent Assembly, many Timorese did not understand that the votes were to make the choice of the members of the Assembly.

In the case of Timor, not all Timorese were able to participate in the process of building the constitution for various problems: many remained in refugee camps, about 5 to 10% of the population; logistical obstacles, here a combination of infrastructure destruction and limited development, among others.

It was established that the Assembly would prepare a draft constitution 90 days after its election, as determined by Resolution 2001/2. This short term did not provide the opportunity to build an alternative provisional model of constitution and the Administrator ruled out the idea of adopting a provisional constitution to allow more popular consultations and civic education, due to the pressures of time and cost of the mission.

Another determination of the Resolution was that the charter should be chosen by the votes of the parties of the Assembly itself and not by referendum. It was also defined that the Constituent Assembly would become the first national parliament, without the promotion of direct elections. The structure of the Timorese process had the same potential for conflicts of interest as occurred in the Cambodian process—an assembly charged with determining its own functions in the future legislature.

Otherwise, there was no prescription on the types of binding constitutional or legal principles, as occurred, for example, in Cambodia and Bosnia and Herzegovina. In Timor, there was "deference" to the sovereignty of the Timorese people, although, mitigated by the presence of international actors. The UN adopted a "*hands off*" *stance*, so that constitutional content would be seen as exclusively the competence of the Constituent Assembly and not imposed by foreign hands. The Transition Administrator did not participate in any session with the National Assembly, since he did not want to be seen as an "influencer" of the project. On the other hand, the UNTAET team monitored and reported the entire constituent process.

As described by Brant, when the draft projections of the constitution violated human rights standards of international standards, the UN political consultants were instructed to meet with members of the Assembly to explain where *the draft did* not maintain the standards.

The election to form the Assembly was held in 2001 and it was sworn in by the Transitional Administrator, consisting of 88 deputies, representing 12 parties and an independent candidacy.[67]

Once the Assembly was appointed, work began. Political parties became the main decision-makers and, in to be part of the discussions, civil society organizations would have to force their entry through the political parties represented there, and there was no provision for popular participation. Also, part of the work were two members

[67] Research conducted by Gouvêa (2016 p. 180).

of UNTAET, a jurist specializing in constitutional law and an expert in politics, on which the task of carrying out the work of the Assembly was to be carried out.

The UN has played two roles in this process: both to "encourage compliance with international standards", and that almost all resolutions contained, in their bulge, the promotion of democracy and human rights; as well as symbolizing a "political actor" with the Constituent Assembly. The process was not followed by a lengthy population dialogue and was restricted behind closed doors.

In the forum held in 2001, there was the suggestion of NGOs to promote an alternative process for the election of a Constituent Assembly, as in the mold of the National Constituent Commission of the South African model, with the broad representation of all sectors of civil society, planning of adequate resources, and a deadline of at least 1 year for consultations.[68] Civil society was the driving force behind the encouragement of wider participation.

UNTAET, for its part, had suggested the creation of a Constitutional Commission in each of Timor-Leste's 13 districts. These mini committees should be tasked with promoting the realization of constitutional civic education on the transition process, with the collection of aspirational content to make up the content of the constitution.[69] The contribution of district committees would be made available to the Assembly. They had only 45 days to educate a predominantly illiterate audience on complex constitutional issues.

The Constituent Assembly challenged the undemocratic nature of the process, although UNTAET continued its planning. District committees held more than 200 public hearings, with at least one hearing in each of East Timor's 67 subdistricts.[70] More than 38,000 people attended district meetings from March 15 to July 14, 2001.

According to Garrison,[71] the executive summary that was transmitted by UNTAET was ignored by the Assembly. The reasons pointed out were that the commissions had not been elected and that they were products of UNTAET and not of the Timorese people, and therefore lacked legitimacy and no reference was made to any of the district reports in the plenary debates.

The UN, the media, and FRETILIN leaders predicted that Fretilin would win a substantial number of seats in the assembly because of its leading role in the struggle for independence from Timor. Despite the probability of monopartisan domination, the process was structured for the elected body to debate and adopt the constitution, without the provision of marginalized groups being part of the process.

FRETILIN had been the winning party of the constituent elections, with a majority of 57.3% of the vote, which made it possible to compose a 55-member bench out of the maximum number of seats of 88. Together with ASDT, the two parties constituted the necessary majority of two-third to draft and get the letter approved.[72] Thus, FRETILIN did not need to be involved in building consensus for the terms that would

---

[68] Garrison (2005, p. 12).

[69] United Nations (2013).

[70] Garrison (2005, p. 19).

[71] Garrison (2005, p. 20).

[72] Ferreira (2000–2006), Simião (2007a, p. 153).

be adopted in the constitution. In other words, this Assembly was not undoubtedly representative of the structure of Timor's political power.

Four projects were presented by the parties that provided for two structures of institutional design with semi-presidential and semi-parliamentary characteristics. With the need for the time held by UNTAET, the main text became the one presented by FRETILIN, and according to Gouvêa the 88 Members had before them a text that for the majority was "strange", not only because it was presented in the Portuguese of Portugal,[73] but also the deputies did not master the legal-constitutional language, clarification given by foreign consultants is necessary.

During the months of the charter's construction, there were daily explanations in the tribune of what popular sovereignty meant, universal suffrage, multipartisanship, participatory democracy, the principle of separation of powers, judicial organization, and democratic legitimacy, among others.[74] These were terms of Western constitutions, knowledge of UN consultants, and very little Timorese. The central work of support and advice to constituent Members in the drafting of the text was in the hands of foreigners.

Gouvêa's[75] concludes that the Charter was approved with 3 months of discussion, with 72 votes in favor and 14 against, with 01 abstention and 01 absence. An additional concern was the fact that the opposition claimed that the Charter was the result of a single party, and this could once again incite violence.

The Timorese Charter, written in 90 days, did not seem to be a national product. The Members had before them a document that for the majority was strange, behold, presented in Portuguese, a language that was not known to all, besides dominated by a language and political-legal influence that was the *responsibility of international experts*, and may therefore not reflect the agreement of stakeholders on nature, the political system, and the future of the state.

According to constitutional theory, this model cannot be considered "democratic" since the power constituted was in foreign hands and the letter was not taken to a referendum. On the other hand, this process did not fully support civil society so that it could be part of the constituent process, so it was not considered inclusive, participatory, and transparent. However, UNTAET has improved constitutional assistance compared to Cambodia, looking better at: planning for the human and material resources needed to meet the Constituent Assembly; support for the development of transparency mechanisms; monitoring the process; and effective intervention to uphold international standards.

Even containing a differentiated panorama, the transitional constitutionalism, which bets on change by constructive effort and that will boost the text, was not perceived in Timor-Leste. Therefore, one problem will be to form a constitutional culture, which is effectively strengthened based on social consensus.

---

[73] Timor-Leste in addition to Tetum has at least 15 other native dialects, such as the Habun, galolen, Wetares, Kawaimine, Bekais. Native languages Mabae and Makasae, in addition to the Tetum, have several speakers exceeding one hundred thousand inhabitants.

[74] Gouvêa (2016, p. 182).

[75] Gouvêa (2016, p. 183).

In this type of intervention, there is no unilateral substantive change in democratic values and principles, but the way of establishing the procedure tends to relate to the use of "abusive constitutionalism" if there is no heterogeneous group of political forces existing in the State in the composition of the constituent, which includes, even, members of minority representation of society.

6.2.4 *Afghanistan*[76]

On December 5, 2001,[77] *through The Bonn Agreement*, the legal basis for Afghanistan's *constitution-making* process was established. The fall of the Taliban presented the opportunity to forge a new consensus among the Afghans to rebuild the state.

Under the auspices of the UN, the Bonn Conference brought together four Afghan political factions, with the aim of securing an agreement for a broad political transition.[78] Brent points out that, unlike the Paris Agreement, the meeting was not fully represented by all Afghan political groups, including the Taliban, which later impacted the peacebuilding process.

The Agreement was intended to end the tragic conflicts in Afghanistan and promote national reconciliation, peace, stability, and respect for human rights in the country. Afghanistan's independence, national sovereignty, and territorial integrity have been reaffirmed, recognizing the right of the people to freely decide their political future in accordance with the principles of Islam, democracy, pluralism, and social justice.

The Bonn Agreement expressed its thanks to the "*Muyahidín Afganos*",[79] who for years have advocated the country's independence, territorial integrity, and national unity, and having a key role in the fight against terrorism and oppression and whose sacrifice has made them heroes of jihad and champions of peace, stability, and the reconstruction of their homeland.

The Agreement recognized, among others, the need to ensure broad representation in the provisional provisions of the term of all sectors of the Afghan population, including groups that were not present or represented in the United Nations talks on Afghanistan.

---

[76] The theoretical basis in this case study is especially focused on the studies conducted by Brant (2005, p. 9). This was a strategically planned choice, considering that the empirical study conducted by the researcher was extremely detailed.

[77] United Nations (2001).

[78] Brant (2005, p. 9).

[79] The invasion of the Soviet Union is a step prior to the emergence of the Taliban movement. This is since most of its members formed part of the resistance against the Russians. The *Muyahidin* Afegons then became anti-Soviet shock troops. From this Afghan-Russian conflict came a second generation of *Muyahidin* that if self-named Taliban, "the scholars of Islam" (Giordana 2018).

The pact also noted that the provisional provisions were intended as a first step towards establishing a broad-based, gender-sensitive, multi-ethnic, and widely representative government.

The Agreement also provided for the establishment of a Provisional Authority, which has held Afghan sovereignty at the time of the official transfer of powers on December 22, 2001. Over the interim period The Transitional Authority was the representative, in its foreign relations and occupied the place corresponding to Afghanistan in the United Nations and in specialized agencies, as well as in other international institutions and conferences.

This Authority would be composed of a Provisional Administration headed by a President, with an *Independent Special Commission to convene an Emergency Loya Jirga*[80] and a Supreme Court of Afghanistan, as well as other Courts that could establish the provisional administration. The composition, functions, and regulatory procedures of both the Provisional Administration and the Special Committee were established by the Agreement.

This authority would cease to exist once *the Loya Jirga* Emergency established a Transitional Authority.

The *Loya Jirga* Emergency, according to the Agreement, should be convened within 6 months of the establishment of the Provisional Authority. His majesty Mohammed Zaher, former king of Afghanistan, declared open *to Loya Jirga* that he would establish a Transitional Authority. This would include a broad-based Transitional Administration to run Afghanistan until a fully representative government could be elected, through free and impartial elections, which should be held before 2 years of convening the "great council" could take place.

According to the Agreement, a *Constitutional Loya Jirga* should be convened within 18 months of the establishment of the Transitional Authority, with the aim of adopting a new constitution. To provide help to *this Loya Jirga* in the preparation of the constitution, the Transitional Administration established within 2 months of its creation and, with the assistance of the UN, a Constitutional Commission.

The UN functions during the transition were established through Annex IV to this Agreement. Thus, the Special Representative of the Secretary-General was responsible for all aspects of the UN's work in Afghanistan, providing and supervising assistance in implementing all aspects of the Agreement.

In this sense, the advisory to the Provisional Authority was focused on the establishment of a politically neutral environment favorable for *the celebration of an Emergency Loya Jirga* in conditions of freedom and impartiality, paying special

---

[80] The *Loya Jirga*, or "great council", is a mass national gathering that brings together representatives from various ethnic, religious, and tribal communities in Afghanistan. It is a century-old institution that was convened in times of national crisis or to solve national issues. Historically has been used to approve a new constitution, declare war, choose a new king, or make broad social or political reforms. According to the Afghan constitution, a *Loya Jirga* is considered the greatest expression of the Afghan people. However, it is not an official decision-making body and the its resolutions are not legally binding and any verdict must be approved by the two houses of the Afghan Parliament and the President to make it official. Bezhan (2013).

attention to the conduct of the organs and administrative departments that can directly influence the convocation and the result *of this Emergency Loya Jirga.*

The Special Representative of the Secretary-General or his delegate could be invited to attend the meetings of the Provisional Administration and the Special Independent Commission on the *convening of the Loya Jirga* Emergency. If there were any controversies at the meetings of the provisional government or the Special Independent Commission, the Special Representative would exercise his good offices to facilitate the exit from the impasse or the adoption of a decision, considering the views expressed in the provisional Government or the Independent Special Committee.

The UN also had the right, according to the Agreement, to investigate human rights violations and, if necessary, recommend corrective measures. He was also responsible for the development and implementation of a human rights education program to promote respect for and understanding of these rights.

The overview of Afghanistan's legal framework, according to Brant,[81] differed from that of Timor and Cambodia in six different ways: *The Bonn Agreement* created a two-front process—a Constitutional Commission to build a draft constitution and a *Constitutional Loya Jirga* to debate and adopt the constitution; the Agreement provided for an 18-month period for the preparation of the project and for *the convocation of Loya Jirga* constitutional, but did not set a deadline for it to adopt the new constitution; the Agreement did not specify the mechanism for the selection and election of members of the Constitutional Commission *or the Constitutional Loya Jirga*; the Agreement did not make the Commission an *independent body; the constitution-making process was* based on a culturally recognized Afghan institutional form; the Agreement did not expressly foresee any constitutional principles that should be included in the constitution.

The Agreement emphasized several objectives and principles of liberal democracy that constitutional exercise could potentially harness, such as creating a policy in accordance with the principles of Islam, democracy, pluralism, and social justice.

In this sense, for the research developed by Brant, the legal framework was "skeletal" and with some serious deficiencies as already mentioned, not establishing a deadline for the approval of the constitution, for its form of composition and election, bem as procedural rules for popular participation. The Afghans leading the process with the help of the UN, in general, were free to lead the process and design the Commission *and the Constitutional Loya Jirga.*

The Transitional Authority, established by *Loya Jirga* Emergency, foresaw the construction of the *constitution-making project* that was structured as follows:

October 2002—formation of nine members of the Constitutional Drafting Committee and Secretariat;
March 2003—submission of the *constitutional draft* to President Karzai;
April 2003—establishment of thirty-five members of the Constitutional Commission;
June and July 2003—civic education program on constitutional issues;

[81] Brant (2005, p. 9).

July and August 2003—public consultation on the key issues of the constitution;
November 2003—launch of the constitutional project for the public;
December 2003—convocation of the *Constitutional Loya Jirga*;
January 2003—adoption of the constitution.

President Karzai, appointed Acting Chairman of the Transitional Administration, appointed the nine members of the Committee for drawing a draft constitution. This Committee did not have a legal mandate and conducted most of its work behind closed doors, conducting few consultations with society and the civilian population. The draft constitution was largely mirrored in the 1964 Afghan Constitution and presented to the President in March 2003. At this point, 6 months have passed from the 18-month period set out in the Agreement.

The President did not name the 35-member Constitutional Commission until March 2003. This Commission was composed of Afghan legal experts, tribal elders, religious scholars, and *experts in* the field of economics and social sciences—among these, seven members were women. In this matter, for Brant, the Commission was quite representative, but there were complaints that the best and brightest of key political groups had been excluded, as powerful political factions were dominating the Commission and thus there would be a greater likelihood of incorporating their own interests.

The Commission's work plan focused on some axes determined by presidential decree:

- Facilitate and promote information for public access throughout the process.
- Hold public consultations in each province and among Afghan refugees in Irã and Pakistan, and, where possible, in other countries, to solicit their views on their national aspirations.
- Receive written prescriptions from individuals or groups of Afghans, inside and outside the family, who wish to contribute to the constitutional project.
- Conduct studies on constitutional project options.
- Prepare a report analyzing the vision of Afghans who were gathered during public consultations and make the report available for public access.
- Disseminate and educate the population about the draft constitution.

One of the fundamental aspects, which was of concern, was related to public participation. Initially, the fear was that the consultative process would be "hijacked" *by dominant factions* and could trigger a high degree of insurgencies.[82] The constitutional advisors emphasized that these dangers could be minimized when well structured and planned for the conduct of the work related to consultations, prescriptions, etc. Experiments from previous interventions had shown that open and ruleless popular participation almost always went wrong, because of the fundamentalist tendencies of certain groups. Thus, the recommendation was to expand the social agenda, the guarantee of rights, including the right to development and a fair distribution of resources.

[82] Brant (2005, p. 9).

After Karzai agreed to undertake a participatory process in March 2003, there were already obstacles to a successful consultative process. First, the public was already quite unaware since the project had been discussed by the Committee behind closed doors. Secondly, the writing committee prepared a project that was not disclosed to the population, which did not feel belonging and became suspicious of the popular consultation process. Thirdly, there was no intention of establishing an independent commission. And finally, there were no funds for carrying out the consultative process, and there was no clear plan for carrying out the work.

The Commission, with the support of the secretariat, had only 1 month to educate the public on constitutional issues, establish the process, and encourage the population to participate. As an aid mechanism, the secretariat allied itself with some Non-Governmental Organizations, totaling approximately one thousand six hundred people, to assist in the process and reach all provinces of the country.

The challenge of conducting civic education and a process of popular consultation were immense, including infrastructure, high illiteracy rate, difficulties in communicating with women and disabled people, as well as overcoming the domains of local leaders, politicians, or land, to promote community meetings. The secretariat was able to distribute more than 450,000 questionnaires on key constitutional issues before commissioners began to travel. Thus, with all the obstacles set, more than fifteen thousand citizens gave their opinions in the advisory processes.

Although these commissioners were tasked with listening to the public, some spent most of their time lecturing or explaining the draft constitution that had been drafted by the committee and slightly revised by the Constitutional Commission.[83]

The secretariat made a Herculean effort to feed a pre-designed database the questionnaires and views collected. Approximately one hundred thousand questionnaires were analyzed and a report was prepared explaining the results and views of the population consulted. According to Brant, the views indicated citizens' concerns about security, a fair distribution of resources, access to education, and praised that, in general, the Afghan population respected the right to freedom of religion.

However, it was left to President Karzai and his influential political members to decide the content of the final version of the constitution and his considerations, according to Brant, were largely based on their political interests. Thus, not much weight was given to popular views on the new draft of the constitution, just as it did in East Timor.

President Karzai approved the final version of the constitution approximately 1 month before the meeting of *the Constitutional Loya Jirga.* The report, explaining the results of the consultations and how the views of the population followed the hands of the delegates of the *Constitutional Loya Jirga.*

The Presidential Decree on the convocation *of the Constitutional Loya Jirga* of July 15, 2003 established the mode of election and appointment, as well as its composition, with a body of five hundred members:

- 50 experts appointed by the President, of which 25 women;

---

[83] Brant (2005, p. 9).

- 344 elected delegates, representing approximately 18,000 members *of loya jirga* emergency;
- 24 refugees elected in Pakistan and Iran;
- 64 women elected, representing 2 women per province;
- 09 Kochis elected, representing the nomadic tribes;
- 06 displaced persons elected, representing three provinces;
- 03 people Hindu and Sikhs elected.

For Brant, the Decree ensured that women, minorities, and marginalized groups, such as internally displaced people, had seats at the table.

The problems arising from the lack of internal security prevented the electoral process for the election of the 344 delegates, as well as occurred for the composition *of the Loya Jirga* Emergency. Many districts were no longer accessible, so *representatives of the Loya Jirga* Emergency formed an electoral group that was assembled in provincial centers to elect their delegates.

The highly detailed rules of procedure were drawn up with the help of constitutional consultants with expertise in comparative studies and the UN and, as these were respected, ended up minimizing opportunities for the commission of fraud or intimidation by political factions. For Brant,[84] despite these efforts, many "warlords" and jihadists were elected to *make up the Constitutional Loya Jirga*, reflecting the political and security reality in Afghanistan.

Almost all elected delegates participated in a 2-day orientation to understand the procedural rules that were participatory and focused on encouraging consensus building and promoting dialogue. Although the rules were agreed in advance, the president *of the Constitutional Loya Jirga* stated that, in this capacity, it could change or circumvent the rules, sometimes to resolve the impasses. This eventually undermined the transparency of the process to some degree.

According to Brant, there was also a certain degree of intimidation, given that "warlords" and jihadists were present. Some delegates did not feel free to express their opinions and when a young delegate protested the inclusion of these members, he was almost expelled *from the Constitutional Loya Jirga* and had to be protected by UN officials.

Plenary deliberations were opened with UN observers attending all sessions. The *Constitutional Loya Jirga* was divided into ten working groups that deliberated observing and analyzing the one hundred and sixty articles of the constitution and presenting suggestions that would be forwarded to a harmonization committee.

This process lasted about 3 weeks and the most heated discussions were represented by key questions about ethnic lines relating to linguistic rights, dual nationality, government structure, and the division of powers. Therefore, these negotiations were held behind closed doors and the UN Secretary-General's Special Representative and a U.S. ambassador helped delegates commit and reach agreement on the final draft on January 3, 2003. President Karzai signed the constitution on January 26, 2003.

---

[84] Brant (2005, p. 9).

For Brant, the representative nature *of the Constitutional Loya Jirga* was achieved in part, which eventually allowed most Afghans to see the Constitution as a positive step towards achieving democracy and good governance, despite failures in the participatory process.

The Secretariat of the Constitutional Commission continued to work for 3 months after the adoption of the Constitution, with the aim of distributing drafts and educating the public about the meaning and scope of the new Constitution.

It was the Afghanistan Transition Administrator who determined the details of the constitution's construction process, consulting the UN Secretary-General's Special Representative Lakdar Brahimi, who was the authority to monitor and assist all aspects determined by *The Bonn Agreement*. The UN Secretary-General's Special Representative (RESG) should ensure that the Afghan priorities that led to the establishment of the UN mission *through the United Nations Assistance Mission in Afghanistan* (UNAMA)[85] were guaranteed, which meant international action with limited powers.

It was determined by UNAMA that the role of the United Nations in the transition process would be that of providing technical assistance, including the coordination of all international actors involved in the process. The aim of this coordination was to ensure that there was no concurrent assistance to the creators of the Constitution.

UNAMA also formed a *constitutional support unit—Support Unit*—initially consisting of a junior UN official and an Afghan administrative assistant with knowledge of the country's political context and with no experience in the *constitution-making process*.

Although the RESG provided general guidance on the constitutional process, it was determined that the constitutional support unit itself could not directly advise the Afghan Director member of the Secretariat of the Constitutional Drafting Commission on options for making the new constitutional charter democratic. The Asia Foundation, funded by the U.S. agency for international development, has secured the presence of two international consultants, both to support UNAMA and the Constitutional Commission, to present constitutional options for the process.

The UN agreed that international consultants should carry out an initial evaluation of the process and prepare reports on how the constituent process could be improved and structured. These reports were drawn up based on the principles set out in the Agreement.

In the list were provided for options for the implementation of a work plan, which included civic education directed at the population, the public consultation process, the process budget, and human resources and material resources to implement the process. Suggestions were also offered for the drafting of Decrees regarding the rules of the procedure and the code of conduct. In this sense, the final decision would be made by the Afghans, the leaders of the process.

After the Transition Administrator agreed to a detailed constitutional roadmap, UNDP was responsible for administering the funds. The Asia Foundation also

[85] Unama Mission Satatement (2017).

provided a financial advisor to the Secretariat of the Constitutional Commission to advise the administration of funds and establish accountability mechanisms.

The UN Secretary-General's Special Representative created a constitutional task force composed of four members of the Afghan Secretariat, a constitutional support unit and two constitutional consultants to coordinate the progress of the process.

It should be noted that the RESG did not have the degree of formal power as it did in Cambodia and East Timor, although it had a strong and prominent role as a political consultant. He met regularly with the President of the Transitional Administration, Karzai.

His position in Afghanistan was prominent as he had a close relationship with Karzai and the Afghan population saw him with good eyes. And, according to Brant, "he used his influence to make sure the process was on the right track".

The RESG also organized consultative discussions with five senior Afghan officials selected by Karzai, who represented key political factions in Afghan territory.

Brant's research indicates that the SRSG ad hoc *advised* President Karzai on a multitude of decisions, such as the election/selection of delegates *to the Constitutional Loya Jirga*, the security and oversight of the electoral process, the role of the UN *in the Constitutional Loya Jirga*, and the role of observers in the process, among others. The results of these discussions were materialized in the form of Decrees or Procedural Rules, revised, approved, and promulgated by Karzai.

As the process progressed, new international actors were incorporated into the process. UNAMA added three additional officials to the constitutional support unit and allocated them to each of the UN regional offices. The Asia Foundation also increased its support and provided the secretariat with a database consultant, media and graphic arts specialists, and logistics and security service providers to assist delegates with preparations for the election of *the Loya Jirga* Constitutional.

It was also guaranteed by UNAMA that the constitutional consultants who advised on the substantive content of the constitutional project were coordinated and that the consultations would be harmonious. Among the members of the group, there was one with deep political knowledge about the struggles of Afghanistan and the other experts in comparative constitutional law. For Brant, it was found that although they had deep knowledge, they had limited access to influence the draft of the constitutional text.

Contrary to the Cambojano and Timorese process, where the UN RESG has stayed away from the constituent process, in Afghanistan his presence was welcome and he had an office within *the Constitutional Loya Jirga*. He was always present in the discussions and used his experience to reconcile opposing views or advise on the position of the international community on the theme.

A UNAMA team also maintained a continued presence *at Loya Jirga* Constitutional to monitor committee discussions, assist with complaints, intimidation or human rights violations that could arise, as well as observe and support the voting process under the baton of the bylaws.

Brant concluded that the UN had a slight influence on this mode of intervention, which did not necessarily translate into less influence from the international community. Their support in the creation of transparent, inclusive, and participatory mechanisms was remarkable, although the deadlines set meant that their impact on the final process was somewhat limited, and serious security limitations and the boiling international and national environment should be considered.

6.3 Hybrid Constituent Power: The Role of the UN as a Political Actor

The *constitution-making process* is defined through the way in which a Constitution is created. This process includes phases that encompass from planning to promulgation and implementation and the substantive aspects that will be contained in the text.[86]

The objective of this analysis is focused on the notion that the study of the original constituent process is extremely important which can influence the ability to legitimize or delegitimize a new constitution. Respect for the theory of constituent power and its semantic nuclei will certainly contribute to the success and stability of the constitutional text. Thus, for Toler,[87] if the writers can follow their own rules, the political community in general tends to see the process of building the new constitution as legitimate and it becomes easier to accept and identify it as a driver for the new constitutional development.

The study described in item 5.2 represents a small sample of the materialization of hybrid constituent power. And this method provides an opportunity for the UN to encourage a process that can promote national reconciliation, build consensus, and create a constitutional culture that will lead the country.

Therefore, the analysis should not be considered as statistical or quantitative research. Comparative case studies are presented as ways of visualizing the operability of hybrid constituent power.

Four different constructions of constituent processes were presented in item 5.2.: Cambodia (1993), located in Southeast Asia; Bosnia and Herzegovina (1995) in Europe; East Timor (2002) in Southeast Asia; and Afghanistan (2004) in the Middle East. These countries were purposely chosen to demonstrate the materialization of hybrid constituent power in different parts of the globe.

It should be noted that all the processes described were implemented after armed conflicts and represented a political transition to the redemocratization of the country in question by the eyes of the UN.

For this analysis have been identified some aspects that will be divided into phases.[88] The topics presented are intended to explore: the process of building the provisional constitution; the convocation of the constitutional drafting body until the

---

[86] Toler (2014, p. 1262).

[87] Toler (2014, p. 1262).

[88] The methodological basis for the choice of phases was based on the studies of Toler (2014, p. 1262).

production of a *first draft* of the constitution; the formal procedures for promulgating the new constitution; and finally the post-constituent aspects.

Many elements will be presented from the analyses of case studies and will also be measured by their quality. This includes civic education,[89] popular participation,[90] the incorporation of this participation, and the dimension of UN[91] influence, among others.

Not all four countries will be represented in the sub-items, since in some studies some data were not found or collected.

6.3.1 Hybrid Constituent Power: Materializing Your Senses

6.3.1.1 Total Constitution-Making Time

In the cases studied, the processes of construction of hybrid constituent power, from the intervention of the UN, ranged from a few weeks to a few years.

Of the cases studied we have:

- Cambodia: 1 year and 1 month;
- Bosnia and Herzegovina: 06 weeks;
- Timor-Leste: 03 months; and
- Afghanistan: 2 years and a month.

It can be said that the process that took place in Bosnia and Herzegovina and Timor-Leste was extremely short. Written constitutions with a tight time frame can mean to the population that they are not a national product.

6.3.1.2 Description of Members in the Constituent Process

The Cambodian constituent process was monitored by the United Nations Transitional Authority in Cambodia. Under the Paris Agreement, an interim eight-member body of Cambodia's Supreme National Council was responsible for overseeing elections for the composition of a 12-member Constituent Assembly. The Nationalist Front came in first place, with 45% of the vote, and the People's Party in second place, with 38% of the vote.

---

[89] Constitutional education is defined as information shared with the public about the constituent process or constitutionalism in general.

[90] Popular participation is defined as the ability of the public to express their opinions in a format that can influence the substantive content of the constitution.

[91] The role of the UN is assessed based on its influence on the *constitution-making*, considering the impact from comparative practices and the theoretical dimension of the original constituent power. The elements will be measured qualitatively and classified on a scale that represents a "weak", "moderate", or "strong" influence.

The Constituent Assembly elected a body of 12 members for the technical drafting of the constitution. A monarchical draft, originally written by French constitutional expert Claude Gille Goure, was defended by the Nationalist Front and Prince Sihanouk and became Cambodia's new Constitution.

The constitution of Bosnia and Herzegovina was drafted by the delegates who were part of the Dayton Peace Agreement. Members of the "Contact Group", representing U.S. Assistant Secretary Richard Holbrooke—along with U.S. mediators and experts—conducted the technical drafting of the Constitution.

The Timorese constituent process was monitored by the United Nations Transitional Authority. The FRETILIN party was the winning party of the constituent elections which allowed for a 55-member bench out of the 88 seats. The main constitutional text presented by FRETILIN became the new constitutional charter.

In Afghanistan, a Constitutional Drafting Commission, composed of nine members selected by the UN and the Transition Administrator, was responsible for the technical drafting of the constitution. The commission was expanded to 35 members (mainly politicians and relevant experts) and convened by the Constitutional Commission. The draft Constitution was reviewed by Karzai's office before being presented to a *Constitutional Loya Jirga* for final ratification.

6.3.1.3 UN Contribution to the Design of Substantial Content of Constitution

In Cambodia, the Paris Peace Agreement, finalized on October 23, 1991, after 2 months of negotiations, outlined eight essential elements for a democratic election and established the timeline and basic principles with democratic bias for the transition and constitutional process in Cambodia.

In Bosnia and Herzegovina, after 3 years of international conferences and peace plans that preceded the Dayton Peace Conference, established the principles for a draft adopted by the Contact Group in the first 3 days of the conference. The focus in Dayton was to establish peace between the warring parties. Bosnia's constitution was established in the Paris Peace Agreement with liberal democratic bias.

In East Timor, the Constitution was inspired by the Portuguese model of liberal democracy by making direct mention of the UN in its preamble, stating that the letter was based on the referenda act of August 30, 1999, implemented under the auspices of the United Nations.

In Afghanistan, the Agreement emphasized several objectives and principles of liberal democracy that constitutional exercise could take advantage of, such as pluralism and social justice, among others.

6.3.1.4 Constitutional Education Pre-elections to the National Constituent Assembly

Perceived only in Cambodia, pre-election constitutional education lasted about 6 months and was carried out by UNTAC along with a human rights task force, which included civil servants, monks, judges, and experts, to develop constitutional literacy using mass communication as a means of achieving. These efforts eventually mobilized some 4.6 million Cambodians to vote in the elections, which included women and the Buddhist clergy.

6.3.1.5 Elections for the Composition of the National Constituent Assembly

Post-conflict elections tend to be highly referential in relation to the previous conflict, with voting concentrated on individual leaders, ethnic groups, or other vestiges that comes from war or representation of struggles. Elections do not in themselves represent a channel through which the nation's constitutional aspirations are represented. Therefore, a strictly democratic electoral model, dependent only on representation through the "electoral ballot", may represent a rhetorical path for the reconstruction of the nation through redemocratization and its catalyst elements.

The elections in Cambodia for the composition of the Constituent Assembly took place 1 year and 7 months after the establishment of the Paris Agreement, with the participation of 90% of the people registered in 21 provinces of the country.

In Bosnia and Herzegovina there was no election, as the Dayton Peace Agreement has already incorporated the Constitution.

In East Timor the election to make up the Assembly was held in 2001 and was sworn in by the Transitional Administrator. Composed of 88 Deputies representing 12 parties and an independent candidacy. FRETILIN had been the winning party of the constituent elections, with a majority of 57.3% of the vote, which allowed to make up a 55 seat.

In Afghanistan, the elections to make up *the Constitutional Loya Jirga* took place in 3 months, from July to December 2003, and 502 different representatives were elected.

6.3.1.6 Composition of Members for the Drafting of the Constitution

Twelve members were appointed in Cambodia to draft the country's constitution. In the second week of writing, the committee made the *draft available*, along with another bill presented by the party, representing the interests of King Shihanouk.

Timor's process highlighted the potential pitfalls of prescribing the tasks of drafting, debating, and adopting a constitution in a single moment, that is, by the constituent national assembly itself. Members of civil society were prevented from participating and a single dominant party presented its project.

In Afghanistan, the Constitutional Commission was composed of 35 members. The selection of members was criticized as non-transparent and not included, eventually leading to the choice of individuals not qualified for the important task of writing the constitutional text.

6.3.1.7 Convocation of the Drafting Members of the Draft Constitution

In Cambodia, the 12 drafting members of the constitution worked behind closed doors, while other members presented their own projects. The choice was the defense of the monarchical project, being ignored the project written by the constitutional committee.

Bosnia and Herzegovina's constitutional project was agreed in the early days of the Bonn Conference and the parties involved continued to negotiate other details during the conferences, which resulted in a final draft allocated in Annex IV to the Agreement.

In East Timor, four projects were presented by the parties that provided for two institutional design structures with semi-presidential and semi-parliamentary characteristics. With the time pressure on UNTAET, the main text became the one presented by FRETILIN.

In Afghanistan, three competing projects were developed. The project presented by President Shahrani, based on the 1964 constitution, was chosen.

6.3.1.8 Establishment of Constitutional Rules

In Cambodia, the drafting procedure included a committee to oversee the work, and the drafting was drafted without debate and discussed in secret with the members themselves.

In Timor-Leste the political parties have become the main decision-makers and to be part of the discussions. Also, part of the work were two members of UNTAET, a jurist specializing in constitutional law and an expert in politics, on which the task of carrying out the work of the Assembly was to be carried out.

In Afghanistan, the rules of the highly detailed procedures were drawn up with the help of constitutional consultants with expertise in comparative studies and the UN.

6.3.1.9 Establishment of Programs and Agendas, Discussion of the Substantive Issues of the Constitutional Charter

In Afghanistan, *the Secretariat of the Constitutional Loya Jirga* was divided into ten subcommittees composed of ten representatives, each of which were intended to discuss the amendments, and, if necessary, any constitutional issues found in the project.

6.3.1.10 Technical Capacity of the Draftsmen of the Constitution

In Cambodia, this capacity was considered weak, since the writers were considered unprepared, lacking technical resources for the prior conception of local constitutional education, which fundamentally affected their technical capacity to produce an effective and integrated constitution to local particularities.

In East Timor, the members of the assembly had no technical capacity to bring the constitutional provisions to an end, with the direct support of two international consultants.

In Afghanistan, members of the *Constitutional Loya Jirga* studied the previous constitutions and those of countries in similar political and cultural conditions. The UNDP and UNAMA Secretariat also provided prior technical advice for the analyses.

6.3.1.11 Role of Local Experts

The role played by *local* experts in Cambodia's constituent process was considered weak. It was represented by the support of five local experts and the meetings were conducted in complete secrecy, which ended up ensuring that other local experts, such as the rest of society, were mostly unable to influence the new institutional design model.

In the Bosnian process, Bosnian experts were severely underrepresented at the conferences, which eventually left them without power of influence over the new constitutional text.

In Afghanistan, advice from local experts was limited and undermined by a combination of competing political interests which are deeply influenced by foreign experts brought in by stakeholders.

6.3.1.12 Role, Power, and Influence of Foreign Experts

In Cambodia, this influence was considered moderate, although the French consultant Claude Gille Goure played a significant advisory role in drafting the constitution. Several U.S. organizations informally offered advice to constitutional writers. As the process was secret, most of the population and non-governmental organizations were unable to participate and influence the process. UNTAC was heavily involved in the early stages of the transition, but its influence dropped significantly in the constituent process, as it considered this to be a sovereign process.

In Bosnia and Herzegovina, international influence was considered extremely strong. The *international experts*, represented by Richard Holbrooke, were at the forefront of the discussions in Dayton, serving as mediators between the factions that were represented, as well as drafting the Peace Treaty and the Constitution of Bosnia. The United States was heavily represented at the conferences and essentially controlled the process by organizing the procedure for drafting the constitution and negotiations.

In East Timor, the central work of support and advice to constituent deputies was in foreign hands, including to end the constitutional wording. Therefore, all political and legal influence was left to these experts who reported directly to the Transition Administrator of UNTAET. The standards of international standards directly influenced the constitutional provisions and this action was considered positive by the UN.

In Afghanistan, UNAMA, to assign the construction of the constitution to local actors, initially blocked most efforts to provide specialized issues that would be incorporated into the constitution. However, procedural issues have received a strong international influence.

The Asia Foundation was funded by the United States to provide foreign experts to work with the Secretariat of the Constitutional Commission to develop the procedural aspects of the constituent process. During the conception of *the Constitutional Loya Jirga*, the Ambassador of the United Nations and the United States established non-negotiable and specific constitutional positions that were adopted. The UN ambassador also used his influence with the king to amend some constitutional provisions before being presented to the *Constitutional Loya Jirga.*

6.3.1.13 Constitutional Education: Pre-constitutional Project

The degree to which a process can incorporate direct participation, typically through constitutional civic education and public consultation, will depend on the context. Political elites play a decisive role in how to structure this process.

In the studies verified, the local community showed a great willingness to participate in the process. In Cambodia and Timor, coalitions of civil society members wrote letters to UN leaders complaining that the level of participation was not enough.

In Cambodia, UNTAC has developed a human rights task force to educate the public with mass communication campaigns. However, this effort happened simultaneously with the secret wording of the constitution; therefore, it can be considered that this effort was devoid of effectiveness, since the population could not influence the process. The role of the public was largely confined to voting and education was basically focused on teaching this procedure.

In Timor, the UN supported direct participation more, but missed the opportunity to establish an effective participatory process. Civic education and popular consultation were carried out together and did not allow the population to understand the constitutional options that would be called into question. On the other hand, these consultations did not promote dialogue with the constituent assembly, and therefore the process was led by UNTAET and thus ignored by the Constituent Assembly.

In Afghanistan, no awareness group or constitutional education for the population had been set up. There was a great push to promote education in conjunction with a popular consultation program, both in rural areas and in refugee camps. Although this education was considered relatively weak due to the time problem and lack of structural planning, this assistance led to greater direct participation. The civic education process was conducted separately from the consultation of the process and was led by national actors.

6.3.1.14 Pre-draft Constitutional: Public Consultation

In Cambodia, a tight timetable for the creation of the new constitution meant that many Cambodians were unable to express their views on the new constitution. It should be noted that UNTAC, together with other NGOs, has made an effort to carry out the consultations, but, already detailed conform, these efforts have been ineffective as they were implemented simultaneously with the drafting of the new constitution.

In Afghanistan, eight regional offices were established by the Secretariat to educate and consult the population. Some meetings were held and some questionnaires circulated through newspapers, but most meetings addressed general and non-specific issues about the project and its substantial elements.

6.3.1.15 Incorporating Public Consultations in the Constituent Assembly

In Cambodia, after the assembly was instituted, there was no consultation or public participation in the constituent process.

In Timor, the National Constituent Assembly challenged the undemocratic nature of the process conducted unilaterally by UNTAET.

In Afghanistan, efforts to incorporate public consultations are hampered by the scheduled agenda of the *Constitutional Loya Jirga*. Ultimately, the impediment of the population's entry into the process was also caused by political differences.

6.3.1.16 Transparency of the Constituent Process

In Cambodia, the transparency process was considered weak, although UNTAC has promoted numerous campaigns through the media. This lack of transparency was caused by the *constitution-making process*. Thus, there was many criticisms regarding the secrecy of the process, among these, some allegations focused on the fact that secrecy eventually allowed those in power to continue to dominate the new constitution in a political way.

The Dayton Agreement, in the case of Bosnia and Herzegovina, was built behind closed doors, with all meetings and deliberations being kept away from popular participation. There was also no provision for popular participation for the recognition of the process, such as a referendum to seal the new constitution.

In Timor, the constituent process was not participatory and was conducted behind closed doors, with all meetings and deliberations being kept away from popular participation. Participation was allowed only to international actors.

In Afghanistan, most public awareness efforts have only provided an illusion of transparency. Most Afghans knew the process, but not the substantive issues of the new constitutional charter.

6.3.1.17 Approval and Promulgation of the New Constitution

In Cambodia, the Constituent Assembly approved the constitutional bill and Prince Sihanouk ratified the constitution, which came into force immediately, transforming the constituent assembly into the new Legislative Assembly.

In Bosnia and Herzegovina, the project was approved and ratified with the signatures of the Dayton Agreements, coming into force after 23 days.

In Timor, the constitution was approved by the constituent assembly with 72 votes in favor, representing an approval of two-third of the members constituted.

In Afghanistan, President Karzai signed the final draft of the constitution which came into force immediately, in accordance with his transitional constitutional provision.

None of the cases studied used the referendum as a mechanism for approving the new constitution. However, for Brant, this is not a requirement to represent the legitimacy of the constitution, if the process led to a constitutional consensus through a participatory, transparent approach and an inclusive process. As this is the result, the new constitution is likely to enjoy legitimacy.

References

Bezhan, F. (2013). Loya Jirga, in Afghan tradition explained. Pub. *RadiofreeEurope RadioLiberty*. Retrieved February 20, 2018, from https://www.rferl.org/a/afghanistan-loya-jirga-explainer/25174483.html

Bologna, C., Rangel, H., & Corrêa, F. (2015). Hyperpresidentialism in Latin America. *Ufpr Law School Magazine, 60*(2).

Brant, M. (2005). Constitutional assistance in post-conflict countries: The UN experience: Cambodia, East Timor & Afghanistan. *United Nations Development Programme*. Retrieved September 24, 2012, from https://agora-parl.org/sites/default/files/Constitutional%20Assistance%20in%20Post-Conflict%20Countries.pdf

Brant, M., et al. (2011). *Constitution-making and reform: Options for the process*. Interpeace.

Caplan, R. (2005). *Europe and the recognition of new states in Yugoslavia*. Cambridge University Press.

Carvalho, N. B. (2017). Latin American Hyperpresidentialisma as a factor of instability of democracies: An inter-relationship with the Brazilian impeachment process. *Brazilian Law Journal, See, 16*(7), 399–411.

Cambodian Information Center. (1991). *Paris peace agreements*. Retrieved October 24, 2018, from http://www.cambodia.org/facts/?page=1991+Paris+Peace+Agreements#annex_1.

Chandler, D. (2000). *Bosnia: Faking democracy after Dayton* (2nd ed., p. 193). Pluto Press.

Coni, L. C. (2006). *The internalization of the constituent power*. Porto Alegre: Sergio Antonio Fabris Editor.

Cottrell, J., Ghai, Y., & Regan, A. (2011). *Constitution-making and reform: Options for the process*. Interpeace.

Ferreira, C. (2000–2006). Bilateral Portuguese-Timorese parliamentary cooperation and the formation of legislative power. In *Silva*

Garrison, R. (2005). *The role of constitution-building processes in democratization: Case study East Timor*. Institute Is Democracy and Electoral Assistance (p. 12). Retrieved April 2014, 13, from www.idea.int/conflict/CBP/

Giordana, V. (2018). *Them Talibanes. Observatory of Conflict Argentina*. Retrieved May, 26, 2018, from https://www.nodo50.org/observatorio/taliban.htm

Gouvêa, C. B. (2016). *As Intervenções da ONU no Processo de Constitution-Making nos Estados em Transição Política: O Papel das Nações Unidas no Resgate da Ordem Democrática* (1st ed., vol. 1, pp. 177–178). Curitiba/PR: Juruá Editora.

Hippel, K. V. (2003). *Democracy by force*: Military intervention by the United States in the post-Cold War world. Trad. Joubert de Oliveira Lyzizid. Rio de Janeiro: Army library.

Keil, S. (2012). Federalism as tool of conflict-resolution: The case of Bosnia and Herzegovina. *I. Europe En Formation, 363*(1), 205–218; 214.

Kelly, C., & Simião, D. S. (Org.). (2007a). *Timor-Leste behind the stage: International cooperation and dialectics of state formation* (p.153). Belo Horizonte: Editora UFMG.

Kelly, C., & Simião, D. S. (Org.). (2007b). *Timor-Leste behind the stage: International cooperation and dialectics of state formation* (p.154). London: Publisher UFMG.

Kings, B. P. W. (1988). Electoral system and campaign financing in Brazil: Misadventures of the Legislative Power under a hyperpresidentialism consociativo. *The Constitution of* 57–90.

Marks, S. (2010). The process of creating a new constitution in Cambodia. In L. E. Miller & L. Aucoin (Eds.), *Framing the State in Times of Transition C: Case studies in Constitution-Making* (pp. 207–244). United States Institute of Peace.

Maziau, N. (2002). L'Internationalisation Du pouvoir constituteant, essai from Typologie: Le point of Vue heterodoxe Du constitutionnaliste. *Revue Générale from Droit International Public*, 549–579.

Mazzone, J. (2005). The creation of a constitutional culture. *Tulsa Law Review, 40*, 671–698.

Oklopcic, Z. (2012). Constitutional (re) vision: Sovereign peoples, new constituent powers, and the formation of constitutional orders in the Balkans. *Constellations, 19*(1), 81. Retrieved February 23, 2019. https://doi.org/10.1111/j.1467-8675.2011.00667.x

Penfold, M. (2010). La democracy subyugada: El hyperpresidentialism Venezolano. *Magazine of Science Politics (santiago), 30*(1), 21–40.

Pulido, C. L. B., & De Freitas, G. M. B. (2015). Fundamental rights, juristocracy constitutional and hyperpresidentialism in Latin America. *Legal Journal of the Presidency, 17*(111).

Ratner, S. (1993). The Cambodian settlement agreements. *American Journal of International Law, 87*, 1–41.

Rosenfeld, M. (2003). *The identity of the constitutional subject*. Trad. Menelick by Carvalho Netto (pp. 22–23). Belo Horizonte: Mandamentos Editora.

Rose Ackerman, S., Desierto, D. A. (2010). Hyper-presidentialism: Separation of powers without checks and balances in Argentina and the Philippines. *Berkeley Journal of International Law (BJIL), Forthcoming*; *Yale Law & Economics Research* Paper No. 418. Retrieved October 24, 2017, from https://ssrn.com/abstract=1709573

Simpson, G. (2004). *Great powers and outlaw states: Unequal sovereigns in the international legal order* (pp. 491–496). Cambridge University Press.

Toler, L. U. (2014). Mapping the constitutional process. *Cambridge Journal of International and Comparative Law, 3*(4), 1262.

Tourard, H. (2000). *L'internationalisation des constitutions Nationals* (p. 11). L.G.D.J.

UN Experience: Cambodia, East Timor & Afghanistan. (2005). *United Nations Development Programme* (p. 9). Available in Retrieved September 24, 2012. https://agora-parl.org/sites/default/files/Constitutional%20Assistance%20in%20Post-Conflict%20Countries.pdf

UN Experience: Cambodia, East Timor & Afghanistan. (2012). *United Nations Development Programme*, 2005. Retrieved September 24, 2012, from https://agora-parl.org/sites/default/files/Constitutional%20Assistance%20in%20Post-Conflict%20Countries.pdf

Unama Mission Satatement. (2017). United Nations Assistance Mission in Afghanistan. *UNAMA Mission Statement*. Retrieved December 15, 2017, from https://unama.unmissions.org/sites/default/files/unama_mission_statement_english_0.pdf

United Nations. (2000). Security Council. Resolution 1325. Resolution S/RES/1325 (2000), October 31, 2000. Retrieved February 12, 2017, from http://www.un.org/ga/search/view_doc.asp?symbol=S/RES/1325(2000)&Lang=S

United Nations. (1991). *General assembly. Increasing the effectiveness of the principles of periodic and genuine elections*. Resolution A/RES/46/137 of 17 December 1991. Retrieved June, 26, 2013, from http://www.un.org/documents/ga/res/46/a46r137.htm

United Nations. (2014). Asamblea General Consejo from security. *Resolution A/50/790; S/1995/999*. Resolution A/50/790; S/1995/999 of 30 November 1995. Retrieved March, 15, 2014, from https://peacemaker.un.org/sites/peacemaker.un.org/files/BA_951121_DaytonAgreement%28esp%29.pdf

United Nations. (2001). Consejo from Security. *Letter closes 5 of diciembre 2001 addressed to the President Del Consejo from Security by El Secretary General. Report Del Consejo from Security* S/2001/1154, from 05 diciembre 2001. Retrieved February 24, 2018, from https://peacemaker.un.org/sites/peacemaker.un.org/files/AF_011205_AgreementProvisionalArrangementsinAfghanistan%28esp.pdf

United Nations. (2001). United Nations Transitional Administration in Timor-Leste. *Regulation No. 2001/2 on the election of a Constituent Assembly to prepare a Constitution for an independent and democratic Timor-Leste.*

United Nations and the Rule of Law. (2017). Retrieved May 13, 2017, from https://www.un.org/ruleoflaw/blog/2017/06/14479/

United Nations and the Rule Of Law. (2017). UNDP annual rule of law meeting: Strengthening the rule of law for sustaining peace and fostering development (12–15 June 2017, UNHQ New York). Pub. 7 June 2017.

UNTAET/REG/2001/2. (2013). Regulation of 16 March 2001. Retrieved January 26, 2013, from http://www.un.org/en/peacekeeping/missions/past/etimor/untaetR/reg20012.pdf

Valenzuela, J. (1991). Camboya Retrieves It peace después of the decades of war. Pub. The country. Retrieved January 13, 2019, from https://elpais.com/diario/1991/10/24/internacional/688258805_850215.html.

Valle, V. R. L. D, Pulcinelli, E., & Maneiro, R. D. M. J. (2016). *Constastation, persuasion and consensus in the Supreme Court: Building democratic constitutionalism* (p. 15). Rio de Janeiro: Gramma.

Verdú, P. L. (1994). La constitución en la encrucijada (palingenesia iuris politici). Madrid: Centro de Publicaciones de la Facultad de Derecho - Universidad Complutense (p. 27).

Chapter 7
Case Study of the UN Intervention in the Political-Legal Structure of the East Timor

This chapter will examine the case of East Timor, which had the direct support of the UN for the development of the constitutional model adopted as shown in Table 7.1 because of the process of transition and reconstruction of democracy. This structure will be better presented according to the phases described in Chap. 4: pre-constituent, constituent, and post-constituent.

Timor-Leste can be considered a paradigmatic case since this intervention has been consummated in three stages. The analysis will make it possible to shape the criticisms set forth in Chap. 4 and explore possible patterns of constitutional resistance. This research allows to focus more systematically on the problem, since it adopts a more descriptive style, aiming to illuminate the previously mentioned concepts.

7.1 East Timor: Characteristics and Nature of Conflict

Located on the smallest and easternmost island of the Malay Archipelago, East Timor, officially called the Democratic Republic of Timor-Leste, is considered one of the world's youngest democratic countries.[1]

The Timorese capital is Dili, and the official languages are Portuguese and Tétum, and there are still about 15 native dialects in the territory. The working languages are English and Bahasa Indonesia.

The declaration of independence took place on November 28, 1975, and democracy was restored on May 20, 2002, and the Constitution has been in force ever since. The system of government is parliamentary, having 13 districts and 67 sub-districts. Its ethnic composition can be described as majority of Malay-Polynesian and Papua origin and Chinese, Arab, and European minorities.

[1] The descriptions of the history of East Timor were taken from the official website of the Democratic Republic of Timor-Leste. Available in: http://timor-leste.gov.tl/?p=29. Acesso em 30 de abr. de 2012.

C. B. Gouvêa and P. H. V. B. Castelo Branco, *UN Interventions and Democratization*, Societies and Political Orders in Transition,
https://doi.org/10.1007/978-3-031-32715-5_7

Table 7.1 UN missions in East Timor

Phases	Mission	Period	Objective
Pre-constituent	*United Nations Mission in East Timor* (UNAMET)	June–October/1999	Aid Mission
Constituent	*United Nations Transitional Administration in East Timor* (UNTAET)	October/1999–May/2002	Transitional Administration Mission
Post-constituent	*United Nations Mission of Support in East Timor* (UNMISET)	May/2002–May/2005	Support Mission
	United Nations Office in East Timor (UNOTIL)	May/2005–August/2006	UN Office Mission
	United Nations Integrated Mission in East Timor (UNMIT)	August/2006–December/2012	Integrated Mission

Source http://www.momentum.tl/pt/cronologia.html

About 90% of the population is Catholic, with minority communities of Protestants and Muslims. The currency is the US dollar.

The western portion of the island of Timor, with capital in Kupang, belongs today to the Republic of Indonesia. The eastern portion, with capital in Dili, had belonged to Portugal since the sixteenth century.

When the first Portuguese merchants and missionaries arrived on the island in 1515, they found populations organized in small States, gathered in two confederations: Easement and Belos, which practiced animist religions. Islam, predominant in present-day Indonesia, had not reached Timor.

Between 1650 and 1675, the first Portuguese Dominican friars arrived in Timor, through which a progressive religious influence was developed, while the Portuguese domination was establishing itself.

The Dutch, in 1651, conquered Kupang, on the far west of the island, and began to penetrate half of its territory. In 1859, a treaty signed between Portugal and Holland established the border between Timor-Portuguese (now East Timor) and Timor-Dutch (West Timor). In 1945, Indonesia gained its independence by passing West Timor to be part of its territory.

During World War II, the Allied forces (Australian and Dutch), recognizing the strategic position of Timor, established positions in the territory, having been involved in hard confrontations with the Japanese forces. In 1945, the Portuguese administration was restored in East Timor.

Between 1945 and June 1974, the Indonesian government stated at the UN and elsewhere that it had no territorial claim to East Timor. Under Resolution 1514 (XV) of December 14, 1960, Timor-Leste was considered by the United Nations as a non-autonomous territory under Portuguese administration.

The UN General Assembly from 1962 to 1973 adopted successive resolutions affirming the right to self-determination of East Timor, just like the other Portuguese colonies. In Portugal, the Salazar regime refused to recognize this right.

The 1974 Revolution, which restored democracy in Portugal, enshrined respect for the right to self-determination of the Portuguese colonies and, to promote this right, the Commission for the Self-determination of Timor was created in Dili. This legislation provided for the formation of a transitional government, which would prepare the elections for a popular assembly in 1976. This law also provided for a gradual transition to Independence for about 3 years—until October 1978.

The creation of political parties was authorized, and three party organizations emerged: the Timorese Democratic Union (UDT), which advocated "the integration of Timor into a Portuguese-speaking community"; the Timorese Social Democratic Association (ASDT), later transformed into the Independent Revolutionary Front of Timor-Leste (FRETILIN), which advocated the right to independence; and the Timorese People's Democratic Association (APODETI), which proposed "integration with autonomy in the Indonesian community".

Since January 1975, the progressive decolonization program was underway, which led to the holding of elections for the regional administration of the Lautém Council. The results of the first popular consultation highlighted the low support for the APODETI party, making it obvious that, by democratic processes, the Timorese would never accept integration with the neighboring country, with cultural differences being one of the main reasons for this refusal.

The animosity between the pro-independence activists and the advocates of integration with Indonesia throughout 1975 led to civil war and, in August of that year, to escape the violence, the Portuguese administration and employees left the territory. Indonesia, to protect its citizens in Timorese territory, invaded the eastern part of the island in December 1975 and renamed Timor Timur, becoming its 27th province. It received tacit American support, which saw FRETILIN as a Marxist-oriented organization.

This invasion was quickly condemned by the United Nations, and on December 22, 1975, the UN Security Council unanimously adopted Resolution 384,[2] which recognized the inalienable right of the people of East Timor to self-determination and independence. The Council condemned the intervention of the Indonesian armed forces and regretted that Portugal had not fulfilled its responsibilities as the administering power of the territory. The Council also called on Indonesia to withdraw all its forces and to Portugal to cooperate fully with the UN so that the Timorese people could freely exercise their right to self-determination. This resolution set the tone for the United Nations position on East Timor over the next 24 years.[3]

---

[2] United Nations Organization (1975). (A Resolução solicitou ainda que o Secretário-Geral da ONU enviasse um representante especial para o Timor com o objetivo de proceder a uma avaliação interna da situação existente com o fim de estabelecer contato entre as partes no território e de submeter uma recomendação à apreciação do Conselho no mínimo espaço de tempo.).

[3] UN Information Department (2000a).

Portugal never relinquished its authority as the administering power, although year after year it was informed by the UN that the conditions in East Timor prevented the country from assuming responsibility for the administration of the territory.

About one-third of the country's population, more than 250,000 people, died in the war. The use of Portuguese was banned and the pro-Indonesian government, which carried out violent censorship of the press and restricted the access of international observers to the territory until the fall of Indonesian President Suharto in 1998, discouraged Tetum.

Indonesia continued to lack international legal recognition of its annexation of East Timor and, in general, the international community remained reluctant on this issue and had not exerted strong pressure towards a diplomatic solution.[4]

The uprising occurred in November 1991, when Indonesian soldiers killed many unarmed protesters in Dili. It was said that 150–270 people were killed, including a foreign journalist who filmed the so-called Santa Cruz massacre. It is known as the event that awoke the turn of the international public opinion, which became favorable to the self-determination of East Timor.

The images of the massacre sparked protests around the world at the embassies of Indonesia, the United States, and England, and at the United Nations, demanding a swift intervention to end the killings. In Portugal, there have never been so many popular demonstrations, from north to south of the country since April 25, 1974. For the first time, the internet was mass-used in the dissemination of pro-Timor campaigns.

7.2 The UN Intervention in the Pre-Constituent Phase

In 1997, then-Secretary-General Kofi Annan opted for a more proactive approach to revitalize the tripartite process involving the UN Secretariat, Indonesia, and Portugal. These talks resulted in a set of three agreements, which laid the groundwork for a popular consultation process, signed at a historical ceremony in New York in 1999. The Republic of Indonesia and Portugal had reached a global agreement on the question of Timor.

The United Nations Mission in East Timor (UNAMET) was established on June 11, 1999. Its main objective was to organize and hold a popular referendum scheduled for August 8, 1999, based on a secret, direct, and universal vote, to verify if the Timorese accepted the proposed constitutional framework: the special autonomy for Timor within the Republic of Indonesia or the rejection of this autonomy, in accordance with the General Agreement.

UNAMET's supplementary structure comprised: a military component aiming at the deployment of civilian police officers to serve as Indonesian police advisors and to oversee the voting escort; a political component to monitor the fairness of the political environment, to ensure access for all non-governmental organizations and

4 UN Information Department (2000b).

others to freely carry out their monitoring and advisory activities of the UN special representative in relation to the political implications; a component responsible for all registration and voting activities; and an information component, responsible for promoting civic education, impartially and objectively, without prejudice to any position or outcome, on the voting process or procedure and explain its implications.

In the spring of 1999, the security situation deteriorated and paramilitary groups, trained and armed by the Indonesian military and operating in the region for years, increased their forces. Human rights organizations have reported murders and other abuses directed not only at pro-independence leaders and supporters but also at students, journalists, activists, priests, and nuns.

The vote was postponed twice for security reasons, and the referendum took place on August 30, 1999. Timorese went to the polls in large numbers, the participation rate was 99% of registered voters, and 78% supported independence.

After the election results, the militias launched a new campaign of terror and more than a thousand people were killed. There were hundreds of people displaced and about 70% of the country's infrastructure was attacked and destroyed.

After 2 weeks of intense negotiation, as members of the Security Council and other governments reluctantly authorized intervention, including from Indonesia, the Council adopted a resolution authorizing so-called humanitarian intervention under this chapter of the Charter as a "response to the grave humanitarian situation resulting from the violence of Timor". The UN had, therefore, sent a multinational peacekeeping task force, International Force East Timor (INTERFET), under the leadership of Australia, which commenced its duties on September 20, 1999 with the aim of restoring security in the territory.

At this stage, the intervention can be synthesized as having the prime objective of conducting a popular consultation. This purpose was further developed in a supplementary structure that included voter registration and voting, civic education, and oversight and monitoring of the electoral process.

7.3 UN Intervention in the Constituent Phase

When stability was restored, a new mission, called the United Nations Transitional Administration in East Timor (UNTAET), was established through Resolution 1272. The Transitional Administration took over all powers in the territory of Timor in February 2000. Sérgio Vieira de Mello was the special representative of the UN Secretary-General and Transitional Administrator, claiming that the tasks in the territory assumed "benevolent despotisms", given that the United Nations had control over all the skills needed to build the new State.

This Resolution made UNTAET the legal sovereign of the territory and a UN protectorate. This mission can be considered the largest of the United Nations in its multifunctional history, with a longer mandate than all previous ones.

The mandate contained the following guidelines:

1. Governing Timor during the transition period;
2. Ensure security and law enforcement and order throughout the territory;
3. Establish effective administration;
4. Assist in the development of civil and social services;
5. Ensure coordination and distribution of humanitarian aid, rehabilitation, and development aid;
6. Support capacity building for self-government;
7. Assist in creating the conditions for sustainable development.

UNTAET was inspired by the model used in the UN Mission in Kosovo, United Nations Interim Administration Mission in Kosovo (UNMIK), although its components were expanded.

Since the beginning of the mandate, a combination of different components has been used, with a focus on multiple approaches to its implementation: political, economic, judicial, military, and police—since creating and empowering sustainable development requires a long—and strategies based on the participation and empowerment of the local community.[5]

The Resolution highlighted the need for UNTAET to "strictly consult and cooperate with the people of East Timor in order to effectively carry out their mandate",[6] but there was no specific role for Timorese within the framework established by the United Nations.

The inability to integrate Timorese into the administrative structures of UNTAET in the political decision-making process created tension between local and international actors and was considered as one of the main shortcomings of the operation.[7]

It should be noted that in the wake of the post-election violence, operational planning, which until then the responsibility of the DPA together with the DPKO, was also assumed by UNTAET. It is interesting to note that the DPKO has no experience in issues related to the institution of democracy and its operations are short-term. The first task of the international community was to ensure security and this goal was largely successful.[8]

Regulation 1991/1[9] regulated the Provisional Government and all executive, legislative, and judicial power resided in one man, the Transitional Administrator, who was also the Special Representative of the UN Secretary-General (SRSG),[10] with a mandate conferred by aliens.

[5] Järvinen (2004).

[6] United Nations Organization (1999).

[7] Järvinen (2004).

[8] Steele (2002).

[9] United Nations Organization (1999).

[10] United Nations Organization (1999).

Any consultation, dialogue or intervention with Timorese leaders was based on a criterion determined exclusively by the SRSG. Every law enacted during the transition period began as follows: "The SRSG … promulgates the following …". Although UNTAET was administered with transparency and accountability, it constituted a government without a constitution.[11]

In addition to preparing Timor for self-government, UNTAET was responsible for all basic government functions: education, health, economic development, property law, public administration, security, defense, border control, transportation, planning, well-being social.[12]

The temporary transition was able to provide the East Timorese, according to Steele[13] after decades of retaliation, a marked improvement in the physical and institutional structures, mainly with the decrease of the violence; however, it was unable to bring the local community together to practice accountability and transparency, which gave the Timorese few chances to experience democratic living. The power of UNTAET was centralized, and there was no freedom of information. The decision-making processes were not open, and there was no understanding of the history and culture of the Timorese people.

UNTAET was not a democratically elected body and, therefore, could not claim legitimacy of the population. Despite the task of developing democratic institutions and the rule of law based on the principles of transparency, accountability, and respect for human rights, this mission did not practice what it preached.[14]

In turn, the problem of forced displacement, covering some 800,000 people, had been effectively managed by the UN and international NGOs, avoiding prolonged hunger and internal displacement.

Regulation 1999/2[15] created the National Consultative Council to set up an advisory mechanism to ensure the participation of the Timorese people in the decision-making process during the transitional period. This was the main dialogue mechanism established by the UN, where the population should present their views, concerns, traditions, and interests.

The Council would be made up of representatives of the people and UNTAET. This may seem paradoxical since the decisions would in no way prejudice the powers set forth by the Transitional Administrator, who held himself as supreme authority over all governmental institutions.

Fifteen members comprised the council, with seven representatives of the National Council of Resistance, three from the Independent Political Group and one representative from the Roman Catholic Church, as well as members of UNTAET and the Transitional Administrator. The latter was responsible for appointing the members of the Council. However, the Timorese members could only be appointed after public

---

[11] Steele (2002).

[12] Steele (2002).

[13] Steele (2002).

[14] Järvinen (2004).

[15] United Nations Organization (1999a).

consultations and their recommendations would be strictly on policy in relation to executive and legislative issues.

This Council should also establish mechanisms for consultation with civil society, including religious groups, women and young people. In addition, it should create sectoral committees—agriculture, education, environment, finance, health, human rights, infrastructure, local administration, natural resources—to increase the capacity to provide advice to the Transition Administrator.

The Judicial Service Commission was regulated by Regulation 1999/3[16] to recommend to the Transition Administrator candidates for the temporary judicial or prosecutorial service, to issue opinions on judicial functions and to prepare a Code of Ethics for Judges and Prosecutors. It consisted of seven individuals, five from East Timorese backgrounds and two international experts.

There was a view that East Timor would represent an "empty shell", a place that would have to be invented by the international community, that is, a United Nations experiment in building a nation.[17] Little attention was given to the planning process for the subtler elements, such as local population expectation, confidence building, and political commitment.

Civic education for the elections was too narrow on the voting process and failed to create an understanding of representation and cooperation among parliamentarians; there was little discussion about how citizens could influence or cooperate with government; the debates had little popular consultation; the decision-making was personalized and restricted.[18]

Another criticism noted by Steele[19] was that, although some consultations were held, the transitional government was not able to accept local contributions, since they had little or no influence over the consultant's decisions. For example, in education, many schools have been rebuilt, but curricula should have been written by local actors, considering the existence of a multiplicity of languages used in East Timor.

After 2 years of transitional governance, the SRSG went so far as to declare to the UN Security Council that "the empowerment of the people has been frustrating and extremely difficult and we, the UN, have been seen as managers rather than mentors", with a view to that the greatest difficulty was to face the lack of people trained to compose and manage the systems of government and social services.[20]

The international community has recognized the Timorese incapacity to deal with military, police, and financial management matters. In this sense, other fields such as national planning, health care and infrastructure, communications, and the judicial system would also be seriously deficient and without international support.

It was national discontent that led to the restructuring of UNTAET, in a note issued by the General Secretary.[21] On October 20, 2000, the National Consultative

[16] United Nations Organization (1999b).

[17] Järvinen (2004).

[18] Steele (2002).

[19] Steele (2002).

[20] Steele (2002).

[21] United Nations Organization (2000).

Council was reorganized to 36 members, exclusively by Timorese members and chaired by FRETILIN leader Xanana Gusmão. Although the Transition Administrator had appointed all new members, retaining power over final decisions regarding commitments, this change reinforced the local role in the decision-making process.

The challenges of East Timor are diverse since colonial rule did little to develop the economy or social services. The years of Indonesian occupation generated a culture of dependency, corruption, lack of cooperation and resistance. According to Steele,[22] the country was considered the poorest in Southeast Asia, with one of the highest child mortality rates in the world. After centuries of underdevelopment, poverty was considered endemic. According to the National Development Commission, 41% of East Timorese lived in poverty, and 48% were illiterate.

In East Timor, the Constituent Assembly elections were held in 2001, under the mantle of UNTAET, and led to the adoption of the Constitution the following year. However, a new Charter does not only concern the content of the legal document but must also consider its drafting process. Any guarantee of human rights in the text may be a stillbirth if the process itself is not based on the principles of democratic and broad participation.[23]

The problems systematized by Garrison[24] brought significant questions to the nature of participation. Not all Timorese were able to participate in the process of building the constitution, since many remained in refugee camps in West Timor.

In March 2001, there was still a population of about 50,000–80,000 refugees who remained in West Timor. This means that 5–10% of East Timor's population was excluded from the constitution-building process simply because of their absence from the territory.

Ultimately, the obstacle to participation was also logistical. Timor-Leste's limited development, combined with the destruction of infrastructure in 1999 in terms of transport and communications, represented significant and practical obstacles for the participation of those outside the capital.

One of UNTAET's main tasks was to prepare for independence and to facilitate the drafting of a constitution. The calendar was formally approved by the National Council and implied the process of constitutional development for East Timor and its future regime. It was established that the Constituent Assembly would prepare a draft constitution after 90 days of its election.[25]

This short term did not provide an opportunity for the introduction of an alternative model through a broad popular representation. The Transition Administrator discarded the idea of adopting a provisional constitution to allow for more civic education and consultation in some suggested communities. Another determination of the UN was that the charter was chosen by the votes of the parties in the Assembly and not by a popular referendum.

---

[22] Steele (2002).

[23] Järvinen (2004).

[24] Garrison (2005).

[25] Garrison (2005).

It would be determined that the Constituent Assembly would become the first national parliament without the promotion of elections. This provision was included in the transitional provisions in Article 167 of the Charter.

The operation was large and extremely burdensome for the UN and international pressure resulted in an early election to accelerate the transition.

UNTAET organized elections to compose the Constituent Assembly on August 30, 2001, exactly 2 years after the referendum. According to Järvinem,[26] the historical and social factors expressed in Timorese reality demonstrated that they were not ready for an election. There was no tradition of pluralism of ideas or opposition in the traditional hierarchical social nature of Timorese traditional culture.

On September 15, 2001, in Dili, the Transitional Administrator took over the House, which was composed of 88 deputies, representing 12 parties and one independent candidacy. In his speech, the Administrator emphasized that the charter should go through several tests and the text should reflect all local points of view and should withstand time.

East Timorese leaders were pushing for a transfer of power to an elected East Timorese body. The National Council had performed the functions of a nascent legislative council, but the appointed members had not been elected. On the other hand, many civil society organizations argued that more time was needed for civic education and consultation about elections, the role of the Constituent Assembly, and the Constitution itself so that elections were "meaningful".

In the forum held in 2001, the suggestion was made by NGOs to promote an alternative process for the election of a Constituent Assembly, as in the form of the South African Constituent National Commission, with a broad representation of all sectors of civil society, resources and a period of at least 1 year for the consultations.[27]

UNTAET, in turn, had suggested the creation of a Constitutional Commission in each of 13 districts of East Timor. These mini commissions should oversee promoting civic education on the transition process, with the collection of aspirational content to make up the content of the constitution.[28] The contribution of the district commissions would be made available to the Assembly.

The National Commission contested the undemocratic nature of the process, even though UNTAET continued with its planning. District commissions held more than 200 public hearings, with at least one hearing in each of the 67 sub-districts of East Timor.[29]

More than 38,000 people attended the district meetings during the period from March 15 to July 14, 2001. According to Garrison,[30] the executive summary that was transmitted by UNTAET was ignored by the Assembly. The reasons given were that the committees had not been elected and therefore lacked legitimacy and no reference was made to any of the district reports in the plenary debates.

---

[26] Järvinen (2004).

[27] Garrison (2005).

[28] United Nations Organization (2001).

[29] Garrison (2005).

[30] Garrison (2005).

FRETILIN had been the party that won the constituent elections, with a majority of 57.3% of the votes, which made it possible to compose a bench of 55 deputies among the 88 seats. Together with ASDT, the two parties constituted the required 2/3 majority to draft and endorse the charter.[31]

It was Regulation 2001/2,[32] which conferred legislative powers on the Assembly, providing for the creation of a specialized committee with powers to approve the regulation, keeping the Transitional Administrator's veto powers unchanged.

Once the Assembly was appointed, work began on the drafting and adoption of a Constitution. Political parties have become the main decision-makers. To be part of the discussions, civil society organizations would have to force their entry through known political parties. Also included were two members of UNTAET, a legal expert on constitutional law and a parliamentary expert, on whom the work to bring good standings to the Assembly[33] was carried out.

The parties presented four draft texts and all were very similar to each other. There were interpreters who translated the texts from Portuguese into Tetum, from Indonesian to Portuguese, from English to Tetum.

All four projects presented by the parties provided for the same structure, with semi-presidentialism or semi-parliamentary characteristics, bringing to the status of sovereign bodies the executive, legislative and judicial powers.

With the pressure on UNTAET, the main text is now only the one presented by FRETILIN. According to Ferreira,[34] the 88 deputies had before them a text that for the most part was strange. Not only because it was presented in Portuguese but also because they did not dominate the juridical-constitutional language, requiring all clarification given by the foreign consultants.

During the months of the Charter's construction, explanations of what "popular sovereignty", "universal suffrage", "multiparty", "participatory democracy", "principle of separation of powers", "judicial organization democratic", among others. These constituted terms of Western constitutions, knowledge of the consultants and very few Timorese, were new words for those deputies. The central work of support and advice to the constituent deputies in the writing of the text was in the hands of the foreigners.

After nearly 3 years of UN administration, 24 years of Indonesian occupation and four centuries of Portuguese colonial rule, East Timor found its destiny on the road to independence,[35] which was finally recognized on May 20, 2002.

The Constitution came into force 2 months later, presenting many similarities with the Portuguese Charter.[36] Xanana Gusmão was elected the President of the Republic in the presidential elections, held on April 14, 2002.

---

[31] Ferreira (2007).

[32] Ferreira (2007).

[33] Ferreira (2007).

[34] Ferreira (2007).

[35] Steele (2002).

[36] Ferreira (2007).

When the East Timor Constitution was passed, the final vote counted with 72 votes in favor and 14 votes against, with 1 abstention and 1 absence, being necessary to reach 60 votes to ratify the project. An additional concern was the fact that the opposition stated that this Charter was the fruit of a single party and that it could once again incite violence.[37]

Despite the close opportunities for public participation in the constitution-building process and concerns about a dominant party position in this process, signs of public acceptance were considered positive, since elections to the Constituent Assembly and the presidential election were free from fraud and corruption.

Despite the close opportunities for public participation in the constitution-building process and concerns about a dominant party position in this process, signs of public acceptance were considered positive, since elections to the Constituent Assembly and the presidential election were free fraud and corruption.

According to Garrison,[38] although the turnout in the presidential election on April 14, 2002 dropped from 91 to 86% in relation to the elections to the Assembly, in both cases, the level of participation is considered high, granting a strong endorsement to the process for any considered standard.

Regarding the delivery of a written document, UNTAET succeeded, as it was able to deliver a new constitution and a democratically elected government in the East Timor within a very short period.[39]

A longer period could have allowed for a more consultative and participatory process with a constitutional commission and a provisional constitution.

7.4 The UN Intervention in the Post-Constituent Phase

According to Freire,[40] the process for establishing the basic structure of the State lasted approximately 2.5 years. There is talk of a technical peace based on liberal assumptions, associated with institutions and mechanisms of governance, such as the organization and conduct of electoral processes or the institutionalization of the procedures of a State of Law.

This was the approach taken by UNTAET, that is, the construction of institutions and mechanisms of a functional State that, although understood as essential, relegated the social and economic dimensions to a secondary plane.

Even with the existing instability and inability to respond adequately to social, political, and economic inequalities, there was a widespread understanding that UNTAET played a key role in creating the structures that serve as the basis for the functioning of the new State despite the various limits which the Mission presented.

[37] Garrison (2005).

[38] Garrison (2005).

[39] Garrison (2005).

[40] Freire (2013).

Following the democratization, the post-constituent m[illegible] called the United Nations Mission of Support in East Timor (UNMISET),[41] was es[illegible] [illegible]th monitoring functions on the various components of the transitional missio[illegible] public administration and internal and external security,[42] for an initial period [illegible] months.

The UN, recognizing the weaknesses of emerging institutions, felt it necessary to create this monitoring to ensure a lasting momentum in the development and strengthening of East Timor's infrastructure—administration, law enforcement, and defense capacity—while noting the concern with the effectiveness of the system which would be implemented gradually. The Mission was led by a SRSG, and it was established that internationally accepted human rights principles should form an integral part of UNMISET training and capacity building.

After a period of 2 years, the Mission would fully return all operational responsibilities to all authorities, and this would be possible without compromising their stability.

The process turned out to be more complex than expected and problems arose, especially in the armed forces and the police, in relation to indiscipline, lack of technical training and the problem of the uncertain situation of former resistance fighters. The UN presence was outcome-oriented with focus on local capacity building.[43]

Security Council Resolution 1473[44] of 2003 decided that the timetable would be readjusted, also including the need to place more emphasis on human rights and the elements that make up the rule of law. The Mission was extended to May 20, 2004.[45]

The successive resolutions[46] issued by the Security Council were intended to extend the Mission—the deadline was extended, again, until May 2005, to address more specifically sensitive areas such as support for administration, justice and the public system; support for security and stability, including more military and civilian experts in the areas of human rights, governance, constitutional law. All the recommendations reinforced, in a systemic way, the appreciation of human rights.

Security Council Resolution 1410 of May 2002 initially employed a contingent of 5,000 military personnel, 120 military observers, and 1,250 civilian police. Also scheduled were 45 foreign civilians, 100 experts for the civilian support group, 241 UN volunteers, and 977 people recruited locally.

At the time of the withdrawal, on April 20, 2005, there were a total of 635 military personnel, including 469 soldiers, 41 officers, and 135 civilian police, supported by 264 foreign civilians, 100 UN volunteers, and 523 civilian employees, totaling a U $ 565,497,900 (five hundred and sixty-five million, four hundred and ninety-seven thousand, nine hundred dollars).

---

[41] United Nations Organization (2002).

[42] Freire (2013).

[43] Freire (2013).

[44] United Nations Organization (2003).

[45] United Nations Organization (2003).

[46] See United Nations Organization (2004).
and the United Nations Organization (2005).

pointed to serious failings in the functioning of the institutions, …s of recommendations aimed at integrating the nation and promoting development of justice, as they strengthen respect for the rule of law and foster community participation in the reconciliation process and justice.

The existence of a credible judicial process discouraged civil attacks for retribution and revenge. The Commission strongly recommended that the UN should establish a mechanism to continue investigations into judicial proceedings with a view to punishing serious human rights offenses. This mechanism would enable the East Timorese government to retain its sovereignty over the justice process and facilitate institutional capacity building by providing channels for the international community to assist in this process.

In May 2005, the Security Council established in East Timor another Mission, called United Nations Office in East Timor (UNOTIL),[48] with the objective of politically supporting the continued creation of national institutions and the police force, as well as promoting democracy and human rights. The Mission assisted the development of important State institutions and provided training on the observance of democratic governance and human rights.

UNOTIL was scheduled to end in May 2006 and the Security Council received recommendations, throughout the period, to extend its term.[49] A series of events that culminated in large political, humanitarian, and security crises from April to June this year prompted the Security Council to extend it to 20 August 2006, considering the need to strengthen the United Nations presence in the country.

The General Secretary later reported that the level of violence had declined and that a new government had been restored, which committed itself to unify the nation. However, he felt that the crisis was far from being resolved and that many ills, such as the government's inability to involve the population, the open wounds of the past, and the high rate of youth unemployment, required long-term attention. The situation of political maltreatment created an opportunity for the outbreak of new crises.

It was also pointed out that the legacy left by the 24 years of occupation gave rise to a great distance between those who fought in the resistance for years, between those who lived in the cities, those who lived in the countryside, and those who went into exile. In addition, there was likely to be a generational gap between veterans and young people. Other causes for the sharp crisis were the old tensions between the Orientals and the West in the armed forces and the police, as well as the poverty and needs associated with it.

The causes of the imbalance of power of State institutions allowed the executive to operate with few restrictions on institutional and constitutional policies.

In June 2006, the President of the Republic, the President of Parliament, and the Prime Minister of East Timor requested the General Secretary to propose to the Security Council the establishment of UN police forces to maintain public order until the police could ensure reorganization and restructuring.

---

47 United Nations Organization (2005).

48 United Nations Organization (2006a).

49 United Nations Organization (2006b).

The Secretary-General, in August 2006, said that since independence, progress had been made in strengthening East Timor's institutional capacity. According to him, the UN and the international community knew from previous experiences that building a nation was a long-term task. This statement was especially accurate as regards the time needed to set up a police service and a new judicial system.

The successive missions had shown that the lack of socio-economic development had subjected the population to poverty and lack of employment. As a result, long-term efforts to improve resource conversion in programs to tackle rural poverty and unemployment were as crucial as anything they could achieve through the new UN mission.

The General Secretary emphasized that the international presence in the security sector and other areas should respect national sovereignty and that the country itself should be responsible for developing and leading the process of national consolidation, and that political leaders should cooperate to create an open and pluralistic democracy, where the whole population felt involved.

A multidimensional and integrated mission was recommended with mandate to: support the country's government and help generate a process of national reconciliation; support in all aspects of the process leading up to the 2007 presidential and parliamentary elections; ensure the restoration and maintenance of public security by providing the UN police with executive power; assist in the work and coordination of the armed forces; strengthen national capacity through mechanisms for monitoring, promoting, and protecting human rights.

The Security Council accepted the request of the General Secretary and established the United Nations Integrated Mission in East Timor (UNMIT).[50] It was determined that this Mission would consist of an adequate civilian component, including a maximum of 1,608 police officers and 34 military officers.

Since its establishment, the mission has worked with the government, with different political parties, and with other interested social actors from inside and outside the country to ensure the fulfillment of the mandate entrusted.

According to UNMIT, in 2007, the situation in the country had improved, although the country's security and political climate remained unstable. The three rounds of presidential elections, finalized in June 2007, were characterized by high popular participation rate, from 80 to 82%, and all political actors, which showed that considerable progress had been made in dialogue and reconciliation since the 2006 crisis, accepted the results. As a result, Prime Minister José Ramos-Horta was sworn in as successor to Xanana Gusmão, and on July 30, a new 65-member Parliament was inaugurated.

In February 2008, rebel soldiers carried out an assassination attempt against the East Timor president, also targeting the Prime Minister. This plot culminated in the death of the rebel leader, Alfredo Alves Reinado, and with Ramos-Horta being seriously injured.[51] Although a state of emergency was decreed for 10 days, due to the seriousness of the incidents, there was no general destabilization of

[50] United Nations Organization (2006a).

[51] Robspierre (2008).

the country, as in 2006. The institutions responded adequately and responsibly, respecting constitutional procedures.

Because of this attack, a new resolution was issued by the Security Council,[52] which expanded the mandate of the mission, condemning the attacks perpetrated and all attempts to destabilize the country, as well as entrusting new tasks to UNMIT.

Efforts were concentrated on promoting dialogue and reconciliation, among others. It, thus, maintained its focus on the unity of the United Nations system, and the joint work of the team was able to promote political, technical, and financial support to help the country achieve its objectives.

In September 2011, the Timorese government and UNMIT wrote a joint transition plan to guide the planned withdrawal of the Mission, scheduled for the end of 2012. The plan, the first of its kind, established priorities and objectives, as well as 129 activities, which should be fulfilled by the UN before its departure.

According to the United Nations, thanks to the strength and determination of East Timorese and their leaders, East Timor has made tremendous progress since 2006 with the support of the international community. The displaced have returned peacefully and since March 2011, the national police have assumed their functions throughout the country.

The media are increasingly strong and make important contributions to the democratic debate. Poverty is declining because of public intervention in infrastructure and services. Primary school enrollment is a key element for stability and economic growth, and the country is well on its way to eradicating adult illiteracy.

On the political side, in 2012, free and peaceful presidential and parliamentary elections were held, and thanks to a quota system, women constitute 38% of Parliament, achieving the highest rate of female parliamentary participation in the Asia-Pacific region.

East Timor started to receive peacekeeping assistance and to contribute personally to United Nations operations in other parts of the world and was a key contributor to the New Covenant for aid effectiveness.

The mandate of UNMIT was extended for a final period until December 31, 2012 by the Resolution dated February 23, 2012.[53]

The Security Council, in its statement,[54] welcomed the progress made in East Timor in strengthening the institutional and human resources capacity of State institutions, including the security, justice, and governance sectors, which play key roles in safeguarding stability and the promotion of democracy.

The closure of the Mission did not mean the end of the United Nations collaboration with the country, since the East Timor continues to face many difficulties and the UN is willing to support the government's proposal to promote the country's development by establishing a working relationship cooperation for the post-UNMIT phase, focusing on institutional strengthening and development.

[52] United Nations Organization (2008).

[53] United Nations Organization (2012).

[54] United Nations Organization (2012).

7.5 The Constitutionalism of Transition, Transformation, and the Democratic and the Legitimacy of the East Timor Constitutional Charter

If the study of constitutionalism is able to find answers and mechanisms that seek to forge a legitimate and democratic constitution and, in addition, to enable the formation of a collective will, the analysis of the Timorese Charter will allow us to understand if in the universe of the categories of constitutionalism transition and transformation—which is based on the ideals of democracy and democratization of the UN, this Constitution finds a refuge to conform the newly democratized nation and to promote its development.

This experience has revealed that there are as many elements of transitional constitutionalism as of transformation in the constitution-making of Timor.

It is already established that the constitutionalism of transition comprises the dimension of the process of constitutionalization, that is, the means of articulation for the projection of the text, and that there is no impediment that this constructive effort comes from both internal and external forces, the introduction of numerous techniques that can form a constitutional culture. Thus, in this category, UN intervention as an external actor finds constitutional support.

Another approach is the fact that the category is also associated with the sensitive context and the legacy of violence whose main objective is the political and institutional reorganization to ensure the stability of the constitutional text itself.

Present in East Timor, the UN has played an active role, both in promoting East Timorese independence and in improving its economic and social development.

The intervention in the pre-constituent phase was connected to the support for the electoral campaigns and was related to the educational campaigns. Within the conception of an aid mission, the referendum held was considered a success by the high rate of popular participation—99% of the voters present.

The operation took place in a hostile environment, with limited infrastructure and under significant pressure, constituting a valuable collaboration to broaden the strengthening of institutions and the system of government.[55] This participation was aimed at reducing the rate of violence and ensuring the smoothness of the electoral process for the local population.

UN action may prove insufficient to overcome the threats, the legitimacy of the outcome, without the existence of a catalyst to help local leaders shape the process, without a form of compensation, leads to those who lose in the polls to have a strong incentive to rebel against the system to overcome the threats. That is what happened—the rejection of the referendum response ended up in a new campaign of terror.

The relativization of the channels of dialogue was used in this category as inductor for the new order. The educational campaign is a competing action that tends to improve the system and enrich the process, but the time devoted to the promotion of

---

[55] Järvinen (2004).

civic virtuality is a compound that must be analyzed. Short timeframes to meet this determination tend not to have any effect.

In East Timor, although UNAMET worked to register the entire population, 76 days did not allow the understanding of the process as an objective of "promotion of democracy", which could simply mean a transfer of knowledge to those who understanding, since the Timorese population had a very high level of illiteracy. Moreover, in this exercise, the UN can be considered paternalistic.

It is extremely important to consider support for electoral campaigns in a coordinated way for the promotion of civic virtuality, paying special attention to the time allocated to this effectiveness so as not to become a symbolic act, as shown in items 4.2.1. In addition, 4.2.2.

The intervention in the constituent order can demonstrate that a charter constructed in contexts with high levels of violence presents several risks and consequences. Twenty-four years of Indonesian occupation in the East Timor represented a critical point for democratization, since the desire to consecrate its power was emerging.

As a theoretical-abstract category, the constitutionalism of transition also has other features, such as the relativization of the process of elaboration of the propulsive charter of consensus.

As stated in item 4.3, too much international influence can be detrimental to a constitutional process because the outcome may be mismatched to local needs. On UNTAET, the figure of the Transitional Administrator in East Timor, exercising all the powers—executive, legislative, and judiciary—was based on a unilateral power structure, since there was no role for Timorese in this composition. It constituted a government without constitution.

The construction of the State must be minimally linked to a horizontality that allows its feedback in the constitutional project, especially on the part of those who live their own experience, given that there is, force to be awakened.

The most successful constitutions, as reported in item 4.2.2, were those in which mechanisms for opening popular participation were significant. In addition, these aspects were often neglected, considering that UNTAET calendars generally had short deadlines, and this eventually prevented coordinated and systemic actions.

In the transitional moment, special attention should be paid to the composition of the advisory council, which also did not enjoy the legitimacy of an elected body, and too much international influence was detrimental to the constitutional process. It is the national authorities that should play a leading role and, in the case of Timor, the SRSG retained power over all final decisions regarding the commitments of the Charter.

The UN represented two strands: both to "encourage compliance with international standards" and almost all resolutions contained the promotion of democracy and human rights; as well as representing a "political actor" at the Constituent Assembly. A lengthy population dialogue, being restricted to the closed room, problems already announced in the previous sub-items, did not follow the process.

The Timorese Charter was written in 90 days and this term did not allow it to be a particular product. The deputies had before them a document that was for the most part strange, presented in Portuguese, a language that was not known to all, and dominated by a language and political-juridical influence that oversaw international experts, and may therefore not reflect the agreement of interested parties on the nature, political system and future of the State.

As example, Article 51, item III, of the Charter, informs us that lockout is prohibited; despite having official languages (Portuguese and Tetum) in the transitional provisions; in its Article 159, Bahasa-Indonesian and English are considered working languages in use and, when necessary, the model of the transitional judicial organization provided for in Article 163, which is composed of national and foreign judges with jurisdiction for the trial of serious crimes committed between January 1 and October 25, 1999, is maintained for the time necessary to the conclusion of the proceedings and investigation.

According to constitutional theory, this model cannot be considered democratic since the constituted power was in foreign hands and the Charter was not taken to a referendum.

Even with a differentiated panorama, the constitutionalism of transition, which bets on the change by the constructive effort and that will impel the text, was not perceived in East Timor. Therefore, a problem will be to form a constitutional culture, which is effectively reinforced based on social consensus.

As a theoretical-abstract category, the constitutionalism of transformation bets on the substantive content of the proposal of constitutionalism manifested in a text that intends to change the social reality.

In addition, for this, it must consolidate the revolutionary efforts; establishing the connectivity of ideological constitutionalism and participation; provide the new design and its preconditions; and represent a continuous and constructive process.

The East Timor Constitution of 2002[56] is quite long, highlighting not only the governance structure but also the social goals of the new nation and the rights of its citizens. It has in its preamble the highlight of the country's history of struggle for independence and the need to build a democratic and independent nation based on the rule of law. Moreover, it makes direct mention to the United Nations, noting that the Charter was based on the referendum of August 30, 1999, which was carried out under the auspices of the UN, confirming the self-determined will of independence.

Its main objective is to guarantee the sovereignty of the country, promote fundamental rights and freedoms and respect for the principles of the rule of law. However, this last objective may have been compromised, given that in the construction process, there was no systemic survey of the norms and customs of East Timor, which are very different according to their different districts. Hence, the great difficulty of finding a fair balance between respect and customary practices—understood in Article 2, as essential to Timorese identity—and the values of democracy and human rights on which the Timorese building is based.[57]

---

[56] This description has been extracted and systematized through studies carried out by IDEA International through the Constitutional Net Project, which aims to support constitutional research in sharing knowledge and building best practices. Available at: http://www.constitutionnet.org. Accessed on: May 15, 2015.

[57] Vasconcelos (2011), p. 23.

The Charter was deeply influenced by the Universalist understanding of human rights and the principles of international law. The UN is primarily concerned with the recognition of the Universal Declaration of Human Rights, adopted in 1948. It was necessary to ensure that minimum substantive rights were respected.

The Charter received, in its Article 9, international law, adopting its general or common principles and conventional law. In addition, all rules of laws contrary to the provisions of conventions, treaties, and agreements received in the internal order are considered invalid. The general or common principles are part of the internal order without the need for any act that expressly recognizes it as a source of law.

This automatic and immediate reception clause expresses an important degree of openness of the Timorese legal system to international law, decisively marking the process of restoration of independence.[58] The right of origin is subject to approval, ratification, or accession by the respective competent bodies.

The interpretation of fundamental rights reflects an open conception, expressly admitting the existence of fundamental rights outside the constitutional context,[59] as expressed in Article 23, since they must be interpreted in line with the Declaration of Human Rights. This opening, for Vasconcelos,[60] raises the question of how to identify the fundamental rights dispersed by the legal order and to determine the extent to which these rights, once identified, could benefit the applicable regime to the fundamental rights formally constituted.

There is, in the Charter, the provision of rights such as equality, life, liberty, security and personal integrity, criminal law enforcement, limit of penalties, habeas corpus, and protection of personal data, among others.

It also mentions the obligation to maintain an independent body with the function of assessing and seeking to satisfy the citizens' complaints against actions or omissions of the public authorities, being able to see compliance with the law, as well as preventing and starting the entire repair process of injustices through a Human Rights and Justice Provider envisaged in Article 27. It was thus aligned with the Paris Principles on the status of national institutions for the promotion and protection of human rights and with the Scandinavian model of Ombudsman, issued after the Second World.[61]

This body has no decision-making power, and its assessment should be forwarded to the competent bodies with the necessary recommendations, which have a duty of collaboration. The Ombudsman is elected by Parliament for a term of 4 years and his activity is independent of the "gracious" and "contentious" means provided for in the Charter and in the laws.

In this document, with a universalist vision of human rights, many principles end up not being consistent with the internal culture, mainly in the definition of its content and scope. East Timor, for example, in addition to Tetum, has at least 15 other native

---

[58] Vasconcelos (2011), p 51.

[59] Vasconcelos (2011), pp. 90–92.

[60] Vasconcelos (2011), pp 90–92.

[61] Vasconcelos (2011), p 109.

dialects, such as habun, galolen, wetarês, kawaimina, bekais. According to Albuquerque,[62] the native languages Mabae and Makasae, besides Tetum, have several speakers of more than 100 thousand inhabitants. In the official sphere, there are four languages: Portuguese, Bahasa-Indonesian, Tetum-Praça[63] (language of most of the population), and English, which was strengthened by UN intervention.[64] Article 13 of the Charter determined Tetum and Portuguese as official languages.

The heterogeneous and complex reality experienced by Timor, especially around phenomena of variation and linguistic-discursive change, is considered intrinsically linked to a dynamic, political reality in which the processes of negotiation of meanings (identity, beliefs) are present in the dialogues intercultural and become increasingly evident and constant, strengthening the processes of hybridization that affect languages, identities, cultures, government.[65]

The heterogeneous and complex reality experienced by Timor, especially around phenomena of variation and linguistic-discursive change, is considered intrinsically linked to a dynamic, political reality in which the processes of negotiation of meanings (identity, beliefs) are present in the intercultural dialogues and become increasingly evident and constant, strengthening the processes of hybridization that affect languages, identities, cultures, government.

In addition, in this sense, the discourse can enter discord with the internal culture, being able to represent a Charter containing symbolic rights and without identity, since it adds a complexity of senses and there is not a clear way to realize its interpretation in this diversity. As stated in Chap. 4, the need to incorporate human rights in the internal order is not denied, but this must be done gradually and must be built by the local population through appropriate political and dialogical channels.

Fundamental rights, such as the right to strike, freedom of association, property, petition, freedom, privacy, universality, and equality, equality between men and women, youth, children, the elderly, citizens with disabilities, among others, are reproduced in general clauses. That is, their rights and obligations are recognized and promoted by the State, to the extent of its possibilities.[66] Fundamental social rights such as security, social assistance, health, housing, education, and culture are also subject to gradual implementation.

It can be seen, as Pulcinelli[67] affirms, that the broad consecration of socioeconomic rights materialized without having at that moment, maturity to promote the precise content definition of such guarantees, and this ends up being a way that ends up expanding the judicialization of public affairs.

---

[62] Albuquerque (2010).

[63] The Tetum language has three dialects: Tetum-Praça, Tetum-Térik and Tetum-Belu. The dialect recognized in the Constitution is the Tetum-Praça, which consists of a Creole that has the Portuguese language as a lexificator language. (Alburquerque 2010).

[64] Severo (2011), pp. 95–113.

[65] Severo (2011), pp. 95–113.

[66] The fundamental rights provided for in Articles 19 (protection of youth); 20 (protection of the elderly); 21 (citizen with a disability); 56 (security and social assistance); 57 (health); 58 (housing) and 59 (education and culture).

[67] Pulcinelli (2015).

The demands of social and human rights ended up assuming a great importance, especially in the centrality of the judiciary. From the 1980s, constitutional courts were considered as protagonists, especially those capable of providing a space for political debate for civil society actors.[68] Klare refutes this role,[69] since for him there is no "transformative award" because it ends up suggesting to the judges the realization of political projects.[70]

Transformational constitutionalism draws the recognition of fundamental rights and is not limited to rhetorical exercise without effectiveness. The commitment is necessarily subject to implementation.

The structure of the power of Timor was divided by organs of sovereignty between the President of the Republic—Head of State, National Parliament, Government—responsible for the conduct and execution of the general policy of the country, and the Courts. It provides mechanisms to neutralize the excesses of concentration of power, including the provision of dialogues and instruments of popular participation, which is coming closer to the category of transformation.

The program of government shall be submitted to Parliament for its consideration. The debate of the program should not exceed 5 days and until its closure, any parliamentary bench can request its rejection, or the Government can request a vote of confidence.

The international concern has advanced in the sense of promoting the political participation of the citizens, besides the representation, being verified a direct approach with the constitutionalism of transformation. Article 6 defends and guarantees political democracy and popular participation in solving national problems; Article 46 defends the right to participation, by itself or by democratically elected representatives, in political life and in public affairs; Article 63 states that the direct and active participation of women and men is a fundamental condition and instrument of the democratic system; Art. 101 guarantees the participation of the members of the government to attend the plenary sessions of the parliament and voice an opinion, and vice versa, and that the parliament may request the participation of members of the government in their work.

The UN, after East Timorese independence, supported the State—through UNMISET, UNOTIL, and UNMIT—for at least 10 years, recognizing the institutional instability and fragility and the State's inability to promote its development, as well as other difficulties mentioned previously.

An "effective post-conflict democracy" is built on a dual basis: a set of structures and procedures that manage the issues that divide society, as well as a set of fundamental relationships between the groups involved.[71]

---

[68] Vieira and Bezerra (2015).

[69] Klare (1998).

[70] In the same sense, Gargarella affirms that the more social and human rights are incorporated, the more power is given to the judges, that is, if new rights are incorporated and the power structure is not modified. (Gargarella 2015).

[71] Instituto Internacional para la Democracia y la Asistencia Electoral (2003).

In this attempt to adjust the directions of direction for a transformative response, the Strategic Development Plan (PED)[72] was coined, which defines a way for the implementation of the national gradual strategy in the period from 2010 to 2030.

This indicates that East Timor, as one of the developing nations, decided to outline its vital choices to go down the path of poverty and fragility and to become a robust, prosperous, and progressive society, with four essential principles being defined: politics, which should create a strong consensus on national cohesion and stimulate confidence in the future; economic potential, since it has valuable resources, including oil and gas; national integration, taking into account that the country is relatively small and with a privileged position for development; dynamism, with a young population, ready to grasp new possibilities, including technological domination.

The priority goals foreseen in this plan are centered on access to free and compulsory education up to the 12th year of schooling; eradication of illiteracy; access to health and basic sanitation; qualifications for citizens; and the eradication of extreme poverty, through universal access to public services and economic development in all regions.

Moreover, in this sense, the path chosen should be harmonized within the regions, applicable to the context of the country and based on the physical and cultural fabric of the country. The PED reflects these choices for the East Timorese. No matter how noble the rationale for promoting development, the structures will not function properly for more equitable and fairer that they are if there is no minimum of cooperation in the interrelationships.[73]

The long-term economic strategy relies heavily on strengthening the pillars of the State to create and maintain a lasting national identity that is unique and exclusive to East Timor.

Encouraging participation increases the potential for the effective implementation of the Democratic Charter and reinforces the sign of legitimacy. Once the tie of recognition has been incorporated, and the more adjusted, the more intense its degree of effectiveness and the constitutional culture that it intends to develop, opening the way to the potential exercise of democratic constitutionalism. The fortification and transparency of the institutions depend on horizontal supervision, in addition to the vertical, and for this, some opening of the institutional design is necessary, mainly to adapt to the local situations.[74]

For Tommasoli,[75] there was excessive reliance on East Timorese governance institutions on the expertise of international experts, and this could jeopardize the development of local capacities—the recommendation was primarily to observe participatory governance mechanisms.

The Timorese people were not allowed to choose the form, basis, term, and character of their constitutional process and the content of their Constitution. This imposition unequivocally generates its illegitimacy.

[72] Integrated Republic of East Timor (2010).

[73] Instituto Internacional para la Democracia y la Asistencia Electoral (2003).

[74] Tomassoli (2010).

[75] Tomassoli (2010).

The Charter can also gain legitimacy through the evolutionary process since its ability to express itself does not necessarily end in its adoption process. It is the permanent process of contestation that allows the development of constitutional living.

During the restoration of democracy, it was possible to glimpse some approximate contours with the category of constitutionalism of transformation, including with the logic of progressive development.

Democratic constitutionalism subordinates the issue of original legitimacy of the text, admitting that this same sign of empowerment of thc Charter comes through practice.

References

Albuquerque, D. B. (2010). As línguas de Timor-Leste: Perspectivas e prospectivas. *Revista Língua e Literatura*, 313–335 (USP). https://www.academia.edu/2121388/As_l%C3%ADnguas_de_Timor_Leste_perspectivas_e_prospectivas

Ferreira, C. (2007). A cooperação parlamentar bilateral luso-timorense e a formação do poder legislativo (2000–2006), Kelly Cristiane Silva, Daniel Schroeter Simião, Timor-Leste *por trás do palco:* cooperação internacional e a dialética da formação do Estado, 153 (Editora UFMG).

Freire, M. R. (2013). As Nações Unidas em Timor-Leste: construir a paz? In Hannah Loney et al., (Eds.), (Vol. I, pp. 101–102).

Gargarella, R. (2015). El constitucionalismo democrático: la sala de máquina de la Constitución. *Politica y Sociedade*. https://youtube/zHCMHQdbEuQ

Garrison, R. (2005). *The role of constitution-building processes in democratization: Case study East Timor* (vol. 12). Institute for Democracy and Electoral Assistance. http://www.idea.int/conflict/cbp

Integrated Republic of East Timor (2010). *Towards peace and prosperity: East Timor strategic development plan 2011–2013* (14th May 2013). http://EastTimor.gov.tl/wp-content/uploads/2010/06/Sumario-PED-Final_PT.pdf

Instituto Internacional para la Democracia y La Asistencia Electoral. (2003). *Reconciliacíon luego de conflictos violentos: resumen de políticas*. Stockholm. http://www.idea.int/publications/reconciliation/upload/policy_summary_esp.pdf

Järvinen, T. (2004). *Human rights and post-conflict transitional justice in East Timor*. The Finnish Institute of International Affairs, UPI Working Papers (vol. 47, pp. 1–16). https://www.google.com.br/search?client=safari&rls=en&q=Human+Rights+and+postconflict+transitional+justice+in+East+Timor&ie=UTF8&oe=UTF8&gf_rd=cr&ei=ckD8VracNIyX8Qeihosw.

Klare, K. (1998). Legal culture and transformative constitutionalism. *South African Journal on Human Rights*, 146–188. http://heinonline.org/HOL/LandingPage?collection=journals&handle=hein.journals/soafjhr14&div=17&id=&page=

Pulcinelli, E. (2015). STF como indultor da mudança no constitucionalismo de transformação. Thesis – Doc. In *Law—post graduate prog* (220). In Law of Estácio de Sá University.

Robspierre, M. (2008). Attack on the Timorese president. *International Environment: Magazine of International Relations*, 7–8. http://www.pucminas.br/imagedb/conjuntura/CNO_ARQ_NOTIC20080226143601.pdf?PHPSESSID=41cc008258b638c00e81255a192fa463

Severo, C. G. (2011). Questões de língua, identidade e poder: hibridismos no Timor-Leste. *Revista Brasileira de Linguistica Aplicada*, 95–113 (Belo Horizonte). http://www.scielo.br/scielo.php?pid=S198463982011000100006&script=sci_abstract&tlng=pt

Steele, J. (2002). East Timor faces post-UNTAET challenges: what is to be done? *The La'o Hamutuk Bulletin*. http://etan.org/lh/bulletins/bulletinv3n4a.html

Tomassoli, M. (2010). Democracia, paz y seguridad: el rol de las Naciones Unidas. *Institute for Democracy and Electoral Assistence, UN, PNUD, 25.*
Un Information Department (2000a). *As Nações Unidas e o Timor Leste: a autodeterminação através de consulta popular* (vol. 4).
Un Information Department. (2000b). *As Nações Unidas e o Timor Leste: a autodeterminação através de consulta popular* (vol. 5).
United Nations Organization. (1975). *United nations security council.* Resolution 384. http://www.un.org/en/ga/search/view_doc.asp?symbol=S/RES/384
United Nations Organization. (1999). United Nations Security Council, Resolution 1264, Resolution S/RES/1272 (Oct. 25th, 1999) (Jun. 26th, 2013) https://documentsddsny.un.org/doc/UNDOC/GEN/N99/264/81/PDF/N9926481.pdf?OpenElement
United Nations Organization. (1999a). *United nations transition administration in East Timor.* On the creation of a National Advisory Council, Regulation UNTAET/REG/1999a/2. http://www.un.org/en/peacekeeping/missions/past/etimor/untaetR/etreg2p.htm
United Nations Organization. (1999b). *United nations transition administration in East Timo*r. On the establishment of a transitional judicial service commission. Regulation UNTAET/REG/1999a/3. http://www.un.org/en/peacekeeping/missions/past/etimor/untaetR/reg3p.htm
United Nations Organization. (1999c). *United nations transition administration in East Timor.* Regulation N 1999c/1 on the authority of the Transitional Administrator in East Timor, Regulation UNTAET/REG/1999c/1. http://www.un.org/en/peacekeeping/missions/past/etimor/untaetR/etreg1.ht
United Nations Organization. (1999d). *United nations transition administration in East Timor.* Regulation N 1999d/1 on the authority of the Transitional Administrator in East Timor, Regulation UNTAET/REG/1999d/1.
United Nations Organization. (2000). *Security council.* Report of the security council mission to East Timor and Indonesia, Report S/2000/1105. http://www.un.org/en/ga/search/view_doc.asp?symbol=S/2000/1105
United Nations Organization. (2000b). *United nations security council.* Resolution 1480, Resolution S/RES/1480. http://daccessddsny.un.org/doc/UNDOC/GEN/N03/363/80/PDF/N0336380.pdf?OpenElement
United Nations Organization. (1999). *United nations security council.* Resolution 1410, Resolution S/RES/1410. http://www.securitycouncilreport.org/atf/cf/%7B65BFCF9B-6D27-4E9C-8CD3-CF6E4FF96FF9%7D/IJ%20SRES1410.pdf
United Nations Organization. (2003a). *United nations security council.* Resolution 1473, Resolution S/RES/1473. http://daccess-dds-ny.un.org/doc/UNDOC/GEN/N03/310/83/PDF/N0331083.pdf?OpenElement
United Nations Organization. (2004). *United nations security council.* Resolution 1573, Resolution S/RES/1573. http://www.securitycouncilreport.org/atf/cf/%7B65BFCF9B-6D274E9C8CD3-CF6E4FF96FF9%7D/POCSRES%201573.pdf
United Nations Organization. (2005). *United nations security council.* Resolution 1599, Resolution S/RES/1599. http://www.securitycouncilreport.org/atf/cf/%7B65BFCF9B-6D27-4E9C-8CD3-CF6E4FF96FF9%7D/POCSRES%201573.pdf
United Nations Organization. (2005). United *Nations security council.* Letter dated 24th June 2005 from the secretary-general addressed to the president of the security council, Report S/2005/458. http://www.un.org/en/peacekeeping/missions/past/unmiset/commission.html
United Nations Organization. (2006). *United nations security council.* Report of the general secretary on East Timor under security council resolution 1690, Report S/2006/628. http://www.un.org/es/comun/docs/?symbol=S/2006/628
United Nations Organization. (2006). *United nations security council.* Resolution 1704, Resolution S/RES/1704. http://www.un.org/es/comun/docs/?symbol=S/RES/1704(2006)
United Nations Organization. (2008). *United nations security council.* Resolution 1802, Resolution S/RES/1802. http://www.un.org/es/comun/docs/?symbol=S/RES/1802(2008)

United Nations Organization. (2012). *United nations security council*. Resolution 2037, Resolution S/RES/2037. http://www.un.org/es/comun/docs/?symbol=S/RES/2037(2012)

United Nations Organization. (2012). *United nations security council*. Statement by the president of the security council, statement S/PRST/2012/27. http://www.un.org/es/comun/docs/?symbol=S/PRST/2012/27

Vasconcelos, P. C. B. (2011). *Constituição anotada da República Democrática do Timor-Leste* (p. 23). Direitos Humanos – Centro de Investigação Interdisciplinar

Vieira, J. R., & Bezerra, R. (2015). Estado de coisas fora do lugar (?). http://jota.info/estado-de-coisas-fora-lugar

Chapter 8
Conclusion

The objective of the work was to verify the institutional capacity of the UN to contribute to the generation of a legitimate constitution order in those countries in stages of re-democratization, based on the way it undertakes of these constitution-making.

Democracy has evolved, over the centuries, expanding its nuclei of adherence. Democratic living is intimately related to the foundations, choices, structures that hold authority and the mechanisms in which these choices can take effect.

If the original aim was to decentralize power, democracy also finds scope for the promotion of human rights and justice, which includes the superiority of the charter, the existence of fundamental rights and their social development, and the cooperation of the formal structures of power. This conceptual evolution allowed us to find materialization, including through external inputs, such as the UN.

As an open system, democracy is unlimited and constructive, not having a single source of interpretation. Its essentiality lies in the cyclical attribute of conforming dissent—being in transformation is its natural and dynamic state.

In this new field created by the UN, it is fundamental that the attributes that involve democracy and democratization are present in the process of forming a new constitutional charter, since they will enable a more participative environment, serving the constitution as a means for its realization.

The main lines of the constitution-making processes that the UN can promote are, in theory, adequate and align with the theoretical-abstract models of the constitutionalism of transition and transformation. The result will be both more democratic and legitimate and more interactive and in tune with the reality where this transposition will take place.

In the matrix of constitutionalism of transition, the constitutional moment is prolonged in time since it invests in how the founding document will be translated. In this sense, it acts as a propeller of the consensus that is constantly evolving—in this profile, the character is instrumental, with progressive incremental logic. Not only does it serve as a basis for political democratization, but it can also create

C. B. Gouvêa and P. H. V. B. Castelo Branco, *UN Interventions and Democratization*, Societies and Political Orders in Transition,
https://doi.org/10.1007/978-3-031-32715-5_8

new institutional possibilities capable of adapting to unprecedented changes that are yet to come. Values, norms, constitutional legitimacy, social and economic development, security are constant demands and present complex characteristics and deep challenges.

The common attributes of the transformative format focus on the constitution as a lever for social inclusion, which is a primary goal in modifying a status quo of political segregation, misery and social exclusion. We are thinking of the reconstruction of the State and, consequently, of society as it goes through the redistribution of resources, as well as the provision of access to essential goods and services. Most of the reforms in transformational constitutionalism draw the recognition of fundamental rights, not limited to rhetorical exercise without efficacy, but rather as a practice that extends the mechanisms of protection and guarantee of these rights, since one intends to "transform reality in which it affects".

The ideas, as all the reflection proposed by the UN show, can be seen as a unique construction architecture, capable of promoting social and human development. They reveal a high potential for generating a legitimate document, a new democratic regime, given that they support a comprehensive political transition, requiring a coherent and multifaceted approach, with a full and prior knowledge of the national situation and the political situation. They should systematically engender compliance with constitutions, with the commitment to implement human rights through dialogues involving all national actors.

It is acknowledged that this process is sovereign and national, so it must be sensitive to the need for counseling, preventing international actors from imposing a foreign constitution. Support for inclusiveness and transparency is stimulated, since participation can promote even the legitimacy of the charter, considering this transformative exercise.

The shifting of the UN idealized guidelines to the reality of a country that is undergoing a process of political transition is not always simple, requiring a connection with the cultural elements and the organization of the society. It demands a more accurate sensitivity, and now, the model can derail, as seen with the experience of East Timor.

The theoretical and empirical dimension, reflected in Chaps. 4, 5, and 6 revealed a high degree of potential to generate an illegitimate document, although it can be recognized that its task in undertaking assistance has resulted in good results.

Intervention in support of promotion and institutional development in electoral campaigns has shown that the use of its expertise assists, among others, in the improvement and strengthening of electoral systems and bodies. In addition, as an impartial body to participate in the process, it ultimately confirms credibility to the electoral process.

About educational campaigns and popular participation, these have proved to be a process under construction. The development of plans to educate the population about the nature of the constituent process, for example, came up against an obstacle—the extremely short time for the completion of these works. The offer to bring together as many groups as possible through an open and participatory environment is still an effort that the United Nations has undertaken together with other actors. Experience has shown that public participation is usually minimal.

What and how to articulate the constitutional project, fruit of hybrid constituent power, for the present and future—included in it the meanings of belonging and identity of the nation? The idea is to go against the universalized liberal project, since the role of the constitution and constitutionalism does not present itself as a finalized project, since it is going through profound changes—nothing more being the product of a new reality that has been imposed.

From this point and based on humanitarian and human logic, we could align a thought that does not aim at the diffusion of a single and finished matrix, but that builds tools to recognize the multinations, common rights, harmonizing and not unifying positions, "*allowing a certain perensity of the constitutional experience as a project of culture committed to the present and future.*[1]"

A real "popular power" has been emerging and a gathering of western states together with the UN, which, united states, are instituting constitutions in independent states, in these cases, in addition to being supported by actions at the military, political or diplomatic level, these countries are now recognized by the United Nations. In this way, we must broaden our theoretical perception of the dimension of the constituent power and how it has operated in the empirical universe. After all, are all constitutions not in any way imposed? Thus, we not only pluralize the unitary concept of "constituent power", but we recognize the existence of constituent powers that exist both inside and outside the State.

Political and legal recognition is among the broad tools that "the great international powers" use to perform their roles as guarantors of the democratic order. Comprehensive undertakings are being imposed, which includes the organic and substantial part of the constitution in the new states.

However, within its ontology, the theory of the original constituent power remains responsive to changes in the geopolitical context and we need to forge mechanisms for the adaptation of its subcategories that has been emerging in the global context, such as the hybrid constituent power. We also need to direct the center of theoretical attention to the political communities that arise from conflicts and that are directly influenced by international actors.

The original constituent power, according to Oklopicic, should not be understood only with a positive aptitude, usually composed of the elements representing the "act, resist, cooperate, nod, choose"; it also has a dark side that represents "control, dominance, co-optation, seduction, resentment, and imposition.[2]"

In recent decades, it has been possible to map an undeniable evolution in the experiences of the United Nations in *the processes of constitution-making and constitution-change* in its most diverse forms: of electoral assistance provided to

[1] BOLZAN DE MORAIS, Jose Luis. *The crises of the State and the Constitution and the space–time transformation of human rights*. 2 ed. Porto Alegre: Bookshop Of Lawyers, 2011, p. 130.

[2] OKLOPCIC, Zoran. Constitutional (re) vision: sovereign peoples, new constituent powers, and the formation of constitutional orders in the Balkans. *Constellations*, v. 19, n. 1, 2012 p. 93. Available in < https://onlinelibrary.wiley.com/doi/full/10.1111/j.1467-8675.2011.00667.x > . Accessed February 23, 2019.

more than one hundred countries; consulting services; advice; logistics; civic and constitutional education; computer applications. The theoretical effort to design instruments capable of promoting a common understanding on the principles, norms, standards and values that are the basis of democracy is also emphasized, with the objective of guiding member states in the development of national democratic traditions and in fulfilling their commitments to human rights and development. Based on these factors, it is understood that, for the UN, the concepts of democracy and democratization are materialized through a constitution.

Constituent Assemblies must contain local experts in the design of their process, since too much international influence can be detrimental because the outcome may be mismatched to local needs. Of the countries in which the intervention took place, the average length of construction of the charters was relatively short, ranging from one to two years. These aspects demonstrate that if the sense of belonging and identity are not intertwined, further destabilization can be triggered.

A constitution is legitimate, that is, recognized not only as a de facto situation, but also as a legal system, when the strength and authority of the constituent power in which its decision rests is recognized by the people. It is valid, because there is a political unity, which is the constitution, representing the subject of the constituent power that can fix the mode and form of its existence. In this sense, it stands out: it is the Constitution, in the political legal sense, a strong agent of social control, responsible for the maintenance and transmission of so-called basic social values; despite suffering limitations in their exercise, in a sociological perspective, the constituent power suffers them in the direct reason of the social values prevailing in society at the time of the elaboration of the constituent text by the Constituent Assembly; and such values are not immutable and serve as an limitations to the exercise of constituent power, which are imposed thanks to the actions of public opinion and so-called interest groups.

The original constituent power has suffered these "fissures" since the decolonization where major powers and international organizations are intervening in *the constitution-making processes in* nations, such as Afghanistan, Cambodia, Timor-Leste, Bosnia and Herzegovina, Afghanistan, Nepal, Haiti, Kosovo, among many others. In these cases, it was not the "people" who used their constituent power to establish their respective constitutional orders. On the contrary, external actors using political power and the interpretation of norms of international law created the possibility that the populations captured within these orders would be recognized as "people".

Some authors have recognized that these phenomena of creating new states are examples of a founding constitutional moment, where great powers break with the "international legal framework", finding normative foundations to justify intervention, such as the maintenance of international collective security, self-defense and the protection of human rights, to rebuild or intervene in the states. It is the self-imposed restriction generated by arguments of great powers that wards off any simplistic notion of popular sovereignty, original constituent power, self-determination, or sovereign equality. And this is the final agency of the legality or legitimacy of the intervention.

The systematic incorporation of human rights in constitutional charters has shown that such insertion may prove insufficient to guarantee desirable levels of effectiveness. This absorption is necessary, since there is no possibility of being compromised with its systemic violation, especially in flagellated nations. However, this process must be constitutive and dynamic, through the exercise that comes from the public autonomy of citizens through the appropriate political channels.

The way a charter is built and who commands this process is as important as its content and must relate to the society it intends to guide. The combination of forces—understood here with an open mechanism of participation, coupled with local needs, functioning as a consultative body—would be able to overcome some substantial and structural problems.

But why does the theory of constituent power remain reluctant to include a kind of external constituent power as part of its constitutional categorization?

For Oklopcic, the "external constituent" power is inevitably intertwined with an unprecedented involvement of external powers in imposing a new political topography. In announcing these axioms, these great powers not only determined who the "peoples" will be by delimiting the borders, but also established a range of options of the fundamental status based on the Western theory of democracy for these peoples. In Bosnia and Herzegovina, Cambodia, Timor-Leste and Afghanistan, the powers determined the identity of the "people" or the "peoples" when they detained the territory and spatial aspect of the constitutional order.

The idea of internationalization of the constituent power, conceptualized in this research as a "hybrid constituent power", represents the approach of the influence of international law on the normative content of constitutional law, making sure that the rules that should order the activities of citizens are not produced only by the national legislature, which creates a problem of legitimacy as to the standards bodies, corresponding to an increasing degree of penetration of international law into constitutional law.

It can be mentioned that the hybrid constituent power causes a shift from the institutional balance of the State because international norms interfere in the formation of internal material or procedural norms, affecting state structures, namely: political organization and the distribution of competencies.

Among the experiences of hybrid constituent power, from the UN interventions already consummated, some lessons were demarcated through the practical perspective by those who were directly or *indirectly involved in peacebuilding operations,* in which one of the objectives was to consolidate democracy. It was intended, for the purpose of delimiting the object of the research and contributing to the construction of the legitimacy and effectiveness of the constitution, to propose some guidelines that can be delineated for the improvement and legitimacy of the hybrid constituent power.

Case studies were also presented that provided a brief overview of the role of UN constitutional assistance in the constituent phase: Cambodia, Bosnia and Herzegovina, East Timor and Afghanistan. Thus, deference was given: the overview of the legal framework; the description of the process, taking into account the degree of inclusion, transparency and participation of the local population; the focus and forms of intervention. The case studies presented do not, however, represent a definitive answer to what the broad set of UN experiences in the field of hybrid constituent power meant.

Nevertheless, the examples set out point to some shortcomings in which it is possible to analyze the compatibility of these interventions with classical theory and, from there, build propositional elements, either for the construction of new semantic nuclei that will make up the old theory, or to attribute reflections that lead the UN's experience in relation to this matter to a more legitimate and democratic path, thus contributing to the recent democracies "not dying" or suffering from the so-called use of abusive constitutionalism.

The countries chosen for sampling were Cambodia (1992), located in the southern part of the Indochina Peninsula in Southeast Asia; East Timor (2002), located in the eastern part of Timor Island in Southeast Asia; Afghanistan (2003), located in central Asia; Bosnia and Herzegovina (2006), located in the western Balkans.

The hypotheses developed focused on the following issues: the overview of the legal framework of the *UN intervention process in the constitution-making process in* the constituent phase; the description of the process considering the degree of inclusion, transparency and participation; the focus, the role of the UN as a political actor, and the UN's mode of intervention.

Thus, it was possible to compare from the theoretical perspective[3] of the original constituent power whether this mode of intervention translates the forge of a legitimate constitution and whether we are dealing with a new theoretical subcategory that comes from the original constituent power, here called hybrid constituent power.

In conclusion, the legal framework that determined the UN intervention in Cambodia was consolidated through the Paris Peace Agreement. The description of the constituent process, considering the degree of inclusion, transparency and popular participation, was extremely weak.

The Transitional Authority, representative of the Secretary-General of the United Nations in the peace agreement, should ensure the implementation of human rights in the constitution in accordance with the Universal Declaration of Human Rights, representing fundamental rights and freedoms; and the construction of a system of liberal democracy. The Supreme National Council, a pre-constituent body created by the Peace Agreement, predicted that in all cases the Transition Administrator would have the power to determine whether the advice promoted by the council or its action would be consistent with the Agreement, with a seat to all meetings.

The main goal of the UN was to ensure that the constitutional construction process was focused on the main objectives of the Agreement which represented an effective bias of liberal democracy. However, as for the creation of the National Constituent Assembly, although its main objective was to respect its sovereign authority – the primary objective of democracy, the lack of transparency and popular access ended

[3] As already explained, the theoretical framework for the definition of what the original constituent power represents enshrines Dantas' doctrine. In this sense, the classical conceptions of Emmanuel's Constituent Power were not analyzed Siéyes and Carl Schmitt. See DANTAS, Ivo. Constituent Power and Revolution: brief introduction to the sociological theory of constitutional law. 2 ed. Bauru: Jalovi, 1985, p. 9; DANTAS, Ivo. *Contemporary State Theory*. Curitiba: Juruá, 2016.

up making the constituent process non-inclusive, having been carried out behind closed doors and under its auspices, which ends up disincorporating the meanings that represent democracy or the representation of a democracy inside out.

The Cambodian constituent process, according to the theory of original constituent power, can be understood as illegitimate. The process was not owned by national, transparent and participatory leadership. And finally, the constituent project approved by the National Constituent Assembly was the one drafted by Prince Sihanouk and strongly influenced by the Transition Administrator.

In the case of Bosnia and Herzegovina, the constituent process was stifled by the Dayton Agreement and a foreign policy agenda was imposed, which included territorial division (federalism) and the structure of the constitutional provision to be implemented. The constitution provided for in Annex IV to the document contained a structure that aligns with the principles defining Western liberal democracy.

The UN intervention in Bosnia and Herzegovina was represented by four distinct phases and at different times, which includes the constituent and post-constituent phase. The constituent process materialized in the Agreement did not provide for any kind of popular participation since the constitution was pre-designed and contained in the Agreement.

The UN High Representative was responsible in the post-constituent phase for coordinating and monitoring civilian aspects for the implementation of the Agreement, promoting elections and monitoring respect for human rights, rehabilitation and return of refugees, facilitating dialogue and reporting the progress of the mission with the United Nations and other international organizations at first, among others.

On the other hand, the UN was also responsible for reforms that contributed to the restructuring of the State with the help of the European Union (EU), such as the removal of ethnic homogeneity as a fundamental constitutional principle and the readjustment of the powers of the State. The later stages were represented by un and EU aid in state reforms, more focused on agreements with local elites. From 2006, in the final phase, the UN's decision was that Bosnian elites should take control of the state without the possibility of further reforms via international imposition.

A central role played by the United Nations in the rebuilding of the new State is envisaged, both as a direct and indirect political actor, even exercising distinct powers in the governmental structure. It should be emphasized the herculean effort of the UN to conform an ethnicity conflicting nation from the imposition of a determined and closed federalist design to national participation. The State of Bosnia and Herzegovina maintains its constitutional structure and the internal crisis is considered permanent. For the theory of original constituent power, this constituent process can be considered illegitimate, already being born with a constitutional hiatus.

The legal framework that determined the UN intervention in East Timor was represented by Resolution 1272, approved by the Security Council. Popular participation in the constituent process can be considered extremely low, with no predictability or mechanism for popular participation in the constituent process.

The National Council was created by the Resolution and appointed by the Transition Administrator to promote its advisory. In its constitution, there were Timorese and UNTAET members, possessing the Administrator, in addition, the power of veto of deliberate decisions.

The main objective of the UN in this transition process was to forge a constitutional charter so that the Timorese people could develop their own constitutional development skills, focusing heavily on the creation of a democratic system and the promotion of human rights. As in Cambodia, the lack of transparency and popular access has made the work of the Constituent Assembly non-inclusive.

As in Cambodia, the Transition Administrator, special representative of the UN Secretary General, preferred to step aside from the work carried out in the National Constituent Assembly, which nevertheless had two members of UNTAET—foreign advisors who specialize in constitution and politics. His tasks were to bring to a term the work of the Assembly and explain the meanings of western terms that represent democracy and democratization. As the works were carried out behind closed doors, it was not possible to show the degree of influence of international actors in relation to the substantive elements of the new Timorese charter. Such influence is shown to be possibly strong, since the Members of the Assembly had little domination of the legal-constitutional language.

In this sense, the Timorese constituent process, according to the theory of the original constituent power, can be understood as illegitimate behold, it was not owned by national, transparent and participatory leadership. Finally, the constituent project approved by the National Constituent Assembly was that fruit of a single political party and possibly strongly influenced by international experts representing the UN.

It was *the Bonn Agreement* that consolidated the legal framework for the UN intervention in Afghanistan. The description of the constituent process in relation to the other countries studied is considered weak, considering the degree of inclusion, transparency and popular participation.

The entire constituent process was monitored by the Representative of the UN Secretary General, from the conception of the Transitional Authority to the establishment *of the Constitutional Loya Jirga.* Its main function was to assist and supervise all phases of the process provided for in Annex IV to the Agreement, i.e. participating in all meetings, investigating human rights violations and recommending corrective measures.

This attribution, as a neutral body in the conflict, allowed access to all organs and departments, paying special attention to their conduct during meetings to facilitate any impasse or the adoption of a decision.

The Transitional Authority, elected by *Loya Jirga* emergency, was influenced directly by the UN through the Special Representative of the Secretary General and its recommendations were materialized in the form of a decree by the Transitional Authority.

The Constitutional Committee, created by this authority to draft the constitutional project, was directly appointed by the Representative of the United Nations, and a support was created specially to advise these works.

The UN also had an office within the *Constitutional Loya Jirga*, created to debate and approve the project. The Presidential Decree that established the mode, election and composition of the members, was carried out by the international organization.

Similarly, UNAMA employees were present at all sessions and in the subcommittees. The Committee on the Harmonization of Constitutional Provisions was held behind closed doors with the presence of the United Nations and the Ambassador of the United States.

The UN exerted direct influence on Afghanistan's constituent process, acting as a political actor, and although the process had a small popular participation, partly due to the fundamental tendencies of certain groups, there was no inclusion and transparency of the whole process. And in this sense, for the theory of original constituent power, the process lacks legitimacy.

We sought to analyze four constituent processes that were carried out, based on the intervention of the UN. These choices were purposeful since the processes had already been mapped in previous research—some even requested by the UN. In this sense, it was possible to test the theory studied in the empirical universe of the case studies presented.

Thus, it can be concluded that both in the Cambodian, Bosnia-Herzegovina, Timorese and Afghanistan constituent process, the UN actively acted as a political actor, directly and indirectly influencing the construction of new constitutions.

This interference may be able to implement certain standards, such as that of western liberal democracy. Its political power can be represented by the economic and structural means it holds, by its technical capacity and, mainly, by the representation of a prestigious moral authority.

Thus, most of the time, the influenced are nations plagued by war, with low development rate, high illiteracy rates and with a high degree of hope in improving the development process of the newly democratized state.

The hybrid constituent power has been consolidating without due theoretical recognition. It incorporates the ideals and meanings of democracy and contemporary constitutionalism, where the UN or any international body or foreign power acts as a political actor, directly or indirectly, in the *constitution-making process* in the constituent phase in states in political transition.

The constitutional letters fruit of this process, for the theory of original constituent power, can be considered illegitimate, since they break with essential paradigms that represent constitutional ideology.

It is said that there is a possibility of ensuring greater legitimacy for hybrid constituent power when it incorporates a means capable of integrating the international and multidimensional expertise of the UN.

The *round table,* as a multistage model and generally used in the post-conflict environment, represents a fundamental innovation in the history of classical constituent power theory, and its characteristics can increase acceptability, adequacy and coherence for the construction of a national constituent assembly more legitimate and compatible with the form of intended democracy.

If, on the one hand, the hybrid constituent power is materialized, its structure and institutional design must be compatible to establish new processes of change, integration and cooperation between the institutions and powers constituted, which will necessarily reduce the negative effects of the imposition and expand the spaces of public vocalizations.

The theory of hybrid constituent power has been consolidating in the empirical universe, dressed with many foundations, such as international collective security, self-defense, the protection of human rights in flagellate nations, even ensuring the "legitimacy" of a unilateral intervention of great powers in these nations.

Admitting that the hybrid constituent power constitutes a theoretical subcategory of the original constituent power can recognize, legitimize and improve the changes in attitudes and circumstances that may arise because of a conceptual change that will occur in the political life of that population. This may represent new efforts to strengthen the theoretical commitment, including betting on the cooperative institutional design for the integration of new policies and political communities.

The recognition of the concept of hybrid constituent power may break with the traditional theoretical bond that represents the relationship of the principle of popular sovereignty with the "constituent power", but the legitimacy of a constitutional order will always be contextual and contingent, and the theory cannot be sustained by a meta-rule of perpetuity.

A constitutional theory that relies on external constitutive involvement must commit itself to a thick normative bill that undermines the legitimacy of the local territorial *status quo*. As a result, we can affirm that this recognition qualifies the normative benefits of the constituent power by betting, for example, on the principle of popular sovereignty as a pillar of support, recommending vigorous popular participation in the issues to be developed by the constitutional project; political projects would be implicated in a web of broader geostrategic legal and political considerations, the development of a constitutional culture.

The problem that has been triggered is that the hybrid constituent power that has been established does not have theoretical precedents capable of establishing checks and balances for the performance of the great powers and international communities. The recognition of the category can limit, restrict and legitimize its performance, including presenting solutions and possible designs so that the "people", holder of state sovereignty, can develop by itself an identity and constitutional culture operationalized through its own steps.

In another sense, the hybrid constituent power may favor the incorporation of a model of institutional design that connects the functioning of the new powers from a cooperative gear, legitimizing in a later way the constitutional charter and promoting the development of constitutional belonging and constitutional culture, reconnecting its performance with national ideals.

Prudently thought at the heart of the theory of original constituent power, this new subcategory may reflect, in political realities, the aspirational promise contemplated by the theory as a framework for reconstruction of a nation.

The constitutionalism of transition and transformation can find answers and instruments that seek to forge a legitimate and democratic constitution and are aligned with the objectives of the UN. In addition, they are conducive to the formation of a collective will, capable of generating a minimum consensus on the charter that is intended to induce transformation.

In summary, this is an account of a result that was not exactly what was expected, and it became clear that the constitutional text, through the intervention of the UN, may not be clothed with the legitimacy intended for the reasons already described. With this conclusion, it is not being predicted that the constitutional text is destined to die. And nothing theoretically prevents the hypothesis of the acquisition of later legitimacy by a constitutional practice more in tune with the concept of democratic constitutionalism of Post and Siegel. But that, only the future will tell.

Finally, this work did not intend to exhaust the subject—quite the opposite. The various conjectures raised here give rise to new research, making clear the need to deepen the study of the phenomenon of UN intervention in the processes of constitution-making, mainly because it is the great representative of human rights and democracy.

Afterword

A few years ago, Sylvia Steiner wrote in a presentation of my work[1] to feel like one of those people whom we consider a brother, given the closeness and commitment to human rights. At that time, we were doing a doctorate at the University of São Paulo, she was a federal adjudicator (desembargadora federal), and in a short time, she would become a judge of the International Criminal Court, a function that she performed with the utmost competence.[2] This condition prevented us from sharing more of our lives in Brazil and doing more work together, although I interviewed her in The Hague around 2006 for a survey that I conducted on the early years of the ICC.

So, I feel about Carina Gouvêa, whom I met about a year ago in Recife, where we live. In the short time of knowledge, we have met frequently, in cafes and restaurants, to exchange ideas, and accomplished academic works of great significance for our lives. The work that Carina Gouvêa asks me to write an afterword is one of those works that fill us with satisfaction over the course of our work reading and when we finish. Empirical research in law has not always found the best paths, which is certainly not the case with Carina Gouvêa and Castelo Branco's work.

I am faced with a significant work not only because its initial basis has been evaluated in a post-graduate *stricto sensu* program in Law but also mainly because of the methodological rigor with which the research was conducted. Not only in the book but also in our conversations, Carina Gouvêa and Castelo Branco's central concern is with democracy and the directions it has taken in contemporary times. In fact, her work begins with a theoretical discussion of democracy in the difficult times we live in. In times that can not be categorized as very democratic, the work makes use of an arsenal of authors who contribute to the theme, especially in English, but also in Portuguese and Spanish languages.

[1] Benvenuto, Jayme (Organizador) Manual de Direitos Humanos Internacionais: Acesso aos Sistemas Global e Regional de Proteção dos Direitos Humanos. São Paulo: Editora Loyola, 2003.

[2] The records of the interviews with judges Sylvia Steiner and Elisabeth Odio Benito were lost since my notebook was stolen in the classroom, shortly after my return from The Hague, The Nederlands.

C. B. Gouvêa and P. H. V. B. Castelo Branco, *UN Interventions and Democratization*, Societies and Political Orders in Transition,
https://doi.org/10.1007/978-3-031-32715-5

Considering the central theme of her work, the concern is directed to the international scene, in which the United Nations is making efforts to democratize national societies in the context of decolonization. There may indeed be more power rhetoric, as well as rhetorical power, in international interventions, which justifies concern from the academic and political point of view. Personally, as I have revealed to Carina in our meetings that I am a defender of international interventions, since they are carried out multilaterally and with the care that the action or the set of actions requires. That is why I prefer the coordinated action of the international community to the inaction of the states or of the international community, in what can be described as the permanence of a state of anarchy compatible with the maintenance of certain national states in a dominant position, and to which national groups not committed with democracy have their spaces extended by the state of anarchy. Even though I am positioning myself, I understand that the debate about it must be pregnant with critical capacity, as Carina Gouvêa and Pedro Castelo Branco's does. As the discussion about constitutionalism evolves, the authors demonstrate enormous ability in the handling of concepts and ideas exposed by the authors consulted. The discussion around the Transitional Constitutionalism seems to stand out for relevance and importance in the context of her work. The same can be highlighted in terms of the interdependence between democracy and human rights. The debate around the typology of constitution-making seems to me of special value in academic spaces committed to the advancement of studies in the theme.

The high point of the paper is certainly the case study on East Timor, whereby the authors fulfill the promise of conducting empirical research on the interface between constitutional law and international law. East Timor is described as a paradigmatic case, since this intervention has been consummated in three stages: pre-constituent, constituent, and post-constituent. This is not an easy task, given the broad scope of coverage of international interventions, and the costs of undertaking empirical research in conflict situations. Carina Gouvêa and Pedro Castelo Branco's demonstrate in her work not only a thematic proximity to the situation under study but also an experience of local context. Carina Gouvêa and Pedro Castelo Branco's work points out important sufficiencies and limitations to the intervention process in the name of democracy. The authors are telling us that democracy is a very important value, so constitutionalism of transition and transformation are capable of "finding answers and instruments that seek to forge the legitimate and democratic constitution".

Jayme Benvenuto

Ph.D. Professor of the Post-Graduate Programs in Law and in Human Rights of the Federal University of Pernambuco. Research Productivity Scholar.

CPSIA information can be obtained
at www.ICGtesting.com
Printed in the USA
LVHW061123090723
751931LV00006B/447

9 783031 327148